real world MACRO

Eleventh Edition

Edited by
Marc Breslow, John Miller, Betsy Reed,
Bryan Snyder, and the Dollars & Sense Collective

REAL WORLD MACRO, ELEVENTH EDITION

ISBN: 1-878585-05-3

Published by:
Dollars and Sense
Economic Affairs Bureau, Inc.
One Summer Street
Somerville, MA 02143
617-628-8411

Real World Macro is edited by the *Dollars and Sense* Collective, publishers of *Dollars and Sense* magazine and *Real World Micro*, *Real World Macro*, and *Real World Banking*.

The 1994 Collective:
Randy Albelda, Rose Batt, Mark Breibart, Marc Breslow, Randy Divinski, Laurie Dougherty, Deborah Dover, Amy Gluckman, David Levy, Dalya Massachi, Gretchen McClain, John McDermott, John Miller, Conrad Miller, Betsy Reed, Rich Rosen, Susan Schacht, Chris Tilly.

Cover Art and Design: Nick Thorkelson
Production: Sheila Walsh

Printed by:
Saltus Press
24 Jolma Road
Worcester, MA 01604

TABLE OF CONTENTS

INTRODUCTION

The eleventh edition of Real World Macro offers an alternative view of national and international economic affairs. While traditional macroeconomic theory assumes that a market economy will produce the greatest number of jobs, goods, and services at stable prices, this collection of articles looks critically at the effects of market forces on people's day-to-day lives.

The articles, drawn from the popularly-written *Dollars and Sense* magazine, share the view that traditional economic policies will not produce the best results for the majority of people. For example, as the opening article explains, the recent economic recovery has benefitted Wall Street at the expense of most Americans.

The rest of Chapter 1, **The Basics: Measuring Economic Performance**, examines some common measures of economic activity: recession, GNP, and consumer confidence. These measures are useful barometers of a capitalist economy's health, but as "A Green GNP" demonstrates, they have a limited capacity to measure people's economic well-being, working conditions, and quality of life.

In the second chapter, **Households and Consumption**, we look at the agents in economic activity. We find financially strapped governments struggling with demands to balance budgets and meet constituents' needs in an era of tax-bashing politics. "The War on Welfare" explains how deficit-cutting mania has posed problems for President Clinton and others who have pledged to overhaul the welfare system. Families struggling to make ends meet in an era of declining real wages and rising personal debt face a range of obstacles. "A Decade of Lost Gains," "What's Work Got to Do With It," and "Gender Gaps Galore" explore the ways in which gender and race influence earning power.

Chapter 3, **Business and Investment**, examines the trends that are shaping the nation's overall economic health. "Generating Affluence" suggests progressive ways to improve the economy's productivity. "Boosting Investment" reveals the results of a study showing that interest rates are not as important to investment as many believe, while "Public Capital, Private Profits" explains why public investment is good for business. "Footloose and Country Free" then reports on the impact of increasing international capital mobility on governments and communities, and

"The Quality Movement" evaluates recent attempts to improve production at U.S. firms.

The articles in Chapter 4, **Fiscal Policy**, discuss the government's taxing and spending policies. "The Clinton Budget" scrutinizes the economic program that President Clinton presented in his first year of office. "Pop Austerity," "Deficits and Our Children," "Deficit Delirium," and "Shrinking the Debt" trace the origins — and project the consequences — of the government's emphasis on deficit reduction. Finally, "Soaking the Poor" explains how state and local taxes favor the rich.

Next we turn our attention to **Banks and Monetary Policy**. Two articles, "Banks in Control" and "Transforming the Fed," examine the ways in which the Federal Reserve determines monetary policy, and two more, "Hard Times for Bankers" and "Spring Cleaning at the FDIC," explain why banks found themselves in crisis at the start of this decade. Throughout, the chapter defines concepts as basic as money — and as central to understanding our economic system.

Chapter 6, **Unemployment and Inflation**, looks at these two villains of macroeconomics. "The Zero-Inflation Ploy" asks how government policies influence these two constants in our economy. "The New Unemployment" and "The Real Unemployment Rate" document the recent rise in permanent job loss and the ways in which government figures understate the problem, respectively. The final article in the chapter, "Policies for Peace," suggests ways the government might ease the pain of unemployment following conversion away from military production.

The last chapter examines **International Trade and Investment**, showing "How Free Trade Fails" and critiquing America's "New Evangelists" who preach the "gospel" of free trade. The European Economic Community is a better model for trade with social justice, says "How P.C. is the E.C.?"

We hope the articles in this eleventh edition of **Real World Macro** render the complexities of today's economy intelligible to you. If they provoke questions about the lessons you have learned from traditional macroeconomic texts, all the better. We welcome feedback from students as well as teachers.

The Editors
April 1994

CHAPTER 1
The Basics: Measuring Economic Performance

May/June 1994

1994

AS THE ECONOMY EXPANDS, OPPORTUNITY CONTRACTS

BY JOHN MILLER

The 1994 economy looks good. Last year it made up the ground lost during the 1990-91 recession, so it's no longer recovering, but expanding. Bolstered by strong consumer spending, the return of corporate investment, and a pickup in factory exports, the economy closed out 1993 with a humdinger of a fourth quarter, posting a 7.5% growth rate, the fastest in a decade.

Economists uniformly doubt that the torrid pace of growth will continue. Still, they expect the 1994 economy to settle back into sustainable growth, around 3.6% according to the 51 economists surveyed by the newsletter *Blue Chip Economic Indicators.* Nor, as they see it, will the expansion end anytime soon. Geoffrey Moore, a leading business cycle expert, doesn't expect the next recession until "at least mid-1996."

Wall Street and Washington have uncorked the champagne. Allen Sinai, chief economist of Lehman Brothers, a Wall Street investment house, celebrated the new year by announcing that "the U.S. economy enters 1994 with the best prospects in years." Not to be outdone, Alan Greenspan, Chair of the Federal Reserve Board, told the House Banking Committee, "The [economic] outlook is the best we have seen in decades." Laura Tyson, the chair of President Clinton's Council of Economic Advisors, was quick to give her boss credit for the economy's performance, saying it is "clearly linked to the president's economic program."

But not everyone is celebrating. After 12 straight quarters of economic growth, 8.5 million people still can't find a job, according to the official unemployment figures. Many more people are out of work according to unofficial estimates. And large corporations are continuing to lay off workers.

Many people with jobs have not fared much better. Workers' wages buy less than they did prior to the recession. By 1992, poverty rates had reached their highest levels since the fierce early 1980s recession. In addition, another two million people were without health insurance, bringing the total to 39 million.

While some parts of the country will enjoy better economic prospects during 1994, most people will live out the year in near-recession conditions. Their long-term economic futures are also dim, holding little hope of a return to the relative prosperity they enjoyed two decades ago.

Why? The light at the end of the tunnel looks so bright in part because it follows a dark five years of economic stagnation. Plagued by the financial excesses of the 1980s, record levels of debt and bankruptcies as well as the collapse of the commercial real estate market, the economy grew an average of less than 1.8% per year from 1989 to 1993. That is its worst performance for any five-year period since World War II.

But even before these years of stagnation, the greed decade of the 1980s had spawned a type of economic growth that benefits the few at the expense of the majority. In fact, economic growth is now predicated on the deepening economic agony of most people more than it has been at any other time since World War II. Profits are improving because wages are not and workers are losing their jobs.

Take Fleet, the largest bank in New England. Already logging record profits — $448 million in net income for 1993 — the bank recently announced a corporate restructuring plan. The downsizing will give profits a healthy boost by cutting $300 million from operating expenses and shedding over 5,000 workers, about 19% of its work force.

The same down-side shadows the rosy scenarios economists sketch of our collective economic future. The very factors that convince forecasters that the economy will grow more rapidly during 1994 and beyond — rising productivity and declining unit labor costs, improved competitiveness, low inflation rates, and a shrinking budget deficit — will mean continued hard times for most workers, people looking for work, and their families.

Even if the economy were to expand robustly enough to spread the benefits of economic growth widely and give those on Main Street, not just Wall Street, a reason to celebrate, economists and policy makers stand ready to recommend that the Fed intervene to maintain price stability by slowing it down. Alan Greenspan, never a party-animal, has already raised interest rates to preempt the inflation associated with rapid growth and higher wages, and to protect the improving profits that are key to sustaining this class-based economic growth.

FROM JOBLESS RECOVERY TO BALLYHOOED EXPANSION

The economic upswing that began in March 1991 has been the weakest since World War II. Compared to other recent recoveries, the economy grew half as quickly and took nearly three times as long to recover the output lost during the recession (despite the mildness of the 1990-91 recession). Already older than most recent expansions, the 1990s expansion is only now in the midst of some sort of delayed adolescence, experiencing its first sustained spurt of rapid economic growth.

The hallmark of the current expansion has been its joblessness. At every stage, this recovery has produced fewer jobs than any other recovery since 1945. By last September, some 30 months into the expansion, employment had grown only 2%. While the typical recovery creates as many as 300,000 new jobs a month, from March 1991 to January 1993 this one created only 40,000 jobs a month. Improved job creation numbers last fall prompted Laura Tyson to announce that 1993 lifted the economy from "jobless recovery to expansion with job creation." Yet the new numbers, ranging between 172,000 and 217,000 new jobs monthly, are still well below the average recovery.

Slower growth alone cannot explain the lack of new jobs. In the first 30 months of this recovery, the economy grew only 6%, but even that should have generated more jobs than it did. In past recoveries, that much growth led to a 2.2% increase in employment. In this one, it has led to just a 1.7% increase.

There are a few reasons for this. For one thing, rather than rehiring laid off workers, corporations have worked those still on the job longer hours. The factory workweek and overtime hours are both at record highs.

Worse yet, corporations have continued the "downsizing" and "restructuring" that began before the recession. Corporate restructuring has cost thousands of mostly white-collar jobs — 600,000 in 1993. Large corporations — Xerox, RJR Nabisco, General Motors, IBM, and others — have continued to lay off workers well into the recovery. In January of this year, large companies announced another 108,000 job cuts.

The combination of layoffs and anemic job growth has left the official unemployment rate at 6.5%, barely lower than during the recession (6.8%). In addition, while these layoffs haven't transformed unemployment into a predominately white-collar problem, they have driven the ratio of white-collar unemployment rates to blue-collar rates up from its usual one-quarter to one-third. What's more, an unprecedented number of those who lost their jobs, more than three-quarters, lost them permanently. These trends prompted *Business Week* to brand the 1990s the era of the "dumpy" — the downwardly mobile professional. "Dumpies and their struggle to maintain middle-class respectability will be as emblematic of the 1990s as yuppies and their flamboyant material excesses" were of the 1980s, according to *Business Week*.

But fallen yuppies and the lack of jobs are not the only problems on the employment front. The kind of new jobs being created is another. Nearly three-quarters of the job growth has been in the service sector, with almost none in manufacturing and construction. In the midst of the recovery, over half of the new jobs were in just three industries: health care, restaurants and bars, and temporary help (for banks, among others). A few of these are good jobs, but the average restaurant job pays only $5.33 an hour. Temporary jobs offer little security and often no health benefits.

In addition, part-time work accounts for 25% of new employment, an unusually large proportion. Over half of those jobs were filled by people seeking full-time work. This is the only recent recovery in which the number of workers forced to work part-time (which typically climbs during a recession) did not decline.

For people who have managed to hold onto old jobs, the recovery has also meant hard times. In addition to working longer hours, many have watched their real wages fall even as the economy has expanded. The real wages of blue-collar and non-college-educated workers continued to fall just as they have since the late 1970s. The real wages of white-collar and college-educated male workers similarly slipped, as they have since 1987. Overall real wages have yet to return to their pre-recession levels; they linger nearly 20% below where they were two decades ago. Median family income, corrected for inflation, is also no higher than it was 20 years ago, even though 20% more families rely on two incomes instead of one.

WALL STREET VS. MAIN STREET

For those pounding the pavement in search of work, or strapped to their desks well after the normal quitting time, this is all bad news. But that is not how Wall Street economists see it.

They point out that the flip side of a jobless recovery is

a productivity-led recovery. On that score, this expansion has outperformed other recent upswings. Corporate restructuring, layoffs, and little rehiring have produced rapid increases in productivity — the economy's output per hour of labor input. For instance, during 1992 the hourly output of U.S. workers rose 4.6%, a 20-year high. This is a far cry from the 0.7% productivity gain the U.S economy averaged from 1973-91.

The combination of quicker productivity gains and meager wage growth has steadily widened corporate profit margins since 1991. By 1993 those larger profits had coaxed more investment into the economy. Capital spending increased 7% in 1993, and a recent Commerce Department survey found that U.S. companies plan to increase capital spending another 5.4% during 1994.

Productivity increases have also helped to keep inflation under control by offsetting wage increases. And lower inflation has in turn helped to keep interest rates low by maintaining the purchasing power of money over time. The Fed's most recent report testifies to the effect of lower interest rates on the economy. During the second half of 1993, the interest-sensitive areas of autos and light trucks, home sales, housing starts and residential construction, and business equipment spending all picked up smartly.

Allan Sinai put it this way: "Positive fundamentals — such factors as higher productivity growth, low inflation, low interest rates, and increased corporate profits — have finally begun to outweigh the negatives." But one man's "positive fundamentals" are another person's negatives. Let's look at a few of his key measures.

U.S. manufacturers have been gaining an edge on their international competitors in holding down their labor costs per unit of output. During 1992, the United States was the only major industrial country to record a fall in manufacturing unit labor costs. In fact, since 1985, U.S. unit labor costs relative to those of the 12 major industrial countries have fallen by 62%. The main reason for this is stagnant U.S. wages, not rising productivity. Since 1985 U.S. output per hour in manufacturing, a measure of productivity, did increase more quickly than in Japan and Germany, 35.8% compared to 33% and 17%, respectively. But in the same period, hourly compensation for U.S. workers barely budged while Japanese and German workers enjoyed 28.2% and 35.3% increases, respectively.

Tepid wage growth and little job creation convince forecasters such as Sinai that low inflation and low interest rates will continue. The "usual forces" that produce higher inflation — such as high wages and high consumer demand — may not arise this next year, even with a step up in growth, according to Sinai.

The prospect of a smaller budget deficit also indicates to Sinai and others that low inflation and interest rates will prevail. Yet the spending cuts that have helped reduce the deficit have hurt millions of people. The cuts have cost government workers their jobs and whittled away the support available to people below the poverty line — from welfare to housing subsidies to fuel assistance. At the same time, poverty rates have continued to rise during the recovery. Deficit reduction is yet another positive fundamental with harsh negative effects.

GREENSPAN TO THE RESCUE

Should the positive fundamental of low inflation show any sign of departing in 1994, Alan Greenspan is ready to rein in spending by pushing up interest rates. In fact, he did so long before most analysts saw any sign of inflationary pressures. In February of this year, he raised the Fed funds rate — the rate that commercial banks charge other banks on overnight loans — by a modest one-quarter percent and warned that further interest rate hikes would follow.

Immediately, banks began charging a higher rate to their prime lenders, and mortgage interest rates increased. The interest rate on 30-year Treasury bonds reached its highest level in nine months, 6.8%, having increased a full percentage point since the economy began to heat up in the fall.

By restricting credit through higher interest rates, the Fed's move should effectively choke off both investment spending and mortgage refinancing, one of the main forces driving consumer spending. Less spending should relieve any real or imagined upward pressure on prices. But with fewer sales and less investment, companies will hire fewer workers and the improving job growth may dry up. This will be no environment in which workers can easily bargain for higher wages. Indeed, the fear that an improving job market would allow workers to demand higher wages was the Fed's real concern, according to *Business Week*.

Greenspan's preemptive strike against inflation showed once again that the interests of bondholders come first. Investors look to the Fed to protect the value of their stocks and bonds by keeping inflation low. If investors believe the Fed is failing to keep a vigilant inflation watch, they could set off a financial panic. And if fighting inflation means keeping a cap on employment growth, so be it.

Even by Greenspan's own standards, however, his actions were unnecessary. There were few indications of accelerating inflation this February. In the fourth quarter of 1993, labor costs — the best gauge of dreaded wage-push inflation — registered the first back-to-back quarterly de-

WITH HIS ECONOMIC STIMULUS PACKAGE IN THE CONGRESSIONAL RUBBISH HEAP, CLINTON SEEMS RESIGN TO PURSUING A PRODUCTIVITY-LED EXPANSION BY CATERING TO THE BOND MARKET.

cline in thirty years. Richard S. Belous, chief economist at the National Planning Association, maintains that, "anybody who see wages ready to take off is in cuckooland." The Congressional Budget Office estimates that the unemployment rate could drop to as low as 5.5% before there would be any significant acceleration in inflation. But the Clinton administration nonetheless endorsed Greenspan's move.

With his economic stimulus package in the Congressional rubbish heap, Clinton seems resigned to pursuing a productivity-led expansion by pleasing the bond market. As the administration sees it, that strategy may cost jobs now but will generate more jobs later as the future benefits of economic growth trickle down, hopefully by 1996.

PUTTING PRODUCTIVITY IN CONTEXT

Even as it ignores the immediate suffering of unemployment, will this strategy nonetheless work? Are the bond market, the Fed, and the Clinton administration supporting sustainable productivity improvements that signal the beginning of a new era of prosperity?

There is real reason to doubt that rapid productivity growth will continue once the spate of layoffs and forced overtime has passed. Robert J. Gordon says the pickup in productivity gains since 1991 is a reaction to the productivity stagnation at the end of the 1980s. To him, the productivity record from 1987 to 1993 doesn't suggest that the United States has broken out of a trend of mediocre productivity growth.

His brother, David Gordon, former economic advisor to the 1988 Jackson campaign, also doubts that recent productivity gains are anything more than a phase. As he sees it, U.S. productivity has stagnated not only because of a lack of investment — in private business capital, public capital, and human capital — but also because top-down labor-management relations browbeat workers rather than cooperating with them. To keep their foot on workers' necks, U.S. corporations employ more than twice as many administrators and managers as German and Japanese corporations.

The current recovery has done little to correct these repressive anti-worker industrial relations. As of 1992, the ratio of supervisory to non-supervisory personnel in U.S. corporations had not changed from its 1989 level, according to David Gordon. In fact, according to several labor economists, such as Massachusetts Institute of Technology's Paul Osterman, corporate retrenchment has continued to interfere with innovative human resource and industrial relations practices by undermining employment security. High-tech corporations such as DEC and IBM had pledged lifetime employment in exchange for workers relinquishing some prerogatives around work rules and embracing rapid innovation in their work. But high-tech has been especially hard-hit by massive layoffs. The promises have been broken, and the techies are out of work.

According to Eileen Appelbaum of the Economic Policy Institute, cost cutting brings short-run productivity boosts but not the kind of continuous process improvements and innovations that are key to long-lasting international competitiveness. One especially despondent economist, Michael Perelman, has dubbed these low-wage retrenchment policies the "Haitian road to development."

In addition, the experience of manufacturing since the 1980s suggests that productivity gains do not necessarily lead to additional hiring. Gordon Richards, chief economist at the National Association of Manufacturing, points out that manufacturing lost 2.6 million jobs during the 1980-82 economic downturn, but recovered only one million of those jobs during the rest of the decade. And after losing more jobs to the stagnation of the 1990s, manufacturing is now down 3.2 million jobs from 1979.

THE FULL EMPLOYMENT GOAL

If this productivity-led expansion won't sustain widely beneficial economic growth, what would? Only a dramatic change in economic policy toward promoting genuine full employment can give those who have suffered through two decades of deteriorating real incomes a stake in an improving economy.

Some mainstream economists have bucked the trend of their profession and rededicated themselves to countering the tragedy of unemployment. For instance, Bill Vickery, president of the American Economic Association in 1992, has devised a plan to promote full employment. He would have the government "recycle savings" through large-scale public investment (from infrastructure to education) and keep inflation in check by controlling corporate profit margins. With genuine full employment in place — something in the range of 1% to 2% unemployment —Vickery foresees a U.S. economy that would "enjoy a major reduction in the ills of poverty, homelessness, sickness, and crime."

Too bad an administration that came to power by promising to create "jobs, jobs, jobs" refuses to take up such a challenge. Instead Clinton has thrown in his lot with the employment-phobic bonds market, tight-fisted Alan Greenspan, and the bulk of the economics profession that is willing to accept continued "underemployment."

This is not just a lament of the left. Even Kevin Phillips, a conservative news analyst, has complained bitterly that Clinton is an inveterate economic centrist beholden to corporate interests and unwilling to support a truly expansionary economic policy. That Phillips can see as much suggests that a populist politics with a clear vision of an economic alternative should be able to find more and more adherents, as fewer and fewer people have a stake in economic growth.

Resources: "The Joyless Recovery: Deteriorating Wages and Job Quality in the 1990s," by Lawrence Mishel and Jared Bernstein, Economic Policy Institute Briefing Paper, Sept. 1993; "Today's Task For Economists," by William Vickery, *Challenge,* March/April 1993; and "The Jobless Recovery: Does It Signal a New Era of Productivity-led Growth?" by Robert J. Gordon, Brookings Papers on Economic Activity, Vol. 1, 1993.

WHEN IS A RECESSION OVER?

SITTING IN A CONFERENCE ROOM, SEVEN SUITS DECIDE

BY JOHN MILLER

Yogi Berra once said about a baseball game, "it ain't over until it's over." If Yogi had been talking about the current recession, he would have said, "it ain't over, even when it's over."

Last December the National Bureau of Economic Research (NBER), a private research organization the Commerce Department has designated as the nation's arbiter of the business cycle, declared the recession officially done. In fact, according to the NBER, the recession ended in March 1991, just eight months after it began. By the NBER's measure, the economy has been recovering for two years.

But most people don't buy it. Last fall, when then-President George Bush told voters the recession had ended, they kicked him out of office. They knew their hard times continued, no matter who said the recession was over.

Take Sylvia Williams. The *New York Times* reported that Boeing, the Wichita, Kansas, aircraft company, laid Williams off, along with 2,000 other workers last June, over a year after the recession had officially ended. Five years before, Williams had started at Boeing as a mail clerk earning $5.60 an hour. When she lost her job, she was earning $13 an hour working on the factory floor. Williams now collects $231 a week in unemployment benefits, due to run out in mid-1993, and holds little hope her job will come back. Like most who lost their jobs during the 1990s, her layoff is permanent.

Can the recession actually have ended almost two years ago if people such as Williams continue to lose their jobs not temporarily, but permanently? The strict economic answer is yes.

A DATE WITH THE BUSINESS CYCLE

The NBER tracks the waves of economic activity that economists call business cycles. A cycle runs its course from the trough of a recession to the peak of an expansion and back down into a trough. In the first stage of the cycle — the expansion — the economy grows as companies produce more goods and services and hire workers. When the economy begins contracting, its second phase, companies produce fewer goods and throw workers out of jobs. The NBER has identified eight such business cycles in the U.S. economy since World War II. (See table below.)

The NBER's Dating Committee, a group of seven economists currently chaired by Stanford University economist Robert Hall, defines which time periods constitute a cycle. By the committee's own admission, the dating process is "fuzzy." The committee has no rigid rules for determining the start or finish of a business cycle. The members rely on developing a consensus among themselves after they study a broad array of macroeconomic indicators. In short, they eyeball the data. The founders worked with 46 indicators; today the NBER publishes *Business Conditions Digest* which lists around 1,000 measures. Among the many indicators the committee's members study are gross domestic product (GDP), the index of industrial production, several interest rates, and personal income. They also study several composite indices, including the index of coincident indicators, which consists of four measures of employment income, output, and sales.

This last recession provides a case in point of how difficult it is dating business cycles. Economists' working definition of a recession is two consecutive quarters of negative real growth, or declining output, as measured by GDP, the most often used measure of overall economic activity. But applying this definition is not easy. It takes time for the federal government to publish official numbers on how fast or slow the economy is producing goods and services. And the committee prefers several indicators to conform to a pattern. The NBER had to wait until spring 1991 before it felt comfortable declaring that a recession had started the previous July. By then most economic indicators — including real growth rates for GDP — finally fit the typical definition. (The graph shows three consecutive quarters of negative real growth as measured by GDP beginning in third quarter 1990.)

Dating the onset of a recession is difficult; dating its end is even harder. Economists agree even less on how to determine when a recession finishes and an expansion begins. They generally divide an expansion, or a growing economy, into two phases. In its first phase, the economy recovers the ground lost — in terms of jobs, output, and other measures — during a recession. When the economy expands beyond its pre-recession levels, it enters its second phase. Economists declare a recession over only when they know a recovery has reached this second phase. They then date the expansion at the point when the economy began recouping the lost output. Should the recovery falter, and the economy lose ground before the first phase finishes, then the recession would have continued.

With this last recession, the expansion began in March 1991. The economy grew sluggishly through the second half of 1991 and the first three quarters of 1992. It grew so slowly, in fact, it took almost two years to replace production lost over the eight months prior to March. And, as of last December, civilian employment, real personal income, and industrial output still had not reached their pre-recession peaks. Nonetheless, the Dating Committee declared March 1991 the official end of the recession when, finally, the third quarter of 1992's GDP grew at an annual rate of 3.4%, driving GDP just beyond its pre-recession level.

A STAGNANT RECOVERY

By the NBER's definition, this past recession was neither long nor deep. Eight months falls well below the average length of a recession. (See table.) The economy lost less real output, as measured either by real GDP or the industrial production index (the Federal Reserve's measure of the nation's mines and factories) than the average post-World War II recession. And the official national unemployment rate never even reached 8%, a number well below the double-digit rate of the 1981-82 recession.

But the end of the recession proper did not halt economic stagnation. The economy is barely growing. Typically, in the first year of a recovery, real GDP growth rates average 6%; this economy registered only 1.6%.

And this barely growing economy has created few jobs. Unemployment rates usually fall only well into an expansion because employers are skittish about hiring too quick-

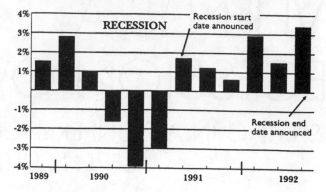

QUARTERLY GROWTH OF GDP
Change from preceding quarter, seasonally adjusted

Source: Department of Commerce, Bureau of Economic Analysis, and *The New York Times*

ly. Still, in a typical recovery, the economy will create as many as 300,000 new jobs each month. But the first nine months of 1992 produced just 340,000 new jobs. Two years into a recovery, the unemployment rate still hovers around 7%. On top of this, an unprecedented number of those who lost their jobs during the recession, around 85%, lost them permanently — the highest permanent job loss since World War II.

Real wages and real income levels, for those who are working, have not only remained far below their postwar peaks, they've also remained below their pre-recession levels. Real wages today are no greater than they were in 1959, some 34 years ago. Real family income is no greater than two decades ago.

No wonder Americans do not believe the recession is over. But officially we are in a recovery, and, unfortunately, this is it. Since 1988, the economy has grown on average less than 1.3% per year. No one expects 1993 to improve much. The consensus forecast of 44 economists the *Wall Street Journal* surveyed foresaw the economy growing no more than 3% this year — too slow to drive unemployment rates much below 7%.

The NBER has not so much misdated the recession as it has demonstrated that its terms are obsolete. The terms measure the ups and downs of a single business cycle, not how the economy affects people's well-being and purchasing power over many years. People's wages and employment opportunities have stopped improving, no matter what the NBER says about the recession and recovery. It is time economic policy makers faced up to that.

Resources: Wall Street Journal, New York Times.

U.S. BUSINESS CYCLES, 1949-1991

Trough	Peak	Trough	Expansion	Contraction	Full Cycle
				Number of months	
Oct 1949	July 1953	Aug 1954	45	13	58
Aug 1954	July 1957	Apr 1958	35	9	44
Apr 1958	May 1960	Feb 1961	25	9	34
Feb 1961	Nov 1969	Nov 1970	105	12	117
Nov 1970	Dec 1973	Mar 1975	37	16	53
Mar 1975	Jan 1980	July 1980	57	6	63
July 1980	July 1981	Nov 1982	12	16	28
Nov 1982	July 1990	Mar 1991	93	8	101

Source: Business Conditions Digest

May 1992

DEFINING CONSUMER CONFIDENCE

A living Charles Dickens might look at the latest Consumer Confidence Index and grumble about this bleak house of affairs. A living William Shakespeare would call it our winter of discontent. They'd be right.

In February, the index — produced by the Conference Board, a business-backed New York City research center — fell to its lowest level since December 1974. In 1974, the country was suffering from a severe bout of "stagflation": The economy was mired in recession, and unemployment and inflation were climbing.

Today's lack of confidence can be traced to the country's bleak labor market. Fabian Linden, executive director of the board's Consumer Research Center, told the *Wall Street Journal* that the "consumer's prime concern [is] job security."

The Conference Board's index is extremely sensitive to public concerns about jobs. It is based on a survey of 5,000 households, conducted by mail, that asks such questions as:

• How would you rate the general business conditions in your areas (good, bad, normal)?

• Six months from now do you think they will be: better, same, worse?

• What would you say about available jobs in your area right now (plenty, not so many, hard to get)?

• Six months from now do you think there will be: more, same, or fewer (jobs)?

• How would you guess your total family income will be six months from now (higher, same, lower)?

• How likely are you to buy a new car in the next six months?

The answers are analyzed and indexed according to a scale with the 1985 confidence level equaling 100. Between January and February of this year, confidence fell almost four points to 46.3.

Tracking the index through the 1980s (see chart) demonstrates just how gloomy Americans are about the economy. During the early 1980s recession, consumer confidence rarely fell below 60. Through much of the decade, the confidence level hovered between 95 and 100, soaring to close to 120 in 1988 and 1989.

Other surveys, such as the University of Michigan Consumer Sentiment poll and one commissioned by *Money* magazine and ABC News show similar, although not identical, trends. The University of Michigan index, which is more sensitive to interest rates than jobs, fell this winter, but had reached lower levels last winter and in 1980.

Government officials find today's numbers quite disturbing. Speaking before the Senate Banking Committee, Alan Greenspan gave his explanation: "When we went into a recession in the past, [workers expected that] a lay-off was merely that, a lay-off, not a job loss. I think there's a different attitude now."

Aside, however, from measuring popular attitudes towards the economy, economists differ on how to use the information provided by the Consumer Confidence Index. The drop in consumer confidence early this year momentarily depressed the stock market, but business analysts didn't expect it to reduce retail sales, noting that the drop in confidence is often greater than the drop in sales. Other economists say the index does reflect consumer willingness to buy expensive items like autos, homes, and the like.

Some economists argue that consumer confidence falls more quickly than the Gross Domestic Product and recovers more slowly. But the confidence index and similar surveys tell a story with a twist: The economy isn't just about numbers, it's also about our reactions, sensibilities, optimism, and discontent.

Resources: The Conference Board, Consumer Price Index, February 1992; *The Wall Street Journal.*

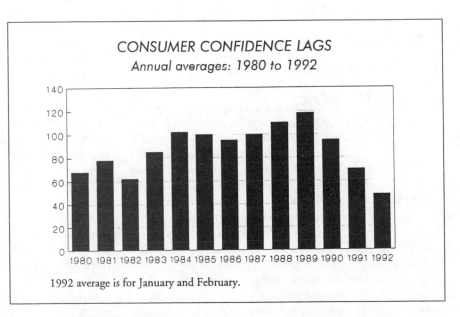

CONSUMER CONFIDENCE LAGS
Annual averages: 1980 to 1992

1992 average is for January and February.

A GREEN GNP

TAKING THE ENVIRONMENT INTO ACCOUNT

BY JOHN MILLER

Indonesia's economy grew rapidly during the 1970s and 1980s — about 7% per year. Oil, natural gas, timber, rubber, and other natural resource exports fueled this apparently healthy economic expansion. Yet not everyone has joined in lauding the country's economic managers.

Robert Repetto, an economist with the World Resources Institute (WRI), is one critic. He says Indonesia has embarked on an "unsustainable course" by depleting its petroleum reserves, destroying its forests, and eroding its soil. The official growth rate does not acknowledge these losses: If it did, annual growth would fall to a modest 4%.

Indonesia's case is not unusual. Many developing nations have exported essential natural resources — denuding forests and milking mineral reserves — to finance short-term growth. And standard bookkeeping practices hide this natural resource drain. Gross National Product (GNP), the established measure of economic well-being, completely ignores the depletion of natural resources in calculating the value of goods and services an economy produces.

> **GNP IGNORES ACTIVITIES THAT DON'T INVOLVE MARKET TRANSACTIONS, NO MATTER HOW USEFUL THEY ARE TO SOCIETY.**

In fact, an expanding GNP (see box) and a sustainable, prosperous economy were never exactly synonymous. But the two never differed so much as they now do. Mounting environmental problems have created today's greater disparity and have led development agencies and economists to consider alternatives to GNP.

In 1987, the U.N.-sponsored World Commission on Environment and Development warned all countries, rich and poor alike, "to take into full account [while measuring] growth the deterioration in the ... stock of natural resources."

Many European countries now do this by supplementing GNP with some form of natural resource accounting. Norway compiles natural resource and environmental accounts for use in economic planning. And "natural patrimony accounts" allow French authorities to monitor the impact of economic activity on the environment.

The World Bank and the World Resources Institute, a private environmental think tank, have worked to develop alternative measures of economic performance sensitive to environmental damage and resource depletion. They hope to replace GNP with a measure that can act as a guide to sustainable development, a practice the WRI defines as "the management of natural, human, and financial assets so as to increase long-term wealth and well-being." Only after factoring environmental impact into the main accounts, these institutions argue, will economic losses associated with environmental damage be taken seriously.

DOES GNP MEASURE UP?

In most countries, governments still consider GNP the most important measure of economic activity. That's the case in the United States. Each quarter, government officials and economists anxiously await the release of GNP figures. A steadily growing GNP, they read as a healthy economy; a decline in the growth rate hints at trouble to come; and a drop in the GNP means a recession.

According to traditional reasoning, GNP — more precisely, real (inflation-adjusted) GNP per capita — measures the level of "potential" well-being for citizens and residents of the nation. More output per person means more national income, and higher incomes allow for greater consumption. These factors can make people better off if a nation provides some equity in the distribution of goods, services, and income.

But GNP leaves out too many crucial factors to effectively measure the full economic well-being of a nation and its people. GNP ignores activities that don't involve market transactions, no matter how useful to society. In addition, it fails to examine income distribution, which is essential to evaluating the impact of economic growth on people's lives.

GNP also fails to provide clues to an economy's long-term potential, especially when applied to resource-exporting Third World countries. To do so, GNP would have to provide a practical guide to the impact of current resource use on future income. In short, it must measure a nation's sustainable income.

GNP, however, only considers sustainability when it accounts for "tangible assets" — like machinery and buildings — that make up business investment. When a business builds a new plant, its expenditures contribute to the investment component of GNP. The new plant is recognized as "productive capital," and its depreciation is written off against the value of production. By accounting for depreciation, GNP recognizes the necessity of maintaining physical assets. Not maintaining assets would lead to declining future output.

This foresight doesn't extend to "biological capital." GNP neither recognizes natural resources as capital nor accounts for their depreciation. As a result, a country could come close to exhausting its resources and irreparably damage its capacity for future growth before the problem is recognized in the accounts. For example, the depletion of Indonesia's forests might not effect GNP until that country can no longer export timber at the current rate.

Repetto of the World Resources Institute shows how GNP can send false signals to policy-makers by treating natural resources as free and unnecessary to renew. He asks his readers to consider the following hypothetical example: Should a farmer cut and sell the timber in her woods to raise money for a new barn? Would she be better off? Most of us would answer yes, if the value of the barn was greater than that of the timber.

No such calculation is made in figuring GNP. Nowhere is the loss — even if it's a temporary loss — of a valuable natural resource, like timber, reflected in the

accounts. In fact, if the farmer builds the barn, GNP would actually increase by the value of the timber and by the value of other products and services used to build the barn. According to the accounts, the timber was worthless as a forest, it only gained value once cut.

TWO PICTURES OF INDONESIA

Repetto uses the Indonesian economy to examine the impact of natural resource depreciation on GNP-based meters of economic performance. He created accounts for the most important natural resources in the Indonesian economy: petroleum, timber, and soil. Together these three resources provide 75% of Indonesia's exports. Repetto estimated the physical destruction of those resources and then assigned a monetary value to those losses, subtracting the total as a "negative" investment. For timber and soil, the two renewable resources, he adjusted his figures for the cost of replacing the assets.

From 1970 to 1984, Indonesia lost 7.2% of its standing timber. Significant soil erosion also occurred during the same period. Increases in farm output in Indonesia's hill country were achieved at the expense of soil quality. And known oil reserves declined each year after 1974.

Resource depreciation has a powerful impact on Indonesia's long-term economic potential. Much of the investment reported by the Indonesian government evaporates after subtracting the depletion of natural resources from official figures to achieve the "Net Domestic Product" (see table). For example, Repetto's measure cut 1984

DEFINING GNP

Gross National Product (GNP) is one of the most familiar economic terms. Economists and government officials use it to evaluate the effectiveness of economic policy and progress. But just what does GNP mean? And how is it calculated?

In the United States, the Department of Commerce calculates GNP through a system known as the National Income and Product Accounts (NIPA). Developed in 1942, NIPA analyzes the economy according to John Maynard Keynes' main macroeconomic categories — consumer spending, business investment, government purchases of goods and services, exports, and imports.

GNP measures the market value of goods and services produced for "final use." "Intermediate goods," or materials used to produce a final product, are not counted. For example, the value of the cloth purchased by dress manufacturers is not added to GNP but is included in the price of the dress sold to consumers. To count it directly would be to count it twice.

GNP includes all the products of U.S. citizens and corporations, even those operating overseas. It also considers the profits on U.S. capital invested abroad.

The "Gross" in GNP means that all "investment goods" — buildings and machinery produced in a given year — are included in GNP, even those that replace worn-out machines and buildings.

Economists say a vigorous economy produces a growth rate of 4% or more and that a growth rate of about 2.5% is needed to keep employment and unemployment rates stable. During the second quarter of 1990, U.S. GNP grew by 0.4%.

investment by about 66%. For 1979 and 1980, the value of depleted petroleum, soil, and timber surpassed the amount of investment in the economy. Repetto's measure reported negative net investment for those years. Accounting for resource depreciation has a similar impact on growth rates. Repetto's gauge cuts the growth rate by close to 50%.

For Repetto, accounting for natural resource consumption flashes an unmistakable warning: Indonesia is on an "unsustainable course." And Indonesia hasn't altered its course since Repetto completed his study. Its rate of deforestation, for example, has actually increased since 1984, and natural resources — oil, natural gas, timber, and rubber — continue to be the nation's leading exports.

DEFENSIVE EXPENDITURES

GNP falls short as a measure of sustainable income in another important way. GNP treats expenditures to counter the noxious environmental and social side effects of economic growth— such as cleaning up after an oil spill— as positive contributions to the economy.

These so-called "defensive expenditures" artificially inflate GNP. Defensive expenditures are in essence costs of production that the debit side of the accounts ignore. Their main function is to neutralize environmental and social damage. They add nothing to the availability of goods and services.

The treatment of environmental damage produces some bizarre anomalies in GNP. For example, the state of Massachusetts spent $202 million cleaning up Boston Harbor in 1989. As government spending, this is added to GNP. On the other hand, Mobil plans to spend tens of millions of dollars over the next several years cleaning up an oil spill that has been seeping into the ground in Brooklyn's Greenpoint section for more than 40 years. Mobil's costs will be considered "intermediate production expenses" and will not be added to GNP. Thus government spending to counter environmental damage seems to add to the wealth of the nation, while private spending on the same thing does not.

In both cases, GNP obscures the link between environmental conditions, quality of life, and economic growth by not accounting for the initial damage. GNP further complicates the Boston Harbor case by considering the cost of the cleanup a positive

contribution to GNP and national income. A more accurate measure would not result in added national income, regardless of who took responsibility for the problem.

ALTERNATIVE MEASURES

Economists have suggested many alternatives to GNP over the years. But the mounting environmental damage of the past decade and the deepening problems of countries pursuing resource-based development strategies have pushed the United Nations, environmental groups, and some countries to develop sophisticated alternative measures of economic performance.

One of the most sophisticated alternatives is the Index of Sustainable Economic Welfare (ISEW — see graph). Developed by World Bank economist Herman Daly and philosopher John Cobb as a replacement for GNP, ISEW makes several adjustments to the accounts. It weights consumption for a degree of inequality; adds the value of

---

THE CASE STUDY OF INDONESIA
World Resources Institutes's Comparison of
Gross Domestic Product and Net Domestic Product

| Year | GDP | Adjustment to Natural Resources | | | | NDP |
		Petrol.	Forestry	Soil	Net	
1971	5,545	1527	-312	-89	1,126	6,671
1972	6,067	337	-354	-83	-100	5,967
1973	6,753	407	-591	-95	-279	6,474
1974	7,296	3,228	-533	-90	2,605	9,901
1975	7,631	-787	-249	-85	-1,121	6,510
1976	8,156	-187	-423	-74	-684	7,472
1977	8,882	-1,225	-405	-81	-1,711	7,171
1978	9,567	-1,117	-401	-89	-1,607	7,960
1979	10,165	-1,200	-946	-73	-2,219	7,946
1980	11,169	-1,633	-965	-65	-2,663	8,506
1981	12,055	-1,552	-595	-68	-2,215	9,840
1982	12,325	-1,158	-551	-55	-1,764	10,561
1983	12,842	-1,825	-974	-71	-2,870	9,972
1984	13,520	-1,765-	493	-76	-2,334	11,186
Average Annual Growth:	7.1%					4.0%

Note: GDP and NDP are measured in constant 1973 Rupiah (billions.) A negative adjustment to a resource signals a decline in the physical reserves of that resource during the year.

Source: "Wasting Assets: Natural Resources in the National Income Accounts," World Resources Institute.

housework; deletes wasteful expenditures, including much of the military budget and national advertising; subtracts defensive expenditures; adjusts for the costs of pollution and environmental damage; and accounts for the depletion of non-renewable resources.

A far different picture of growth and economic welfare emerges after application of ISEW to the modern United States. Both real GNP per capita and ISEW per capita increased rapidly in the 1960s as output boomed and the income distribution grew somewhat more equal. Beginning in the 1970s, however, the two measures moved in opposite directions. Real GNP per capita increased by 2% per year in the 1970s and 1.8% per year between 1980 and 1986. But ISEW per capita stopped its steady increase in 1973 before tumbling by 1.3% per annum between 1981 and 1986. Daly and Cobb attribute the decline to slower growth in domestic investment, a worsening distribution of income, the exhaustion of oil, natural gas, and coal fields, and long-term environmental damage caused by corporate dumping of industrial waste.

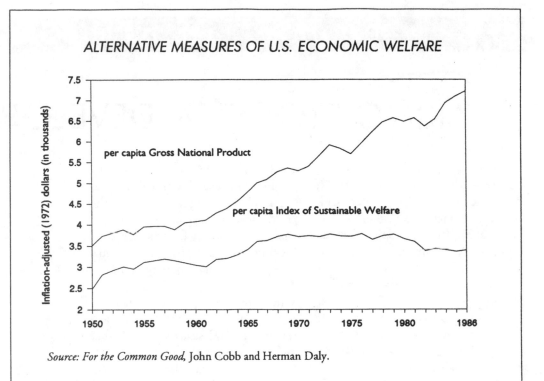

ALTERNATIVE MEASURES OF U.S. ECONOMIC WELFARE

Source: For the Common Good, John Cobb and Herman Daly.

MEASURING UP

Measures of economic performance that take into account both economic and ecological factors are prerequisites for making sound public policy. Misleading information — like that provided by the GNP — can only contribute to the making of bad policy. Better gauges — like Daly and Cobb's ISEW, Repetto's natural resource accounts and the U.N. Development Programme's Human Development Index — wouldn't automatically lead to progressive policy, but they would allow us to assess more accurately the state of our economy, ecology, and world. Better measures would give us the information needed to take stock of the complex relationship between economic growth, environmental health, and social welfare. Only then might the rid-

dles of sustainable development be addressed in a knowledgeable fashion.

But investment decisions hold the key to halting the degradation of the environment in today's world. Investment remakes the technology of today and decides the technology of tomorrow. In the United States, lasting improvements in environmental conditions have only come in those few instances where alternative technologies have replaced those inimical to the environment. The classic example is lead-free gasoline, which has dramatically lowered levels of lead pollution.

These kinds of changes can only take place on a large scale when investment decisions are not private affairs guided solely by the pursuit of profits. Public pressure from citizens and consumers and economic incentives have forced limited improvement in corporate environmental practices and government policy. But to score more important victories, investment decisions must be subject to public control where they could be guided by accurate measures of sustainable growth, a sound environment, and a healthy economy that favors the economic welfare of the entire population.

Resources: Robert Repetto, *Wasting Assets,* 1989; Herman Daly and John Cobb, *For the Common Good;* World Commission on Environment and Development, *Our Common Future,* 1987.

November 1990

TAKING STOCK OF DEVELOPMENT

The United States is no longer the world's wealthiest nation. In 1987, that honor belonged to Switzerland, the nation with the highest Gross National Product per capita. But the second-place ranking the United States earned in the GNP sweeps actually masks how poorly our nation does in providing for its people.

Seeking a more accurate measure of "human attainment," the U.N. Development Programme (UNDP) created a Human Development Index (HDI) and used it to rank 130 countries. The index considers life expectancy, adult literacy, and a measure of a nation's purchasing power to present an alternative gauge of economic and social well-being.

The table at right compares HDI rankings to those based on GNP per capita, listing the top 10 countries according to HDI, 38 selected countries, and the bottom 10 nations. A ranking of 130 signals the best rank, one the worst. For example, in the HDI rankings Japan has the best rating while Niger has the worst. The third column in the table shows the difference between each listed country's GNP ranking and its HDI rank, with positive values suggesting a quality of life higher than the country's GNP would indicate and negative values revealing a lower quality of life.

Using the HDI, the United States falls from second to 19th place, or last among the developed nations. It ranks just ahead of Israel and the now defunct East Germany. A relatively low literacy rate (96% compared to 99% for most developed countries) sets the United States back. And according to educator Jonathan Kozol, the official U.S. literacy rate may be vastly overstated, so the country might belong even lower on the scale.

It is worth noting that the only other Western industrialized country that sees its ranking fall to a comparable degree is South Africa. Apartheid's effects reduce that country's ranking 14 points.

In the developing world, socialist or once-socialist nations tend to do better on the HDI scale. China, Cuba, and Vietnam, for example, all performed far better when ranked by HDI than GNP. Even Ethiopia did better, rising 18 places from its bottom ranking on the GNP list. High literacy rates and somewhat longer life expectancies tend to explain these gains.

As a group, the oil-rich Arab states fell farthest when comparing HDI to GNP. Saudi Arabia plunged 43 spots, Oman 56, and Kuwait 34 on the list. Strikingly low literacy rates — especially female literacy rates — explain this phenomenon.

Despite its efforts, the UNDP hasn't created the perfect scale. It was unable to consider income distribution, regional and urban-rural discrepancies, and political freedom. It also had to rely on sometimes unreliable government statistics. Nevertheless, the agency utilized the HDI in making several policy recommendations including: reducing military spending, increasing social subsidies, reducing and refinancing debts, and giving top priority to sub-Saharan Africa — the least developed region according to both GNP and HDI scales — in planning aid programs.

Resource: Human Development Report 1990, U.N. Development Programme, 1990.

RE-RANKING NATIONS

	HDI rank	GNP per capita rank	Change in rank
Top ten countries			
Japan	130	126	+4
Sweden	129	125	+4
Switzerland	128	130	-2
Netherlands	127	117	+10
Canada	126	124	+2
Norway	125	128	-3
Australia	124	114	+10
France	123	119	+4
Denmark	122	123	-1
United Kingdom	121	113	+8
Finland	120	121	-1
Other selected countries			
West Germany	119	120	-1
United States	112	129	-17
Israel	111	108	+3
East Germany	110	115	-5
Chile	107	73	+34
Czechoslovakia	106	102	+4
USSR	105	101	+4
Hungary	101	87	+14
Yugoslavia	100	90	+10
Poland	98	83	+15
South Korea	97	92	+5
Singapore	96	110	-14
Cuba	92	66	+26
Mexico	91	81	+10
Kuwait	88	122	-34
Albania	84	61	+23
North Korea	82	67	+15
Brazil	80	85	-5
UAE	77	127	-50
Iraq	76	96	-20
Nicaragua	71	54	-17
South Africa	68	82	-14
Libya	67	103	-36
China	66	22	+44
Philippines	65	46	+19
Saudi Arabia	64	107	-43
Iran	61	97	-36
Vietnam	56	16	+40
Indonesia	54	41	+13
Zimbabwe	52	45	+7
Oman	48	104	-56
Egypt	45	49	-4
India	37	25	+12
Pakistan	36	33	+3
Tanzania	35	12	+23
Nigeria	24	36	-12
Angola	22	58	-36
Ethiopia	19	1	+18
Bottom ten countries			
Benin	10	28	-18
Afghanistan	9	17	-8
Mauritania	8	40	-32
Somalia	7	23	-16
Guinea	6	31	-25
Chad	5	4	+1
Sierra Leone	4	27	-23
Burkina Faso	3	13	-10
Mali	2	15	-13
Niger	1	20	-19

November/December 1993

THE WAR ON WELFARE

CLINTON'S CARROTS AND STICKS

BY TERESA AMOTT

Stumping the campaign trail, "New Democrat" Bill Clinton vowed to end "welfare as we know it." Clinton pledged to make welfare "a second chance, not a way of life" by imposing a two-year limit on recipients of Aid to Families with Dependent Children (AFDC), the major cash assistance program for poor families. With these words, Clinton joined the long list of presidents, going back to Lyndon Johnson, who have proposed ambitious plans to reform AFDC.

Richard Nixon proposed a negative income tax and a national minimum benefit. Jimmy Carter sought to provide guaranteed public employment at the minimum wage for all welfare recipients. Ronald Reagan signed into law a plan that attempted to make work rather than income support the centerpiece of the AFDC program. But none of these plans has addressed the problems at the heart of welfare: a shortage of good jobs with adequate wages and benefits; the absence of a national family policy that would provide paid parental leave, subsidized child care, and income supplements to single parents; and continued race and gender discrimination in the workplace.

As articulated during the campaign, Clinton's plan is to provide carrots — education, training, and supportive services such as child care and help with transportation expenses — for two years, after which the stick would be applied: the recipient would be forced off the rolls and into private employment or a public sector job. The combination of carrots and sticks is quintessential Clinton: a queasy mixture of liberal policies seeking to address inequalities of access and opportunity, and conservative policies that blame the victim for presumed failures in moral character.

By adopting a get-tough attitude toward welfare recipients, Clinton sought the votes of Reagan Democrats, placing himself in the rhetorical camp of Reagan-Bush attacks on the welfare state. But by promising education and training, Clinton committed himself to additional spending that will prove difficult to obtain in the current atmosphere of deficit-reduction mania. During the campaign, Clinton played both the welfare and the deficit cards, but now he's left holding a bad hand.

THE LURE OF THE CARROT

In late June, Clinton announced the formation of a 26-member Inter-agency Working Group on Welfare Reform, Family Support, and Independence, consisting of government officials from the Department of Health and Human Services, the Department of Labor, the Internal Revenue Service, the Treasury Department, the Department of Housing and Urban Development, and various other agencies. The group's proposal will most likely not be available until early next year, but its contours can already be discerned from Clinton's campaign rhetoric and from the writings of two of the working group's members, liberals David Ellwood and Mary Jo Bane.

Before Clinton appointed them to the Department of Health and Human Services, Bane and Ellwood had collaborated on influential studies measuring the length of time recipients spend on welfare. They found that the majority of recipients leave the rolls within two years, but that most people on welfare at any point in time are in the middle of a long stay. Imagine a 13-bed hospital in which 12 beds are occupied throughout the year by chronically ill patients who do not leave the hospital. The 13th bed, though, is occupied by a series of 52 patients who stay for one week each. At any one point in time, 12/13 (roughly 85%) of the patients would be in the midst of a long spell of hospitalization. Over the course of the year, however, over 80% would have been hospitalized for only a short spell. The same dynamic operates in welfare. Bane's and Ellwood's work has helped to identify this pattern, but it has not only been used to debunk myths about the prevalence of long-term welfare stays. It has also been used to focus attention on the small share of recipients who do stay on for long periods of time.

Ellwood, a Harvard economist whose writings on welfare had captured Clinton's attention years ago, is the father of the time-limited proposal that has become the core of Clinton's plan. The Ellwood plan, spelled out in his book *Poor Support: Poverty in the American Family*, proposes four major policy shifts: An increase in the earned income tax credit (EITC) in order to make work pay; publicly-provided education, training, and support services for a limited period of time; a requirement that after that period recipients find work, either in the private sector or in a government job; and a tightening of child support enforcement, including a government guarantee of child support when the noncustodial parent is unwilling or unable to make a minimum payment.

It is clear from the administration's statements that it sees welfare reform as a package of carrots and sticks modeled on Ellwood's work. Ellwood himself has noted that the administration is already reforming welfare, with the recent expansion of the EITC as the first step. Under the EITC, low-wage workers get a tax refund that acts as a supplement to wages. As a result of the Clinton budget, a family with two or more children will receive a credit of $4 for every $10 of the first $8,425 they earn — amounting to $3,370 if the family has one full-time year-round minimum wage earner. The credit phases out around maximum earnings of $26,000. Another key element of welfare reform that Ellwood continues to stress is universal health coverage, but the prospects for a speedy resolution of health care reform — and the prospects for universal coverage at a price affordable to low-wage workers — are looking increasingly dim.

Additional carrots that the administration hopes to provide are access to education, job training, child care, and assistance with work expenses. There is increasing evidence that these items will carry a high price tag, but no one wants to foot the bill. Indicative of such a trend has been the experience of the Family Support Act, the 1988 welfare reform plan that required states to provide some of these services to a targeted share of their welfare recipients, and provided some federal funds to match state spending. Shortly after the bill was passed, the recession hit. Facing fiscal crisis, most states cut their welfare budgets, and some resorted to draconian measures. Michigan, for instance, eliminated its general assistance program, cutting off checks to 80,000 poor people. Under those circumstances, additional spending to educate and train welfare recipients was definitely not on the agenda. States have come up with funds to match only three-fifths of the $1 billion in federal funds set aside for the program and only one in

WELFARE MYTHS

1. The average family on welfare has more children than the average family that does not collect welfare benefits.
2. A growing share of poor children is receiving AFDC.
3. The more generous a state's welfare benefits, the more female-headed families you are likely to find in that state.
4. If families leave the AFDC rolls and find a job, chances are good that they can move out of poverty.
5. Welfare creates an inherited dependency, with generation after generation on welfare.
6. Since most mothers work outside the home, it is only fair to expect welfare mothers to support themselves.
7. The U.S. welfare system is more successful at ending poverty than that of other countries.

REALITIES

1. The average welfare family has two children — the same as the national average. Seven out of 10 AFDC families have two or fewer children.
2. In 1990, only 59% of poor children received AFDC, compared to 84% in 1973. The combination of rising poverty but roughly constant AFDC rolls has meant that the program serves a falling share of poor children.
3. Studies have shown no correlation at all between the level of benefits and the prevalence of female-headed families. During the 1980s, when the share of poor children receiving AFDC fell, the share living in female-headed families rose.
4. Millions of jobs pay less than poverty-level wages. In 1989, 40% of women

working full-time year-round earned less than $13,500. In 1991, 5.5 million people lived in working poor families with children, where at least one wage earner worked full-time year-round.

5. Studies suggest that AFDC is rarely received by successive generations of dependent families. One study found that four of five daughters from families that were dependent on welfare did not go on to receive AFDC as adults. And, studies suggest that welfare-dependent children are no more likely than other poor children to receive AFDC later in life.

6. While the majority of married mothers with children do work for pay, they work only part-time or part-year. Is it reasonable to require AFDC mothers, who are solely responsible for child-rearing and whose children are significantly less healthy than more affluent children, to work full-time or full-year?

7. The U.S. is significantly less effective at raising children out of poverty than other countries, and our record is getting worse. In 1986, U.S. government programs reduced the poverty rate for children in single-parent families by only 4 percentage points — from 58% to 54%. In contrast, in Great Britain, the rate was reduced from 71% to 9%. In 1979, U.S. government programs raised almost one in five poor families with children out of poverty; by 1991, only one in eight was lifted out of poverty.

Sources: New York Times, 7/5/1992; U.S. House of Representatives, Select Committee on Hunger; Children's Defense Fund, *The State of America's Children 1992*; U.S. House Ways and Means Committee, The Green Book 1992; David Ellwood, *Poor Support: Poverty in the American Family*; Child Trends, *The Life Circumstances and Development of Children in Welfare Families*.

nine recipients is receiving services. Ellwood's plan, in comparison, might cost as much as $30 billion a year.

And the evidence from decades of job training programs for welfare recipients is not encouraging anyway. In San Diego, a program that provided education, training, help with job searches, and unpaid work experience boosted participants' earnings by less than $700 a year compared to a control group that didn't receive any of these services. The administration and others have hailed another program, in Riverside, California, as extremely successful because participants averaged a 65% increase in earnings over the control group — but the average participant still earned less than $3,000 a year!

STICKING IT TO THE POOR

In contrast to these carrots that seek to make work pay or improve recipients' skills, welfare reform sticks presume that recipients have flawed moral characters and that AFDC benefits encourage them to bear children out of wedlock and depend on the state rather than seek employment. The sticks come in two forms: time limits that would force recipients off welfare after a certain period, and behavioral restrictions, which are rules and regulations aimed at controlling recipients' lives. Clinton has gone on record in favor of a two-year cutoff, and early hints from the Working Group indicate that this cutoff is not negotiable. This is one campaign promise that Clinton won't break.

The idea behind time-limited welfare is simple: recipients learn dependency after years on the system, and some sort of "shock" is necessary to push them out into the real world of jobs, financial responsibility, and socially acceptable behavior. The idea appeals to conservatives who wish to punish recipients and force them into the workforce at very low wages and unsafe working conditions, as well as to low and moderate income taxpayers who have been led to believe that welfare is taking a huge tax bite out of their paychecks. (Actually, the average state spends 2% of its budget on AFDC, and the federal government devotes less than 1% to it.)

The major flaw in time limits is that they try to solve a problem that isn't there. Welfare is not a narcotic and recipients don't need to go cold turkey to lose their addiction. As the hospital bed analogy shows, the typical AFDC client leaves the system on her own within a relatively short time. Fewer than one in seven recipients stay on welfare continuously for more than five years. Those who do remain for longer periods of time tend to be in poor health, live in areas where unemployment is high (rural and central city), have low educational attainment, and little work experience. In today's job market, in which workers without advanced education cannot earn a living wage, it is impossible for them to leave AFDC and support their families, particularly once child care costs and the loss of Medicaid benefits (federal health insurance) are figured into the calculations. For these recipients, many of whom had their first child when they were teenagers, it is economically rational to stay on welfare until their children are older and they can return to school and find jobs.

Moreover, implementing a time limit would be a nightmare. How would we count the time on AFDC? Most recipients move on and off the system as they enter or leave low-wage, temporary jobs, when a child is born or becomes 18, when they marry or a relationship ends. The most stringent versions of the limit would impose a lifetime cap. Others suggest two years in any one spell or two years after the birth of a child. Each of these proposals involves complicated tracking of recipients and will be an administrative mess.

And what will happen after two years? Clinton's language has been vague on this point — recipients must "get a job," but no one knows what kind of job. Most analysts believe that between one and a half and two million adults — the vast majority of them women — will reach a two-year cutoff. With official unemployment hovering around nine million people, there simply will not be enough jobs for those pushed off AFDC, and all the estimates of job growth over the coming years are gloomy. During the 1930s, this problem was solved with the Works Progress Administration, which employed nearly three million workers at its peak in 1938-39. But public sector job creation, estimated to cost $20 billion for welfare recipients, is too expensive for the current political climate. With deficit reduction mania epidemic in the Capitol and the rest of the country, it is hard to imagine how a major public sector jobs program could come about.

> THE AVERAGE STATE SPENDS 2% OF ITS BUDGET ON AFDC, AND THE FEDERAL GOVERNMENT DEVOTES LESS THAN 1% TO IT.

That leaves workfare, a plan in which welfare recipients continue to collect their checks but "work off" their benefits by performing volunteer community service work. There is absolutely no evidence that participation in workfare plans increases people's employability, and Ellwood has gone on record warning against a nationwide workfare plan. It would be extremely expensive, since child care, transportation subsidies, and administrative costs could amount to $3,500 per workfare placement. For one and a half million people to participate could cost over $5 billion in new money. Since total state and federal spending on AFDC is roughly $20 billion, this would constitute a huge expansion in spending without providing any new services to recipients.

In addition, it is hard to imagine how the government would find millions of placements for workfare participants. Some public sector offices are so crowded that there will literally not be any room for welfare recipients. Public sector unions also fear that a program of this scale will displace their members, especially over time as county

and city governments slow their hiring and replace new workers with unpaid workfare participants. (That may be part of the attraction of the plan for antiunion local legislators.) House Republicans have proposed a simple cutoff with no workfare and no public sector jobs, but the prospect of catastrophic homelessness and hunger is so real that it is extremely unlikely that their plan will go anywhere.

COERCIVE CONTRACTS

The other sticks wielded by welfare policy planners are behavioral restrictions that punish recipients by cutting benefits if they don't fulfill certain requirements. A number of states have applied for federal waivers that would permit them to experiment with these restrictions. Perhaps the most popular such program is Learnfare, the name given to a number of state plans that link the size of a family's grant to the school attendance of children or teen parents. Learnfare plans are currently in place in six states, and 15 states considered plans in 1992 but failed to adopt them.

Wisconsin's plan was the first and has received the most attention. An evaluation found that it has not had positive effects on school attendance (in Milwaukee, truancy actually increased after implementation of Learnfare), and it has resulted in a number of "sanctions," the AFDC's euphemism for cuts in benefits. After one year of the program, over half of the students sanctioned for truancy had dropped out of school. The plan's administration, moreover, has been a disaster. One mother, for instance, found her family's grant cut because her daughter failed to show up at the local public school — but the child was not enrolled in public school and had perfect attendance at a nearby parochial school! Her experience was typical: one review found that over 80% of the sanctions were erroneous.

One problem with the Learnfare model is that it is based on the idea that children in welfare families are less likely to attend school than those from families not on welfare.

WE'VE GOT TO STOP THE HANDOUTS, THE SOMETHING-FOR-NOTHING ATTITUDE...

... THE DEPENDENCY THAT PASSES FROM ONE GENERATION TO THE NEXT!

SO YOU'RE FOR CUTS IN WELFARE CHECKS?

I'M FOR HIKES IN THE INHERITANCE TAX

While the national evidence on this point is sketchy, a Wisconsin study found that welfare children attend school an average of 169 days, compared to 172 days for non-welfare children. In addition, the president of the Milwaukee Teacher Association believes that "Learnfare sanctions have undermined [his] ability to develop a positive relationship with some of [his] students," and speculates that "Learnfare has been an attempt to help the career of politicians and not a help for poor families."

In fact, a U.S. District judge temporarily suspended Learnfare in Milwaukee because he argued that poor people "should not be made homeless and hungry in the name of social experimentation." The real problem with Learnfare is that it ignores the reasons kids don't go to school. Cutting their families' incomes when they cut school won't improve the physical condition of schools or make them safe and drug-free, provide up-to-date, multicultural textbooks, or create alternative schools and apprenticeship programs for kids whose needs aren't met by traditional curricula. In short, Learnfare is no substitute for educational reform.

A second popular behavioral restriction is the family cap, which eliminates the grant increase that under current law is provided to a family as the family's size increases. Proponents of family caps argue that these grant increases provide an incentive for additional births, and that cutting the increase will hold down welfare family sizes. Seventeen states rejected family caps in 1992, but they are in place in California, New Jersey, and Wisconsin. Like Learnfare, family caps are based on stereotypes about welfare recipients. The facts are that AFDC families are on average the same size as non-AFDC families, that high-benefit states do not have larger AFDC families or higher teen birth rates than low-benefit states, and that fertility rates of AFDC mothers are lower than rates for the general population. A New Jersey study found that 70% of AFDC children were conceived *before* the mother became a welfare recipient. According to Jodie Levin-Epstein and Mark Greenberg, attorneys at the D.C.-based Center for Law and Social Policy, "there appears to be no empirical support for the family cap approach. The only effect that we know will occur is that very poor families will be made poorer."

A host of other behavioral restrictions have been proposed in various states, including plans to cut a family's benefits if children do not receive their immunizations or family members do not receive annual health checkups, to decrease benefits to recent migrants from lower-benefit states, to require teen parents to live with their parents or another adult, and to require that recipients use the Norplant contraceptive after they have a certain number of children (this was proposed in South Carolina and Mississippi, but rejected by the legislatures in both states). A few states rejected proposals to offer cash incentives for sterilization ($10,000 for a tubal ligation in Washington, or $500 for a vasectomy in Tennessee).

Although Clinton and his welfare policy experts have not endorsed any of these proposals, behavioral restrictions may sneak into the administration's proposals through the back door. Clinton's past experience as a governor left him deeply committed to state experimentation, so he is philosophically inclined to permit states to devise their own versions of a national welfare reform plan. Budget cutting may also drive him toward state-level "laboratories" for welfare reform, since small demonstration projects are far less costly and carry less political risk for the administration than a national plan.

One additional component of the Clinton plan will be child support enforcement. The 1988 Family Support Act began to require that states determine paternity at birth and withhold wages from "deadbeat dads." In addition, a delinquent father's federal income tax refunds are now channeled to mothers owed child support. There is little evidence that child support enforcement will help welfare mothers since the fathers of most children receiving welfare have relatively low incomes, and because at present, AFDC recipients only get to keep $50 of any child support collected on their behalf each month. (The state keeps the rest as "reimbursement" for AFDC payments to the mother.)

In his writings, Ellwood has called for a child support assurance plan in which the government advances the money to the custodial parent regardless of the father's ability to pay. A few child support assurance bills have been introduced into Congress that would provide a guaranteed payment of approximately $2000 for one child, $2500 for two, and $3500 for three. AFDC recipients would have their grants reduced by that amount, so they would see no net increase in income. However, if they took a paying job, their child support assurance payment would not be reduced dollar for dollar with earnings (as are AFDC payments). Child support assurance, then, would remain as a supplement to wages and would help to "make work pay." Several states have begun demonstration projects of the concept, but again, uncertainties about the cost of the program mean that the Clinton administration is unlikely to propose a nationwide plan.

PLAYING THE WELFARE CARD

The political stakes for welfare reform are high for Clinton. He wooed conservative voters by promising to get tough on recipients, defining welfare as a major domestic problem and not-so-subtly suggesting that as a New Democrat, he would place the concerns of white, middle-income taxpayers above those of poor people and people of color. Said Clinton, "It's time to honor and reward people who work hard and play by the rules. That means ending

BEHAVIORAL RESTRICTIONS MAY SNEAK INTO THE ADMINISTRATION'S PROPOSALS THROUGH THE BACK DOOR.

welfare as we know it.... No one who can work should be able to stay on welfare forever." These lines, and phrases such as "welfare as a way of life," were the Clinton version of a Willie Horton ad, conjuring up false images of welfare recipients having more children to get bigger checks.

Now the administration wants to implement a plan that will cost tens of billions of dollars and guarantee services to welfare recipients that are not available to low and moderate income households, such as child care and transportation subsidies. Budget cuts in discretionary domestic spending will be harsh in the next three years, so any new spending initiatives must take place now. But the administration's implicitly racist and sexist rhetoric will continue to undermine the political will to make any investments in poor families. As Lucy Williams, a lawyer and welfare advocate on the faculty of Northeastern University Law School, points out, "While a white may support income transfer programs for the elderly because she or he anticipates growing old someday, whites know they will never be African American, fourteen years old and pregnant." Conservatives in Congress can hardly wait to denounce the plan as yet another spending initiative that will drain the hard-earned tax dollars of virtuous, traditional families who play by the rules into the pockets of bad mothers who have chosen welfare as a way of life. No one will describe this transfer in racial terms, but the subtext will be clear.

With health care reform bogged down, and the mid-term elections looming ahead, Clinton needs to deliver a welfare reform program soon. The danger is that the conservative momentum in Congress that Clinton has fed will lead to a program consisting only of sticks, with no carrots. Progressives working on welfare reform find themselves once again in a defensive position, warding off punitive attacks on poor people and supporting anemic policies because they are the lesser evil.

A large coalition of Washington, D.C.-based advocacy groups is gearing up for the coming welfare reform battle, including the Children's Defense Fund (whose president, Marian Wright Edelman, is a personal friend of the Clintons), and organizations representing women, unions, and people of color. Most of these groups are now urging increased spending on education and training for welfare recipients, even though such programs rarely produce adequate increases in earnings. At the state level, though, remnants of the National Welfare Rights Organization, an organization of past and present welfare recipients that

played a key role in broadening access and improving benefits in the early 1970s, have regrouped as the National Welfare Rights Union (NWRU). The NWRU defends AFDC recipients' entitlement to long-term benefits, arguing that women on welfare already have a job raising children and that the government has an obligation to support them, especially since there aren't enough decent jobs to go around.

The real issues in welfare reform involve the subordinate status of women and people of color in the labor force, women's responsibilities as primary caretakers of children, and the lack of good jobs at good wages — none of which are adequately addressed by the welfare reform plans put forward so far. According to the Institute for Women's Policy Research, 45% of women would earn too little working full-time and year-round to bring a family of three to the poverty threshold, including day care costs for one child. Without reform of the low-wage labor market, welfare reform will do nothing to lessen poverty.

Imagine instead a system in which paid family leave, child allowances and extended unemployment benefits provided cash assistance to poor families who also were covered under a national health plan and had access to affordable and high-quality dependent care. And imagine that union organizing and a living minimum wage transformed the low-wage labor market, with comparable worth policies ensuring gender and racial equity in pay, and other regulations ensuring wage and benefit parity for temporary and part-time workers. Unless the values implicit in these policies motivate welfare reform, rather than racist and sexist myths about the failings of welfare mothers, the coming debate will surely provide more relief to conservatives with pent-up hostility than to families in need of support.

Resources: Richard A. Cloward and Frances Fox Piven, "The Fraud of Workfare," *The Nation,* 5/24/93; Lucy Williams, "The Ideology of Division: Behavior Modification Welfare Reform Proposals," *The Yale Law Journal,* vol. 102, 1992; Roberta M. Spalter-Roth, Heidi Hartmann and Linda Andrews, *Combining Work and Welfare: An Alternative Anti-Poverty Strategy,* Institute for Women's Policy Research, 1992; Mark Greenberg and Jodie Levin-Epstein, *The Rush to Reform,* Center for Law and Social Policy, 1993; U.S. House Committee on Ways and Means, Green Book 1993; Ruth Conniff, "Cutting the Lifeline: The Real Welfare Fraud," *The Progressive,* February 1992.

March 1993

DECADES OF LOST GAINS

THE CONSERVATIVE ERA AND RACIAL INEQUALITY

BY EDWIN MELENDEZ

In 1963, Martin Luther King's dream of a multiracial society of free and equal citizens electrified millions of Americans. In the decade that followed, black Americans and other people of color made significant political and economic progress. But now, some 30 years later, the United States is moving not nearer to, but further from, making King's dream a reality.

Economic, social, and political reversals for people of color began in the mid-1970s. They are the result of trends that predate the Reagan era, particularly the dissolution of the civil rights movement, the end of the postwar economic expansion, and the persistence of racist ideologies.

But conservative economic strategies — including an assault on the public sector and the use of unemployment to discipline labor — have dramatically accelerated the economic decline of people of color. Furthermore, conservative rhetoric has heightened a dog-eat-dog ideology that holds that people of color can advance only at the expense of whites.

In short, while progress toward racial equality slowed before 1981, the Reagan and Bush administrations played a critical role in worsening the economic position of people of color. As a result, race relations have deteriorated and the United States is becoming a nation ever more deeply divided.

REVERSING A DECADE OF GAINS

The political pressure exerted by the civil rights movement and economic trends in the 1950s and 1960s improved the relative living standards of people of color. The ratio of black to white individual median income was relatively constant during the first three business cycles of the postwar period, but increased sharply during the long expansion of the 1960s (see table). Between 1959 and 1969, black men increased their median income by 9% relative to white men. Unemployment among all people of color dipped from two to 1.8 times that of whites.

During the early 1970s, many economists and others, including the Nixon administration, heralded the imminent end of racial discrimination. They claimed that economic gains by people of color were the result of long-term historical trends, built into the very structure of liberal capitalist America. The gains were attributed to the joint effects of growing racial tolerance and a capitalist economic system in which competition forces cost-conscious businesses to hire the most qualified and productive workers at the lowest price, regardless of race.

Trends since the mid-1970s do not support this assessment, however, and cast doubt on the claim of a positive role played by the capitalist system in promoting racial equality and harmony. Most of the income gains made by black men in the 1960s were lost by 1979, after the 1974 recession. During the Reagan and Bush years, income gains for black men stagnated and black women actually lost ground relative to white women.

Despite the gains in median income for both black men and women relative to whites before the 1980s, overall family income ratios have barely budged since the Civil Rights Act of 1964 became law. In part, this is because gains for black households have been offset by the rapid increase in white women's labor force participation and with it the increase in white family income. Black men's labor-force participation has also fallen more quickly than that of white men.

Moreover, the improvement in relative incomes for people of color prior to 1975 masks what can only be called an ongoing disaster on the jobs front. Since the mid-1970s, the employment picture for both whites and people of color has worsened considerably. But people of color have suffered disproportionately higher and growing rates of unemployment. Since the late 1970s, the gap has grown between overall black and white unemployment. Between 1959 and 1974, black male unemployment was 2.2 times that of whites; between 1976 and 1990, it grew to 2.4 times that of whites. For women, the corresponding unemployment ratio rose from 1.9 to 2.4.

DOES THE MARKET PROMOTE RACIAL EQUALITY?

Contrary to conservative claims, the improvements in black income before 1975 stemmed not from "competitive labor markets" but from two quite particular and time-bound events.

First, many blacks migrated out of the agricultural South and into the industrial North during the 1950s and 1960s. Migration was responsible for most of the gains in black male income relative to white male income and changed the nature of male employment dramatically. In 1950, nearly 25% of employed black men held jobs in agriculture. Another 25% were employed as laborers. By 1970, less than 4% worked in agriculture and only 16% were laborers. Instead, black men moved into jobs in the higher-paying industrial sector.

The second factor raising the economic standing of people of color relative to whites was a changing occupational structure for women of color. Black women, in particular, were drawn from work in private households to jobs in the service sector, especially government employment or clerical work. Over 42% of employed black women worked in private households in 1950. By 1991, the figure had fallen below 3%. In 1955, full-time female workers of color earned 54% of what white female workers earned. By 1965, this number had jumped to 73% and peaked at 93% in 1979. The income ratio has since dropped, to 85% in 1991. While all women continue to earn substantially less than men, the improvement for women of color helped to narrow the earnings gap between whites and people of color generally.

Progress toward racial economic equality sputtered in the late 1970s. A prolonged period of recession and stagnation coupled with the start of a decline in manufacturing jobs had a negative impact on people of color.

RECONSTRUCTING THE RACIAL ORDER

Since 1979, three particular aspects of federal government policy have intensified the attack on the economic status of people of color: macroeconomic policies, spending priorities and tax reform, and civil rights policy.

The ability of the Reagan administration to gain political support for a macroeconomic policy of high unemployment may have been connected to the fact that the costs of unemployment and underemployment are heavily concentrated among people of color. One Bureau of Labor Statistics study found that while both black and white workers were thrown out of work during contractions in the postwar period, unemployment grew faster for black than for white workers during those contrac-

tions. All workers are subjected to the discipline of unemployment in the capitalist economy, but the unequal impact of the business cycle upon people of color makes them a "buffer" against the full effect of the cycle upon other workers.

The second prong of the de facto assault on the economic status of people of color was the shift in spending priorities from social programs to military procurement. The first phase of cuts in federal social programs, initiated during Reagan's first term in office, hit people of color especially hard. According to studies released in Reagan's second term, the average black family lost three times as much in income and benefits as did the average white family in 1981. The average Latino family lost twice as much.

Most of the programs with the largest budget cuts directly or indirectly subsidize the working poor. Poverty rates for people of color who work are substantially higher than for other sectors of the population. The largest cuts have been for programs such as the Comprehensive Employment and Training Act (CETA), which directly affect the functioning of the labor market and the training available for the working poor. While the Reagan and Bush administrations' rhetoric proclaimed that the alternative to welfare must be employment, they all but eliminated the programs that support this alternative.

The reorganization of the budget toward defense and away from social needs also altered the structure of employment and the position of people of color in the labor market. Defense spending rose from 23% of the budget in 1980 to 36% of the total federal budget by 1990.

A REVERSAL OF GAINS

Postwar trends in the economic status of people of color*

	1953	1956	1959	1969	1973	1979	1986
Ratio of black to white median income							
Men	.59	.56	.58	.67	.69	.62	.63
Women	.49	.45	.53	.79	.90	.91	.85
Families	.56	.53	.52	.63	.58	.57	.57
Unemployment rates							
White men	2.5	3.4	4.6	2.5	3.8	4.5	6.0
White women	3.1	4.2	5.3	4.2	5.3	5.9	6.1
Black men	4.8	7.9	11.5	5.3	8.0	11.4	14.8
Black women	4.1	9.0	9.4	7.8	11.1	13.3	14.2
Labor force participation rates							
White men	86.1	85.6	83.8	80.2	79.5	78.6	76.9
White women	33.4	35.7	36.0	41.8	44.1	50.5	55.0
Black men	86.2	85.1	83.4	76.9	73.4	71.3	71.2
Black women	43.6	47.3	47.7	49.8	49.3	53.1	56.9

*Data from 1963 to 1969 refer to "blacks and others." Data from 1973 to 1986 refer to blacks only. Years represent peaks of postwar business cycles.

Source: Reprinted from *Mink Coats Don't Trickle Down.*

Although the overall effect of military spending on employment is controversial, there is less doubt about its employment effect upon people of color. Most of the increase in military spending under Reagan and Bush was concentrated in capital-intensive industries largely closed to people of color — weapons procurement, research and development, and military construction. The shift in U.S. government spending priorities from human services to military procurement decreased job opportunities for people of color. Blacks and other people of color, as well as white women, are significantly under-represented in the major military procurement industries. They are instead disproportionately employed in human service occupations.

Using 1980 employment data, a hypothetical shift of a million jobs from health services, education, and social services to aerospace, communications, and electronics (prime military industries) would generate a net loss of 320,000 jobs for white women, and 66,000 jobs for black women. By contrast, white men would gain 386,000 jobs. The job losses of black men, who have more employment in the military-related industries, would be almost exactly offset by job gains.

Equally important is that government employment has slowed and leveled off. Federal government employment as a share of total employment dropped from 3.9% in 1979 to 2.7% in 1990. Because the government at all levels employs a higher proportion of people of color than the private sector, the recent shift in jobs from the public to the private sector of the economy has tended to reduce employment opportunities for people of color.

The first term of the Reagan administration reorganized not only government expenditures but the tax structure as well. The 1981 tax act offered tax-cutting tailored to the affluent taxpayer. The "supply-side" reform package ended a tradition of regular revisions to the tax code that benefitted low-income families. The net result of changes in federal tax policies has been a shift in the tax burden to middle- and low-income groups. Since blacks and Latinos are heavily over-represented in low- and moderate-income groups (given their limited access to business ownership and financial assets), tax reform aimed at affluent taxpayers benefits them very little. Income losses per household in 1982 due to tax changes averaged $575 for Latinos and $457 for blacks.

Reagan's budget and tax policies generated a substantial redistribution of income, not just from poor to rich, but also from people of color to whites. The Congressional Budget Office estimated that under those policies households with incomes under $20,000 per year lost $19.7 billion between 1983 and 1985 alone. Conversely, households with incomes above $80,000 per year gained $34.9 billion. Some 60% of Latino families and 63% of black families are in the under-$20,000 income category. On a per capita basis, this redistribution of income represents an average loss of $1,100 for families below $10,000 and a gain of $24,000 for families over $80,000.

THE ASSAULT ON AFFIRMATIVE ACTION

One of the most important accomplishments of the civil rights movement was the legal promise of equal employment opportunity and affirmative action policies. The impact of affirmative action on the employment of people of color, particularly black males, was generally positive. Affirmative action encouraged the demand for black males in white-collar and craft occupations, particularly in large and expanding corporations. Blacks found better-paying jobs, and the demand for low-skilled blacks increased as others moved up the occupation ladder.

The Reagan and Bush administrations vigorously opposed affirmative action on the grounds of "reverse discrimination," the idea that using affirmative action to eliminate racial discrimination creates discrimination against whites and results in less efficient production. According to this view, racial oppression is over and our generation should not be forced to pay for our ancestors' mistakes.

Contrary to Reagan/Bush beliefs, there is no evidence supporting a decline of workers' productivity due to changes in racial composition (as would be the case if less qualified workers were hired). In many cases, the cost to firms and losses to whites from affirmative action are very small. Often the gains from affirmative action benefit all workers. Affirmative action programs can improve access to better jobs and education for everyone in the workplace.

In addition to their attacks on affirmative action programs, the Republican administrations tried to alter the very definition of racial discrimination, seeking to disallow the use of simple statistical evidence of discriminatory hiring patterns. Rather than evaluating claims of racial discrimination based on hiring outcomes, the Reagan and Bush administrations argued that intent to discriminate must be proven and "quota" systems avoided.

In 1985, a California federal appeals court upheld the use of statistical evidence, writing, "Since the passage of the Civil Rights Act of 1964, the courts have frequently relied upon statistical evidence to prove a violation. In many cases the only available avenue of proof is the use of racial statistics to uncover clandestine and covert discrimination by the employer or union involved."

The Reagan/Bush era is history. The administrations that promised to balance the budget, make U.S. products more competitive in international markets, and raise the standard of living for average Americans generated the largest budget and trade deficits in the nation's history, and the average family is worse off today than it was in 1980. People of color, however, paid an even higher price for the conservative economic experiment.

Can a new civil rights movement be kindled to counter this assault? Much depends on coming to terms with the thorny question of who benefits from racial discrimination. Mobilizing a mass movement against racism in the United States will involve confronting the perceived interests of some whites in perpetuating the racial order.

WHAT'S WORK GOT TO DO WITH IT?

WORK ALONE WON'T LIFT POOR FAMILIES OUT OF POVERTY

BY RANDY ALBELDA AND CHRIS TILLY

Conservatives offer a simple explanation for why some families end up in poverty while others don't: Poor men and women don't work hard enough, and poor women don't manage to get married and stay married. "The requirements for getting out of poverty in this country are...minimal," maintains neoconservative sociologist Charles Murray, and the top requirement is to "get a job, any job, and stick with the labor market."

"That's ridiculous!" says Diane Dujon of the National Welfare Rights Union, a ten-year veteran of the welfare rights movement and a former welfare recipient herself. "There's structural reasons why people are poor: They have the worst education and the lowest-paying jobs. Single mothers end up poor because women just don't earn what men earn on the job market. Plus they have the additional problem of taking care of children."

Our research shows she's right. We recently completed a study in which we looked at why certain types of families are especially likely to be poor. For example, why did 43% of families headed by single mothers fall below the poverty line in 1987, compared to only 5% of families with two adults and no children? We found that hard work is not a route to prosperity for most poor families, because these families lack sufficient workers to place in the labor market, and because those who do find jobs find only low-wage jobs.

Conservatives have called for welfare "reform" — including reduced benefit levels, tightened eligibility rules, and stricter work requirements — and Congress has enacted many of these proposals over the last ten years, most recently in the Family Support Act of 1988. But our research suggests that since the majority of the poor are not in a position to work their way out of poverty, such policy changes simply leave poor families worse off.

Particularly critical to a family's income level are family members' gender and age, the total number of working-age adults, and the number of children. To find out just how family makeup affects income, we grouped U.S. families into seven types (see box). Using data for 1973, 1979, and 1987, we adjusted family income to correct for family size and inflation. The income adjustment means that we measure income in "need" units rather than dollars — with one unit equal to the poverty line for a given family type. Unless otherwise stated, all income comparisons in this article are made on the basis of these need units rather than raw income.

As might be expected, the income differences between family types are stark. *DINC* households (double income, no children) pocketed more than three times as much adjusted income as single mothers — *Moms*. How much of the gap is due to effort, and how much to disparate numbers of working-age adults and wage levels? The answer comes from a closer look at families' sources of income.

BRINGING HOME THE BACON

Family income includes both earnings (wages and self-employment income) and unearned income (property income, alimony and child support, and government assistance). Differences in earnings provide the key to income disparities among the seven family types, since earnings account for 77% of the average family's income.

Earnings differences among family types have been large and stable during the 1970s and 1980s. In fact, the ranking of family types from highest- to lowest-earning did not budge between 1973 and 1987.

Earnings are largest for families with working-age male adults (see graph). This includes husband-wife families (*DINCs* and *Ozzies*) as well as families headed by a single man (*Guys* and *Dads*).

The presence of children reduces adjusted earnings. Two-parent families with children earn only 70% of what those without children earn. Among female-headed households, *Moms* (single mothers) earn much less than *Gals* (single women with no children).

Finally, *Elder* families, headed by people over 65, have the lowest earnings, although not the lowest incomes. Of all the family types, their incomes are supplemented most by unearned income, mainly government transfers.

Most of the differences in earnings between family types result from the different amount of labor families supply. When we broke down those differences, we found that family types who work less do so because they have fewer available workers — not because of laziness or welfare dependence.

We calculated the number of available adults for each family by adding up the number of adults under age 65 and then subtracting one half an adult if there are children under the age of six. Subtracting half an adult takes childcare needs into account.

When we compared the average number of available adults with the number of person-weeks actually worked by family members, we found that they were closely related. On average, for every additional working-age adult, a family adds about 30 weeks of paid labor per year.

The second factor affecting earnings is the average wage family members can obtain. This wage depends on the sex and age of paid workers in the family. In our sample, working men earned about twice as

FAMILY TYPES AND INCOME SOURCES

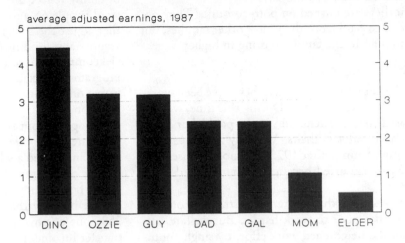

average adjusted earnings, 1987

In this article, we examine family income by type of family and by source of income using Census Bureau data from the Current Population Survey. To allow meaningful comparisons between families and over time, we adjusted income to take into account family size and inflation. We looked at 1973, 1979 and 1987 because these three years correspond roughly to the last year of the economic boom over the last three business cycles in the United States, making them the most appropriate years to compare during the 1970s and 1980s.

Income sources

We distinguished four sources of income: earnings from work or self employment; income from property, savings, and pensions; child support and alimony; and government-provided income. The above graph shows adjusted earnings by family type for 1987.

Family types

We divided the families into seven types, distinguished by the number of adults, the presence of children under 18, and the age and gender of the head of the household. The percentage of families in each type in 1987 are in parentheses.

DINC — two or more adults, no children, head under 65 (short for "Double Income, No Children") (21%)

Ozzie—two or more adults of any age, with at least one child (named in honor of Ozzie and Harriet) (28%)

Guy — one male adult under 65, no children (13%)

Gal — one female adult under 65, no children (11%)

Mom — one female adult, any age, with at least one child (6%)

Dad — one male adult, any age, with at least one child (1%)

Elder — head of family 65 or older, no children (20%)

Income adjustment

In order to adjust for inflation and take into account different income needs based on family size, we divided each family's income by its poverty line. The Census Bureau calculates the poverty line for a family based on the number of adults, children, and persons over 65, and adjusts the line annually by the average inflation rate. For example, in 1987 the average poverty line was $8,282 for DINCs, $11,871 for Ozzies, and $9,164 for Moms. A family with an adjusted income of 2.0 has a dollar income equal to twice its poverty line.

much as working women on a weekly basis. So, for example, even though single men and women worked almost identical numbers of weeks, the women ended up earning far less than their male counterparts.

Single mothers are burned on both accounts. They not only provide less paid labor than most other families, but also have no man in the family to bring in higher wages.

WHO'S WORKING NOW

We also looked at which family members have been working more since the early 1970s. During this time, women have increased their participation in the paid labor force, while men have reduced theirs. Virtually all increases in average family earnings after 1973 — among households with women — occurred because women worked more weeks per year.

Conservatives argue that tightening restrictions on welfare will spur the poor to work harder. But welfare cuts don't explain the heightened work effort by single mothers, who make up the main welfare population. *Moms* increased their work effort only between 1973 and 1979 — before Congress enacted the major welfare cuts. Between 1979 and 1987, on the other hand, single mothers worked fewer hours.

In any case, changes in family work effort over the 1970s and 1980s made only a small dent in the earnings differences among family types. The large gaps wrought by disparate amounts of available adults and levels of wages dwarf the small changes in earnings over time. The earnings gap between *Ozzies* and *Moms* is narrowing, but at the current rate *Moms* will take 581 years to reach even half of what *Ozzies* earn.

SLICING THE INCOME PIE

The glaring inequalities in earnings between families would be less serious if other forms of income (property, alimony, child support, and government aid) offset those inequalities, but that isn't the case. Only *Elders* receive enough unearned income to raise their total income figure substantially.

Property income adds little to earnings, making up less than one-twelfth of the average family's income. Child support and alimony also barely affect total income, even for *Moms*, since two-thirds of single mothers receive no alimony/child support at all.

Government transfers such as social security and Aid to Families with Dependent Children (AFDC) represent the income source of last resort for families. The average family collects less than one-tenth of its income in transfers, but *Moms* and *Elders* benefit far more than the average.

Although the government assists both single mothers and elders, the size of the public commitment diverges sharply between the two groups: elder households receive five times as much as single mothers. This doesn't mean the government guarantees the good life for elders, but it does mean that public assistance to single mothers is small indeed. What's more, overall government aid to single moth-

ers fell steadily between 1973 and 1987 in real terms, while transfers to elders increased.

The changes in government transfers for these two types of family reflect the divergent paths of public policy toward people 65 and older versus single mothers. Policies that adjust the social-security program for inflation and secure stable funding demonstrate that society has a financial commitment to elders. But means-tested government programs, especially AFDC, have suffered from a conservative onslaught. Benefit levels have fallen: adjusted for inflation, the average monthly benefit for an AFDC recipient dropped from $150 in 1975 to $125 in 1987. Federal and state governments have tightened eligibility requirements and placed a whole new emphasis on the "responsibilities" of poor people who receive means-tested transfers.

The bottom line: Of *Elders* whose pre-transfer income left them below the poverty line, government aid lifted 75% out of poverty. Of *Moms* with poverty-level pretransfer income, the government lifted only 10% out of poverty.

TIME FOR A DATING SERVICE?

The evidence is clear: Some families have less income than others not because their work effort is inadequate, but because they lack the necessary available labor time and have access only to low-wage jobs.

As a result, cutting means-tested transfers has effects that Diane Dujon calls disastrous. "Instead of decreasing the burden on poor people," she declares, "they are adding to their burden." Welfare cuts will do little to make the poor work harder, because so many of the poor have little extra time to work. Even when work requirements are coupled with child care, single mothers don't stand to gain much, since the wages available to them are low. Over the 1970s and 1980s, welfare cuts have canceled out the small earnings gains single mothers made, leaving them with lower incomes than before.

In fairness to conservatives, they do look beyond hard work. They seek to assist single mothers by collecting child support from absent fathers — but we find that the amounts of income involved are very small. And conservatives call for single women to marry — which we find does make a big difference in family income. Maybe the next conservative proposal will be a national dating service for single mothers.

But women shouldn't be forced into marriage by poverty. An alternative is a concerted policy to reduce poverty by providing adequate government assistance. This *has* worked in the case of elders. Thus, the most direct way to reduce poverty is to increase government aid to the poor. Despite its political unpopularity, this policy makes sense — not just for elders, but across the board.

Resources: Albelda and Tilly, "Resources, Opportunity, and Effort" (working paper); Isabel Sawhill, "Poverty in the U.S.," *Journal of Economic Literature*, September 1988; S. Danziger & D. Weinberg, *Fighting Poverty: What Works, What Doesn't* (1986).

December 1992

GENDER GAPS GALORE

Median income of full-time, year-round workers, age 25+, 1989

Male high school grads:	$26,600
Female high school grads:	$17,500
Male college grads:	$38,600
Female college grads:	$26,700

Median income of single-parent families, 1989

White male-headed:	$30,500
White females:	$18,900
Black males:	$18,400
Black females:	$11,600
Hispanic males:	$25,200
Hispanic females:	$11,700

Rates of home ownership for single-parent families, 1990

White males:	53%
White females:	40%
Black males:	39%
Black females:	22%
Hispanic males:	29%
Hispanic females:	21%

Ratio of median housing costs to median income for single-parent families, 1987

Male owners:	17%
Female owners:	19%
Male renters:	31%
Female renters:	43%

Median net worth of single-adult households, 1988

White males:	$16,600*
White females:	$22,100*
Black males:	$1,500
Black females:	$800
Hispanic males:	$3,000
Hispanic females:	$700

Poverty rates of single-parent families with children, 1989

White males:	15%
White females:	36%
Black males:	34%
Black females:	54%
Hispanic males:	27%
Hispanic females:	58%

*Older single white women pull up the median net worth of all single white women. Because a married woman often outlives her spouse, she inherits the couple's accumulated wealth.

Source: Paula Ries & Anne Stone, eds. (for the Women's Research and Education Institute), *The American Woman 1992-93: A Status Report.*

January 1993, updated April 1994

MOMS WITH JOBS

Over the past 20 years, an eroding male paycheck and an emerging feminist ethic have brought the nation's mothers into the paid work force in droves. But employers, private and public alike, have barely begun to properly accommodate these new workers. Not only do working moms and their kids suffer from the same inequities in pay and benefits that all women face, they usually also lack the special supports they need: child-care assistance, paid maternity leave, flexible work schedules, etc.

By historical standards, the recent flood of mothers into U.S. offices, shops, and factories has been spectacular:

• Whereas in 1975 only 38% of those with children under six had paying jobs, by 1990 over 58% did.

• Still greater numbers of mothers with children between six and 17 are now working — about three-quarters of them.

• And even women with babies under the age of one are joining or rejoining the labor force: 50% by 1986.

But even these figures do not fully reveal the far-reaching transformation of family and work life now under way. For one thing, the number of married moms with jobs jumped from 37% to 59% between 1975 and 1990. In the same period, a growing number of the nation's moms found themselves on their own financially. By 1991 nearly a quarter of all families with children under 18 were headed by women, up from 15% in 1974. Among blacks the percentage rose even more, from 33% to 58%.

Moreover, these hard-pressed mothers are not just working when it's convenient. By 1990 nearly 40% had full-time jobs, an increase of 10 percentage points in just 10 years. And, not surprisingly, divorced mothers — even those with children under six — are far more likely to work full-time than are married ones. In 1990 about 54% of them did, compared to only 38% of the married.

What kind of reception has society given its newly working moms? Like all working women, on average they bring home a paycheck about 30% less than that of men. This is frustrating enough for moms in two-parent families; for single mothers (especially the never married), it's often disastrous. On average, they struggle along on an income less than a third that of the average two-parent family ($13,000 vs. $42,500). Almost half of these families live in poverty.

While the 1980s brought some improvement in women's pay, they also brought a marked deterioration in their health-plan coverage (and in men's). In 1980 about 68% of the women working full-time and 18% of the part-timers had employer- or union-sponsored health insurance. In just the next seven years, those percentages fell to 63% and 15%, respectively. Moreover, even women with workplace health insurance increasingly found themselves paying part of the premiums.

As for essential benefits like maternity leave and child-care assistance, very few mothers as yet enjoy them. Only a small number of even medium- and large-size U.S. firms provide family leave: in 1989 just 3% offered paid maternity leave, though the 1992 Family Leave Act now requires unpaid leave. The picture regarding child care is just as dismal. In 1987 fewer than 5% of all private employers provided any direct form of such assistance (see table).

Overall, government is doing only slightly better than the private sector:

• About 12% of all federal and state government employers offer some form of child-care assistance.

• The governments of most large industrial countries have mandated family leave with pay for all public- and private-sector workers. The U.S. law calls only for unpaid leave.

• In 1990 the federal government enacted a bill appropriating $2.5 billion over three years to the states to help them subsidize child care.

• The federal government now offers parents $4 billion worth of tax credits annually for child care. However, a third of that sum goes to families with annual incomes over $50,000, and only 10% to 15% to those with incomes under $15,000.

What about the future? Working moms can only hope President Clinton means to keep his campaign promises about jobs and health insurance.

Resources: Paula Ries & Anne Stone, eds. (for the Women's Research and Education Institute), *The American Woman 1992-1993: A Status Report.*

EMPLOYERS WHO PROVIDE CHILD-CARE BENEFITS, 1987
(in percentages)

	Private Sector	Government
Employer-sponsored day care	1.6%	9.4%
Assistance with expenses	3.1	2.9
Information or referral services	4.3	15.8
Flextime	43.6	37.5
Voluntary part-time work	35.3	26.7
Flexible leave time	42.9	43.7
Number of employers	1,128,000	74,000

April 1992, revised March 1994

SPIRALING DOWN
THE FALL OF REAL WAGES

Do you feel like you have less money in your pocket than 5, 10, 20 years ago? Yes? Well, you aren't alone. Since reaching their peak in 1973, real wages have fallen a dramatic 21%. In fact, wages are no better than they were in 1958, over 35 years ago.

Future paychecks may not improve either. If the 1990s recovery looks anything like the 1980s, wages will not boost most Americans' standard of living. Even when the economy has grown, workers' paychecks have not grown with it.

Real wages are measured by average gross weekly earnings, corrected for inflation. They include the money paid to production and non-supervisory workers in the private sector, approximately four-fifths of all those employed. (Excluded from this measure are agricultural and public-sector employees.) Real wage figures do not include the earnings of professional workers and managers, usually called salaried personnel.

The graph below depicts the changes in workers' purchasing power by comparing real wages from 1955 to 1993. Prior to 1973, economic growth and improving real wages moved together. From 1955 to 1973, the heart of the post-World War II boom, real wages rose almost every year. They didn't rise in 1958, the only sharp recession of the early post-war years.

After 1973, real wages plummeted beginning with the stagflation recession of 1974-75, that not only put the kibosh on workers' wages but also brought higher prices too.

A rather long but sluggish expansion during the late 1970s restored some of the purchasing power workers had lost to stagflation. But by 1978, a growing economy no longer improved workers' wages.

On the heels of that sluggish expansion came the double-dip recession from 1979 to 1982, the worst contraction since the Great Depression. Double-digit official unemployment rates and anti-worker corporate and public policy robbed workers of their bargaining power, and real wages fell sharply to only 85% of their 1973 peak.

When the recession ended, for the first time since World War II the slide in real wages did not end as well. By the end of the 1980s expansion, workers' wages had slid to less than they had been in 1982. How did this happen? When the economy grew quickly during 1983 and 1984, real wages improved. But as growth slowed, wages declined in all but one of the subsequent years of the Reagan-Bush administrations.

What this graph doesn't show is how falling real wages squeeze families. Americans have coped by working more hours and taking on second jobs. More family members are working. In part to keep family incomes from plummeting, women have joined the work force in increasing numbers. Compared with 20 years ago, women work considerably more hours per week and more weeks per year. Even the exit of women from the labor force during childbearing years has dropped off sharply. Women bear fewer children and return to paid work when their children are still young to keep the extra paycheck coming.

The history of wages over the last 30 years bodes ill for the 1990s. Families that can't boost their income with the help of a second or third wage-earner are likely to fall further behind.

Sources: Economic Report of the President 1994, Table B-45; Council of Economic Advisors and Joint Economic Committee, Economic Indicators.

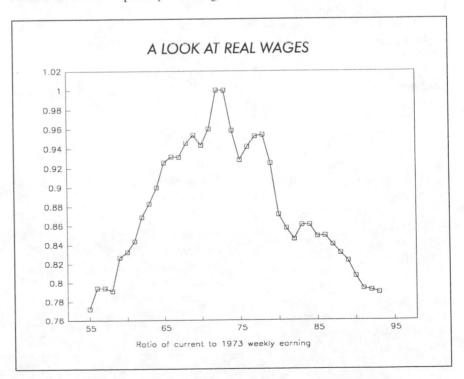

A LOOK AT REAL WAGES

Ratio of current to 1973 weekly earning

July/August 1992

U.S. AMONG WORST IN INEQUALITY

Among 21 top industrialized countries, only Australia has a higher rate of income inequality than the United States, according to recently published figures from the United Nations Development Programme (UNDP).

For 21 countries that had the highest rankings on the UNDP's "Human Development Index," a measure of social and economic well-being, the United States finished next to worst by two measures:

• The richest 20% of U.S. households make about 10 times as much as the poorest 20%.

• The poorest 40% of U.S. households earn only 16% of national income.

Former Eastern Bloc nations Hungary and Poland performed best on equality, but such capitalist powerhouses as Japan and Germany were also far more egalitarian than the United States. The gap between the top and bottom Japanese households was less than half as wide as in the United States. The lowest 40% of Japanese households received about one-third more of the national income than the same group here.

The data shown in the table must be regarded with some caution. They are for varying years between 1980-88 depending on the country, and the quality of the data varies from one nation to another.

The gap between rich and poor Americans is not only large, it's also growing. Between 1983 and 1989, according to U.S. government sources, the share of total wealth owned by the top one-half of one percent (0.5%) of U.S. households increased from 24% to 29%.

Lower earnings among workers go a long way toward explaining income inequality. According to the Census Bureau, between 1979 and 1989, the percent of full-time, year-round employees earning "low wages," defined as less than $12,195 a year, increased from 12% to 18% of the total work force.

The rise in the proportion of low-wage workers took place mainly among men, whose percent rose from 13% to 18%. Rates for women were much higher than for men in both years but stayed relatively constant, varying from 29% in 1979 to 30% in 1989. The percentage earning low wages rose substantially for Latinos, from 30% to 37%, and for whites, from 11% to 16%, but stayed approximately constant for African-Americans, going from 30.5% to 31.0%.

One popular explanation among mainstream economists for wage rates is worker productivity. Yet, at least in manufacturing, productivity trends fail to explain what has happened to U.S. wages in recent years. According to a study by Andrew Sum of Northeastern University, from 1979 through 1989 real hourly earnings for manufacturing workers fell by 8.3%, despite growth in output per hour of 26.3%. This contrasts sharply with the three previous decades. Productivity rose by around 30% a decade from the 1950s through the 1970s. In the 1950s wage gains were slightly greater than productivity increases, but in the 1960s wages rose by only half as much as productivity. And in the 1970s wages rose only 6.1%.

Resources: United Nations Development Programme, *Human Development Report*, 1992; U.S. Bureau of the Census, "Workers with Low Earnings: 1964-1990," May 1992; *Business Week*, "Would the Economy Gain From Spreading Inherited Wealth?" May 18, 1992; Andrew Sum, "Broken Promises: Rising Labor Productivity in Manufacturing and the Decline in the Real Earnings of Production Workers Over the 1979-1989 Period," Northeastern University Center for Labor Market Studies, 1992.

RANKINGS OF INCOME INEQUALITY
For industrialized nations, 1980-1988

	Ratio of highest 20% to lowest 20%	Income share of lowest 40%
Hungary	3.0	26.2
Poland	3.6	23.9
Japan	4.3	21.9
Sweden	4.6	21.2
Belgium	4.6	21.6
Netherlands	5.6	20.1
Germany*	5.7	19.5
Spain	5.8	19.4
Norway	5.9	19.0
Finland	6.0	18.4
Italy	6.0	18.8
France	6.5	18.4
Israel	6.6	18.1
United Kingdom	6.8	17.3
Yugoslavia	7.0	17.1
Canada	7.1	17.5
Denmark	7.1	17.4
Switzerland	8.6	16.9
New Zealand	8.8	15.9
United States	8.9	15.7
Australia	9.6	15.5

*Former East Germany not included.

November/December 1993

GENERATING AFFLUENCE

PRODUCTIVITY GAINS
REQUIRE WORKER SUPPORT

BY DAVID M. GORDON

For more than 25 years the U.S. economy's productivity performance has been dismal. Reversing this record is essential to improving the wages and working conditions of American workers.

The Clinton administration has appeared to grasp the magnitude of the problem. "Increasing productivity growth will have a direct and positive impact on living standards," declared the White House in its original economic program, *A Vision of Change for America*. "We simply must do better." But Clinton's analysis of the productivity problem is incomplete. His initial program focuses primarily on machines and skills — on the technical components of production. So far he has paid little attention to the concerns and struggles and incentives of the workers whose labor is essential for production.

In order to revive productivity growth in the United States we must analyze all the sources of its stagnation. We must pay attention not merely to machines and bridges and training, but also to the people and institutions which make production happen.

WHY DOES PRODUCTIVITY GROWTH MATTER?

Much of our economic welfare depends on the rate of productivity growth. Labor productivity measures an econo-my's output per hour of labor input. Productivity growth measures the change in an economy's hourly output from one year to the next.

If the pace of productivity growth increases, firms can produce the same output with fewer hours of work. This makes it possible for companies to raise wages without increasing their prices and undermining their competitive positions. More rapid growth also makes it possible for people to take advantage of the lower labor-time requirement by increasing their leisure time.

Many workers and trade unionists, however, fear that productivity growth will threaten their jobs. But this does not have to be the case. For example, unions can negotiate to turn some of the dividends from enhanced productivity into reducing the average workweek from, say, 40 to 35 hours. If each worker puts in fewer hours, then employment levels can remain high. Or, if productivity growth contributes to improved competitiveness of U.S. firms, net exports may increase. This in turn could generate higher output, potentially enhancing employment despite greater output per hour.

Fears of productivity growth are likely to be acute in economies like the United States where workers, if they have any job security at all, have it only in their current job but lack any more general promises of employment. If automation boosts productivity and thereby eliminates specific jobs, the workers holding those jobs have no guarantee that they will find other work in the same firm or anywhere else in the economy.

In Japan and many European economies, by contrast, workers' security is more likely to be tied to employment in general, not to a specific job. As a result, workers have often cooperated in promoting more rapid productivity growth because of the prospects for enhanced earnings and leisure time.

SLUGGISH U.S. PRODUCTIVITY

Recent history leaves little doubt about the sluggishness of productivity growth in the United States and the seriousness of the problems our economy currently faces. During the long boom period from the late 1940s through the mid-1960s, the growth rate of hourly output in nonfarm businesses averaged 2.6% a year. In the next business cycle, from 1966 to 1973, output growth slowed to 1.8% a year. It then plummeted to 0.6% a year from 1973 to 79.

One major symptom of failure during the Reagan-Bush era was that productivity growth remained sluggish, scarcely increasing to only 1.0% a year during the 1979-1989 business cycle. Productivity growth during the 1980s remained stuck at a pace less than two-fifths as rapid as during the 1948-1965 boom.

Recent U.S. productivity performance also pales in comparison to the major competing economies. As Figure 1 shows, among the seven major advanced economies during the 1980s, overall productivity growth in the United States ranked dead last. It averaged one-third the pace in Japan and only three-fifths the average of the remaining

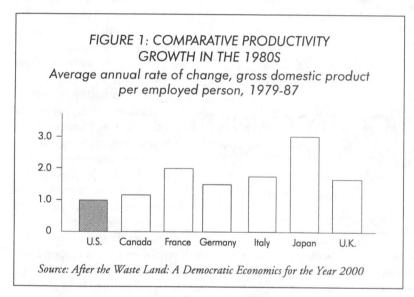

FIGURE 1: COMPARATIVE PRODUCTIVITY GROWTH IN THE 1980S

Average annual rate of change, gross domestic product per employed person, 1979-87

Source: *After the Waste Land: A Democratic Economics for the Year 2000*

five. This sluggish relative performance contributed to declining U.S. competitiveness on international markets.

THE VIEW FROM THE WHITE HOUSE

For the Clinton administration, the productivity problem is primarily an "investment problem." We have not contributed enough resources, they argue, to building up the skills, technology and infrastructure necessary to sustain more rapid productivity improvements.

"The slowdown in productivity growth is partly mysterious," Clinton's *Vision* document concludes. "But no one doubts that part of the cause is that as a nation we have underinvested: in private business capital, in public capital, and in 'human capital' — the skills and capabilities of the American workforce."

This leads to Clinton's emphasis on substantial new "investments" to improve the economy's performance. "More investment is vital to raising the growth rate of productivity and boosting living standards," the White House insists. "We must invest more in business capital, in public infrastructure, and in the skills of our people....The

Clinton program will do precisely that."

This commitment led to proposals in the original program for a cumulative total of $144 billion in "new investment" outlays over the 1994-98 period. These investment proposals spanned a broad spectrum of initiatives in transportation, environmental protection and conservation, energy development, community development and defense conversion, revitalizing technology, and "lifelong" skills training.

MORE THAN MACHINES

Clinton's analysis is useful, but it does not go nearly far enough. It views production as a technical process, with skills, machines, and supporting capital mechanically combining to produce final output. Production is fundamentally a social process, however, not a technical one. How people relate to each other and their bosses in production influences productivity at least as much as how many skills they have acquired or how many machines they can mobilize.

This leads us inevitably to basic questions of labor-management relations. How much power do managers and supervisors wield over workers and how do they wield it? What role do labor unions play either in promoting cooperation or in insulating workers from conflict? Are workers slaves to the division of labor, monotonously fulfilling the same boring task day in and day out — or are they encouraged to develop and apply a continually expanding set of productive skills? Are workers subject to the capricious decisions of their bosses about job security, promotion and benefits, or do they have some basic rights which cannot be violated without just cause and due process?

Once we look at these dimensions of production, it becomes clear that U.S. workers suffer from an archaic system of labor-management relations. Workers are goaded in the United States with the stick, not the carrot. Millions have little or no employment security — threatened with layoffs, downsizing, or outright job dismissal for inadequate performance. Fewer and fewer workers share the "voice" provided by union representation.

These heavy-handed worker-management techniques in the United States are out-of-date. Many other successful advanced economies are more likely to stimulate their workers with the carrot, seeking cooperation rather than conquest.

One recent study of the seven largest advanced economies, by Robert Buchele and Jens Christiansen, provides a vivid illustration. It develops two indices of the degree to which working conditions support workers in production. One index, of worker cooperation, includes such features as profit-sharing to encourage worker involvement. The second index is of workers' rights — such as union representation rates and protection against layoffs. Japan scores highest on the worker cooperation index, with Germany highest on worker rights. The United States comes in last on both. And, as Figure 1 shows, the United States is last in productivity growth as well.

Also important is the bureaucratic burden imposed by archaic production relations in most U.S. corporations. By the late 1980s, corporate bureaucracies had assumed gargantuan proportions in the United Sates. As Figure 2 shows, the proportion of total civilian employment in managerial or administrative occupations had reached more than 12% in the United States by 1987, at least three times as high as in Germany, Japan, or Sweden.

This massive spending on corporate bureaucrats matters for productivity growth since it goes hand in hand with the lack of worker cooperation and worker rights. When worker-management relations rely on the stick, corporations require battalions of stick-wielders. If U.S. corporations rewarded their workers rather than clubbing them, millions of bureaucrats could eventually be freed for more productive tasks.

Some managerial cutbacks have finally begun to occur in the past couple of years, but they appear to be a defensive and haphazard reaction to mounting competitive pressure, rather than a systematic effort to transfer leverage and influence to production employees.

CHANGING THE U.S. WORKPLACE

This analysis suggests that we need much more than investments in equipment, skills, and infrastructure to revive productivity growth in the United States. We also need to scrap our outmoded labor-management relations and invest in dramatically new systems appropriate for the 21st century. What changes should we pursue?

In order to commit themselves to enhancing their firms' performance, U.S. workers need dramatically expanded rights: They should enjoy greater ease and less risk in forming trade unions to protect their interests. This would occur, for example, if union representation were automatically certified once a minimum of, say, 55% of employees in the bargaining unit sign union cards — rather than enduring the contentious, expensive, and typically unfair elections currently required in the United States. They need enhanced protection against arbitrary dismissal or plant shutdown, as could be partially provided by requirements for advance notice of any plans for shutdowns or mass layoffs. They also urgently require access to a decent and enforced federal minimum wage; universal health care benefits they can carry to another job; and expanded rights to vacation time and other key fringe benefits.

We also need mechanisms to provide workers greater voice in production: through expanded worker participation, and direct worker influence over critical management decisions.

In its rhetoric, the Clinton administration sometimes acknowledges such imperatives for a more productive U.S. economy. Secretary of Labor Robert Reich, for example, has written frequently about the need for greater worker involvement in production.

But so far, Clinton's attention to these dimensions of workplace transformation have amounted to little more than towel-waving and cheerleading. At a major Clinton conference on the Future of the American Workplace in July 1993, for example, administration spokespeople pointed to promising examples of visionary corporations which had improved their competitiveness by involving their workers. But they said nothing about the kinds of policy changes which would be necessary to push the less "visionary" to follow these examples.

More than cheerleading will be necessary. As long as there are so many workers in the United States who have no alternatives to low-wage, low-benefits, low-skill, low-rights, and high-insecurity jobs, then U.S. corporations will continue to take advantage of these pools of inexpensive workers by goading them with the stick, not the carrot. We need to eliminate the option for corporate recourse to 19th-century work practices before we can build a 21st-century production system. Without such pressure, the administration's "new investments" in machines, skills and infrastructure may have little success in reviving U.S. productivity performance, or improving working conditions and living standards.

Resources: "Industrial relations and productivity growth: a comparative perspective," Robert Buchele and Jens Christiansen, *International Contributions to Labour Studies, 1992; After the Waste Land: A Democratic Economics for the Year 2000,* Samuel Bowles, David M. Gordon, and Thomas E. Weisskopf, 1990.

> PRODUCTION IS FUNDAMENTALLY A SOCIAL PROCESS, NOT A TECHNICAL ONE.

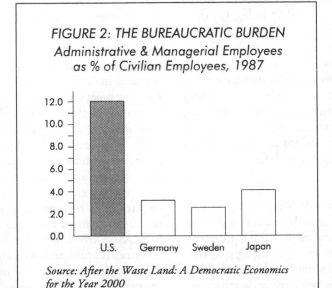

FIGURE 2: THE BUREAUCRATIC BURDEN
Administrative & Managerial Employees as % of Civilian Employees, 1987

Source: After the Waste Land: A Democratic Economics for the Year 2000

BOOSTING INVESTMENT

THE OVERRATED INFLUENCE OF INTEREST RATES

BY GRETCHEN MCCLAIN AND RANDY ALBELDA

Imagine for a moment that you have been voted in as the president of a large country. Also assume that your country has sluggish growth, a shrinking pool of high wage jobs, and that a decreasing proportion of its physical assets is being replaced with new plant and equipment (i.e., buildings and machinery). What would you do to secure the long-term economic health of your country and the majority of its citizens?

Politicians, the media and mainstream economists have a remarkably simple answer: reduce the deficit. They argue that U.S. government borrowing reduces the pool of available credit and therefore pushes up long-term interest rates. These higher rates, as they see it, crowd out private investment. Get rid of the deficit and interest rates will fall, causing investment to flourish.

The Economic Policy Institute, a progressive Washington think tank, has released a report by economist Steven Fazzari that shoots this argument full of holes. Of three possible determinants of investment — interest rates, sales growth, and how much cash a firm has on hand — Fazzari finds that interest rates have the weakest impact.

The policy implications of this assertion are profound. If Fazzari is right, the most important types of fiscal policy that the current administration can pursue to promote private investment in new plant and equipment will be those that directly increase demand for products and services, not those that aim to reduce the deficit.

WHY INVEST?

Few economists or politicians would disagree that an economy's prospects for long term growth depend on the productive capacity of its people and its physical equipment. But what to invest in — and how to get the appropriate economic actors to invest — is a matter of much debate.

All economies face a choice between using their productive resources to produce goods and services to be consumed now, and forsaking today's consumption to produce more goods for the future. While catering to consumption today may be more satisfying for wealthier countries and absolutely vital for poor countries, it fails to provide for future growth.

Investing in new plant and equipment can stimulate growth over time, as it provides the physical capacity for new production. Moreover, new plant and equipment tend to be better designed than the existing capital stock, and the improvement usually helps to boost output per worker. If this new productivity translates into higher wages, investment can also increase a country's standard of living and improve employment possibilities. In turn, improving human productive capacity — through training and education — can lead to growth and increased productivity in the long run.

Investment, and the consequent increase in productivity, is critical for international economic success. The more efficiently a country can produce a product, the more competitive that country will be in the world market. Since international markets provide an avenue of demand for our goods, the more domestically produced products and services we can sell abroad, the more jobs we can support here.

Investment can also help stimulate the economy in the short run. During an economic downturn, increased investment will yield more jobs and income for workers who would otherwise be unemployed. They will then return their income to the market when they purchase goods and services, which will boost demand for those products. Economists call this the "multiplier effect." The increase in demand in turn encourages firms to invest more so that they can meet that demand — known to economists as the "accelerator effect." All in all, such a cycle creates more jobs, income, and spending.

While few economists dispute the importance of investment, many disagree on what type is needed, which sectors of the economy are best able to provide it, and what the best ways to encourage investment are. Typically, these debates have revolved around the government's role in encouraging private investment in new plant and equipment. Recently, a focus on the role that public investment in infrastructure and education plays in promoting not only our economic well-being and growth, but also in encouraging private investment, has widened the terms of the debate.

THE BACKDROP

The traditional economic argument about investment — and the prevailing conservative line espoused by elected officials at the federal level — has been that the most important fiscal policies to encourage privately-owned firms to invest are those which boost profits. If the government helps provide the conditions for profitability, the argument goes, firms will be encouraged to make the right types of investment.

Government tax and spend policies designed to promote investment over the last decade and a half have tried to boost profits by reducing corporate taxes and by stimulating savings. Such measures were supposed to leave firms with a bigger bottom line, in the hope that they would turn profits into new plant and equipment. Cuts in personal income tax rates — especially for the wealthiest — were intended to leave people with more after-tax income that they could save. Higher savings, says this supply-side logic, translates into lower interest rates which in turn lead to more investment. While these policies were very effective in redistributing money from the poor to the wealthy, they did not do much for investment. The amount of new fixed investment (i.e., new plant and equipment) relative to the total amount of plant and equipment sank to its lowest post-WWII mark between 1989 and 1991.

Merely providing the conditions for profit-making does not mean that private firms will plough those profits back into new plant and equipment. Speculation on real estate markets, the value of foreign currencies, or the price of silver and gold could easily eat up new profits. Much of the money generated for investment in the 1980s financed mergers and acquisitions, which generally resulted in less employment and little new physical productive capacity. And, perhaps even more important, new investment by U.S. firms may not take place in the United States. Investing abroad has been the trend since the 1970s. Finally, even if there is domestic investment and it increases productivity, unless workers share in those gains it may not promote robust growth or increase the standard of living of the country as a whole.

In the face of the failure of the past decade's policies to promote investment, conservatives have come up with a new explanation of why the economy is so sluggish: the deficit. Ironically, the conservative policies mentioned above are largely responsible for the $4.4 trillion public debt, but nonetheless Republicans, along with many Democrats galvanized by billionaire Ross Perot, have latched onto deficit reduction as the most important fiscal policy of the 1990s.

The deficit, argue people like Senate Republican leader Bob Dole and Treasury Secretary Lloyd Bentsen, has been keeping long term interest rates high because it creates competition for precious funds. The result is that federal borrowing, necessitated by debt-financed government spending and tax cuts, has been "crowding out" private investment. The best solution, they say, is to reduce the deficit and bring down long-term interest rates so that private investment will thrive.

IDENTIFYING INFLUENCE

Fazzari tackles their assumptions in his study of the influence of the federal government's taxing and spending policies on private investment. Using a rather large data base from Standard and Poor's on over 5,000 manufacturing firms from 1971-1990, Fazzari tested three different factors for their effects on levels of investment in plant and equipment: interest rates, the business cycle, and the financial conditions of the firms.

According to Fazzari, these three "channels of influence" shape patterns of investment. First, he takes on the traditionalists, by addressing the costs associated with investment: the price of borrowing money (i.e., interest rates), depreciation (how fast the new piece of equipment or building will lose its value), and taxes affecting both corporate profits and dividends. To measure this channel, Fazzari employs the interest rate on one type of corporate bond.

Next, he considers the influence of the business cycle by looking at sales growth. Traditional economic theory tends to assume a ready market, but Fazzari suggests instead that firms may make investment decisions based on their perception of their ability to sell their products. The more robust current sales are and are expected to be, the more likely firms will be willing to risk new investment — regardless of the interest rate. Since the general condition of the economy influences sales levels, it also has an impact on investment.

In Fazzari's examination of the third channel of influence — the financial condition of firms — he again questions conventional wisdom, this time about the supply and demand for loans. Most economists assume that if the

IN THE FACE OF THE FAILURE OF THE PAST DECADE'S POLICIES TO PROMOTE INVESTMENT, CONSERVATIVES HAVE COME UP WITH A NEW EXPLANATION OF WHY THE ECONOMY IS SO SLUGGISH: THE DEFICIT.

expected return on an investment exceeds the interest rate, then the project is profitable and will be undertaken. This is most likely to be true when the firm in question has enough cash on hand from prior profits to make the investment without asking a bank for a loan. Many firms, though, need to borrow money, and some are unable to persuade banks to loan it to them. Banks often refuse loan applications from new businesses with few assets, or charge them prohibitively high interest rates. Even if a young firm finds a potentially profitable investment, severe constraints on raising capital may prevent the firm from pursuing it. A firm's financial condition—not the projected rate of return on the new investment — can thus end up determining whether or not investment takes place.

> CONCERNS ABOUT INVESTMENT SHOULD NOT STAND IN THE WAY OF POLICY INITIATIVES THAT ARE IMPORTANT FOR SOCIETY, SIMPLY BECAUSE THEY MAY CAUSE INTEREST RATES TO RISE.

PERFECTING POLICY

After looking at the importance of interest rates, the business cycle, and the financial conditions of firms in determining investment, Fazzari found that interest rates exert the weakest influence of the three factors. He concludes that there is no evidence that interest rates significantly affect investment for the fastest growing firms in his sample. Based on these findings, Fazzari claims "it would be speculative to base policy on the assumption that interest rates drive investment to an important extent, especially for growing firms."

So, what kinds of fiscal policies should we adopt? If we believe Fazzari's results, we should be looking for those that attend to the financial conditions of firms and stimulate demand for products. The worst fiscal policies for generating investment would take money out of the economy — like deficit reduction. The negative effect of such policies, he contends, would likely outweigh any boost to investment that might result from lower interest rates.

Though long gone the way of the campaign trail, Clinton's "middle class tax cut" would probably have given investment at least a temporary boost by generating increased consumption. Increased sales from a temporary tax cut create the illusion of a permanent increase in demand, and the multiplier and accelerator effects discussed earlier come into play. In order to meet what firms believe is a permanent increase in demand for their goods, they make investments in more equipment, more factories, and more employees.

Another means of encouraging investment that Fazzari evaluates is cutting corporate income taxes. Such cuts increase firms' after-tax profits, leaving them with a larger pool of funds to invest if they so choose. Since there is no guarantee that they will invest the savings from reduced taxes, though, Fazzari prefers investment tax credits (ITCs) to cuts in taxes for all firms. Only if firms invested would they be able to reduce their corporate tax bills. In Fazzari's view, ITCs will effectively encourage investment whether it is sensitive to interest rates or not.

The most important lesson from Fazzari's analysis is that concerns about investment should not stand in the way of policy initiatives that are important for society, such as spending on education and job training, simply because they may increase the federal budget deficit and cause interest rates to rise. Government investments in public works and education will likely increase productivity in the long run, and this can only be good for investment. Moreover, if investment is not sensitive to interest rates, then the deficit's much-discussed "crowding out" effect on private business is bound to be very small. And as Fazzari points out, if unemployment is high, the stimulative effects of deficit spending on sales may far outweigh the impacts of the rising interest rates.

Clinton's focus on the goal of deficit reduction should be tempered by a thorough analysis of what his policy implies for society's immediate and long-term welfare. When we underinvest in the economy during a recession by eliminating educational and social investments, the foregone technical innovation resulting from this underinvestment may lead to less efficient workers, and lower productivity, for many years.

Fazzari's results not only repudiate the traditional answer to lagging investment — tax cuts for the wealthy and the lowering of interest rates — they also suggest that the current preoccupation with lowering the deficit is completely misguided. Instead, the government should be trying to stimulate the economy, which will boost not only sales but investment and incomes.

PUBLIC CAPITAL, PRIVATE PROFITS

PUBLIC INVESTMENT BENEFITS BUSINESS

BY CATHERINE LYNDE

Lower taxes, reduced government spending, and less government intervention in the economy have been the rallying cries of U.S. business interests for more than a decade now. They have achieved concrete successes in all of these areas, helping firms reduce costs and thus maintain profitability in the highly competitive, low-growth U.S. economy of the 1980s.

But beware of unintended consequences. Over the longer term, business may be shooting itself in the foot by taking a hard line against government taxing and spending policies. Recent studies find a connection between the decline in U.S. profits during the 1970s and early 1980s and a similar decline in public spending on the economy's infrastructure — roads, sewers, bridges, and other public works.

This relationship between private profits and public investment suggests that a blanket attack on all government spending may backfire. If the stock of public capital is not adequately maintained, it may become increasingly difficult for private businesses to sustain their profitability.

Contrary to popular notions, many government expenditures bolster and maintain the profitability of private investment. Public infrastructure investments make it easier for businesses to operate profitably by providing useful resources or services that individual firms would find difficult to

finance themselves. For example, public expenditures on interstate highways reduce transportation time and costs for firms; public power plants reduce energy costs; flood-control projects improve the profitability of agricultural production; and public transit systems allow workers to reach central-city jobs.

Alternatively, when highways deteriorate, truck maintenance costs rise. When public transit systems are not maintained, workers may frequently arrive on the job late or look for jobs closer to home. Deteriorating public schools will have an impact in the future when businesses can't find educated workers.

Since the 1970s, the stock of public capital has been growing at slower and slower rates. The government-owned non-military fixed capital stock (which includes roads, buildings, bridges, subways, etc.) grew by an average of 4% annually before 1970, but has averaged only 1% since 1981 (see graph). As a consequence, the value of government-owned capital as a percentage of the gross national product (GNP) fell from 66% in 1964 to 51% by 1985.

Meanwhile, U.S. profit rates began a pronounced slide in the early 1970s, after rising through much of the 1950s and 1960s. Net rates of return to business (taking depreciation into account) have fallen from an average annual rate of 11.5% during the 1950s and 1960s to 8.2% since then (see graph). Attempting to explain the decline of profits in

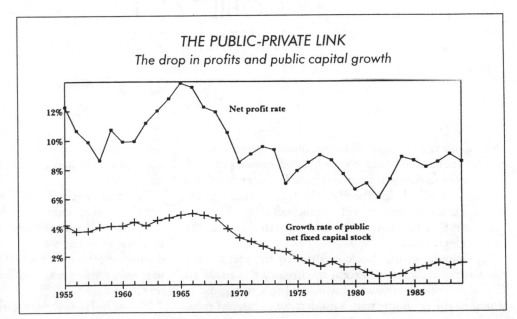

THE PUBLIC-PRIVATE LINK
The drop in profits and public capital growth

Net profit rate

Growth rate of public
net fixed capital stock

the United States, economists point to numerous factors that have influenced business profitability: increased international competition, the oil price shocks of the 1970s, high interest rates, and inflation. Most agree that government spending and taxing policies have also affected private profitability.

The recent studies, such as one by the new Assistant U.S. Treasury Secretary, Alicia Munnell, attempt to quantify the relationship between private profit rates and public-sector investment. When public capital and private profit growth rates are compared, it becomes clear that the two statistics have declined in tandem. One study finds that a 1% annual increase in the public's net capital stock corresponds to a 2.2% annual increase in net private profit rates. This suggests that an extra $20 billion expenditure in 1989 — only 2% of yearly government purchases — would have raised net profit rates from 8.5% to 8.8%. That might not seem significant enough to lead capitalists to agitate for higher public spending on roads and schools, but add $20 billion over a few years and profit rates grow noticeably. For example, a five-year impact would add about one full percentage point, driving up net profit rates to 9.5% in 1989.

Declining profit rates over the last 15 years have put businesses in a serious bind, and cutting costs is one way to keep profits up. Successful recent attempts to shore up profits by cutting wages, taxes, and environmental controls are all too familiar. And capitalists have cut costs in another way — through "deferred maintenance" on their own plant and equipment. As a result, the private capital stock is depreciating at a faster rate now than it was in the 1960s.

Similarly, in their attempt to maintain profit rates, businesses have been forced to support policies that reduce public capital, thereby hurting profitability over the long term. They face the contradiction that if they don't earn enough profits in the short run, they won't be in business to care about earning profits in the long run.

Resources: D.A. Aschauer, "Government Spending and the Falling Rate of Profit," *Economic Perspectives,* May/June 1988; C. Lynde, "Private Profit and Public Capital," *Journal of Macroeconomics,* Winter, 1992; A. Munnell, "Is There A Shortfall in Public Capital Investment?," *New England Economic Review,* May/June 1991.

March 1991

FOOTLOOSE & COUNTRY FREE

MOBILITY IS KEY TO CAPITALISTS' POWER

BY RON KWAN

During last fall's budget crisis, speculation raged over foreigners' increasing leverage over U.S. economic policy. A previously intransigent President Bush had abandoned his "no new taxes" pledge shortly after U.S. representatives signed a trade agreement with Japanese officials. The pact called on the administration to take steps to eliminate the U.S. budget deficit.

For Canada's central bank, events early last year left less room for speculation — except by currency traders. With Canada's economy slowing down, the bank attempted to stimulate the economy with a modest cut in interest rates.

But the wealthy, seeking higher returns, began selling their Canadian investments and their Canadian dollars. The currency's value dropped three cents within a matter of days. To halt the capital flight, the central bank had to raise interest rates well above their previous levels, stifling consumer spending and business investment in plant and equipment. Canada fell quickly into a recession. By December, unemployment had risen more than two percentage points to over 9%.

Have the U.S. and Canadian governments lost the autonomy to determine their own monetary and fiscal policies? To some extent, yes. Does Japan now rule? No, capital rules.

Owners of capital have always been able to move their wealth across national boundaries, but they can now do so more freely than at any time since the end of World War II. This internationalization of capital markets and production increasingly constrains all governments, including those accustomed to calling their own shots on the international scene.

It also hurts ordinary citizens in more direct ways.

Workers are pressured to accept lower wages or lose their jobs, as capitalists seek more favorable conditions elsewhere. Their communities are robbed of income, and their local governments are deprived of an adequate tax base. And taxpayers everywhere are left to foot the bill as transnational corporations (TNCs) use their global reach to shelter their profits.

While workers, communities, and government officials most commonly direct their wrath at foreign capitalists, particularly those from Japan, investors' nationality is not the most pressing issue facing U.S. communities or policymakers. Despite significant national differences in corporate styles and structures, capitalists tend to behave similarly regardless of their country of origin. German, Japanese, and British capitalists are generally just as anti-union when operating factories in the United States as their U.S. counterparts. And they are just as quick to sell off any government's bonds if the interest rate dips. All want the highest possible profits wherever they are, or wherever they have to go.

As capitalists gain greater power to go wherever they please, the key issue facing people in all countries is how to control capital to make it work for the whole population.

AGILE, MOBILE, AND HOSTILE

Since the 1960s, capital increasingly has flowed across borders. The movement of capital has jumped dramatically, both as diversified purchases of stocks and bonds known as portfolio investment and as direct investment— controlling interest in physical assets like factories and real estate.

In 1970, U.S. citizens owned $166 billion in assets abroad (both portfolio and direct investment). By 1988 this had risen to $1,254 billion, an increase from 16% to 26% of the value of the U.S. gross national product. Foreigners, meanwhile, increased their ownership of U.S. assets from $107 billion in 1970 to $1,786 billion in 1988, a jump from 11% of U.S. GNP to 37%.

This globalization of capital makes it very difficult to even define capital's nationality. For example, with competition from other industrialized countries, exporters producing in the United States have lost much of their clout. But international companies headquartered in the United States have suffered no competitive decline at all. While the share of world manufactured exports produced in the United States dropped from 17.1% in 1966 to 13.4% in 1985, U.S. corporations' share increased from 17.3% to 18.3%. They hadn't lost business; they had simply shifted much of their production to their subsidiaries in other countries. With U.S. corporations producing less and less in the United States, the gap between their interests and the interests of the U.S. people are now more glaring than ever.

Why has capital become so footloose? Most simply, the U.S.-dominated postwar capitalist economy gave way to a more pluralistic world order, with other capital centers and other significant markets. The economies of Japan and the European countries regained their prewar strength, and newly industrialized countries like South Korea and Brazil began to compete in international markets. Capital began to surge across national boundaries seeking new markets and profits.

Perhaps the most commonly heard explanation for the increase in capitalists' freedom of movement is technological change. While technology's impact is often overstated, satellite communications permit portfolio investors in global financial markets to trade around the clock, making it almost as easy for a U.S. investor to trade German as U.S. bonds. This has increased the overall mobility of financial capital and permitted the rapid transmission of market crashes like the one in October 1987.

More important, faster and cheaper communications and transportation have allowed owners of TNCs to more closely control their direct investments in their far-flung foreign affiliates, enhancing their power. Lower transportation costs, combined with lower tariffs, have made it profitable for corporations to produce further from the products' ultimate destination. This permits them to shift or threaten to shift production when local labor unions or government officials act contrary to the company's interests.

Still, technology only facilitates capital mobility; it doesn't cause it. One of the most overlooked reasons for the increase in capitalists' freedom to move their wealth is the political dominance of international capitalists, who have used their power to implement free-market policies around the world.

> AS CAPITALISTS GAIN GREATER POWER TO GO WHERE THEY PLEASE, THE KEY ISSUE FACING PEOPLE IN ALL COUNTRIES IS HOW TO CONTROL CAPITAL TO MAKE IT WORK FOR THE WHOLE POPULATION.

DECONTROLLING CAPITAL

Since World War II, governments have reduced or repealed much of the legislation designed to control capitalists' actions. At the end of the war, most countries had substantial restrictions on the movement of capital across borders, for conducting trade, to make investments, or simply to hold foreign currencies. While dominant U.S. financiers and large corporations favored unrestricted capital movement, weakened European capitalists sought to protect themselves from U.S. domination with a variety of policies designed to limit capital mobility. (See box.)

Such controls had a macroeconomic rationale as well.

They allowed progressive governments the autonomy to pursue full-employment policies and set appropriate interest rates free of the fear that the wealthy would take their capital abroad.

As large Japanese and European corporations recovered from the war, they sought to expand their investments beyond their own borders, and the alliance between domestic capitalists and advocates of progressive economic and social policies broke down. By the late 1970s, governments began to fully deregulate the movement of capital, urged on by the free-market ideology of monetarism and the ascension of Prime Minister Margaret Thatcher in Britain and President Ronald Reagan in the United States. The U.S. government had already removed most capital controls by 1975. The United Kingdom and Japan did so by 1979, and Australia followed in 1985. Members of the European Community are committed to eliminating all internal controls on capital movement, leaving the industrialized capitalist countries with the fewest limitations on capital since before World War I.

FASTER AND CHEAPER COMMUNICATIONS AND TRANSPORTATION HAVE ALLOWED OWNERS OF TRANSNATIONAL CORPORATIONS TO CONTROL THEIR DIRECT INVESTMENTS IN FAR-FLUNG FOREIGN AFFILIATES MORE CLOSELY.

CAPITAL CONSTRAINTS

One consequence of capitalists' growing international freedom is the constraint on national governments' ability to stimulate their economies through expansionary fiscal and monetary policies. If a government tries to spur economic activity by loosening monetary policy, expanding credit, and lowering interest rates, foreign and domestic owners of financial capital, seeking higher interest rates elsewhere, can leave. This limits the funds available in credit markets, raising interest rates and reducing or eliminating the intended effect of the original policy. Such capital flight also lowers the value of the domestic currency, which fuels inflation by raising the costs of imported goods. In the face of capital flight, most central banks back away from expansionary monetary policies, as the Bank of Canada did within hours of its modest interest-rate reduction early last year.

Fiscal policy is also constrained. When governments raise taxes on corporations and on the wealthy or they ex-

pand social programs, the rich can simply move their money elsewhere. In 1981, the newly elected French government of Socialist Francois Mitterand felt the sting of international capital. The government increased spending on social benefits to families, the unemployed, and retirees; announced plans to expand public employment and investment; and moved to nationalize some major industries. This led to faster growth in France. But the wealthy began to take their money out of France, forcing the government to devalue the franc three times in 18 months. By June 1982, the French government effectively gave in, limiting social transfers and public spending in favor of policies to promote business investment and household saving. A similar dilemma now faces Bob Rae, the newly elected socialist premier of Ontario.

Facing recession, U.S. policy-makers now find themselves boxed in on both fronts. If the Federal Reserve Board lowers interests rates too far, financial capital will go elsewhere. And if Congress catches a sudden case of populism and tries to stimulate the economy through increased deficit spending, it will have to answer not only to a hostile Bush administration but to the deficit's financiers, foreign and domestic.

Another consequence of the globalization of capital markets is the rise in currency speculation, which increases the volatility of both interest and exchange rates. Currency trading now measures in the hundreds of billions of dollars *per day*, as speculators seek to profit from short-term shifts in exchange rates. Even before Canada's central bank lowered interest rates, currency speculators forced the Canadian dollar down a full cent by selling off their Canadian holdings in anticipation of the move.

Governments are further limited in how they can tax corporations. If they raise tax rates, capitalists can easily shift their profits elsewhere. TNCs often illegally evade taxes by recording profits in low-tax jurisdictions such as Panama. Moreover, since overseas profits are only taxed by the U.S. government when they are received by the U.S. parent, TNCs can legally avoid paying U.S. corporate income taxes in two ways. They can reinvest the profits abroad, or they can judiciously time the so-called repatriation to coincide with losses from their domestic operations, reducing their total tax bills.

Data in a recent study by economists James Hines of Princeton and Glenn Hubbard of Columbia show that in 1984, 69% of foreign subsidiaries of profitable U.S. corporations paid no dividends, interest, rent, or royalties to their U.S. parents. As a result, they paid no U.S. taxes on profits from abroad.

Such corporate tax avoidance has helped persuade governments all over the world to lower their corporate tax rates in an effort to get TNCs to report and retain profits in their respective countries. Between 1984 and 1990, the U.S. government cut the corporate income tax rate from 51% to 39%. The average rate for the United States, Japan, Germany, France, Canada, and the United Kingdom fell from 51% to 43% over the same period.

Foreign-owned companies also pay little in U.S. taxes on their U.S. operations. A February 1990 *New York Times* investigation reported that U.S. subsidiaries of foreign companies have doubled their gross income in the 1980s but have seen virtually no increase in their U.S. tax bills. According to a congressional investigation last year, foreign-owned companies commonly engage in transfer pricing: One foreign parent charged its subsidiary $250 per television set, but charged only $150 to an unrelated company. According to the *Times*, foreign companies may owe the IRS as much as $13 billion.

Such corporate tax evasion leaves the rest of us holding the fiscal bag, with higher payroll taxes and reduced social services.

Who Is Us?

Political economist Robert Reich, in a *Harvard Business Review* article entitled "Who Is Us?," concluded that, contrary to popular opinion, "us" should not include U.S. corporations producing abroad, but it should include subsidiaries of foreign companies producing in the United States.

In fact, neither type of transnational corporation is "us." U.S. and foreign corporations that operate globally have fewer long-term interests in common with the U.S. communities in which they produce than they once did. TNCs now have less stake in a community's infrastructure, education, training, or health care. And they are less concerned with maintaining good labor relations. If the local community and work force don't ante up with direct or indirect subsidies or contract concessions, then the TNC can shift production elsewhere. The threat

CONTROLLING CAPITAL

The term "capital controls" refers to any government mechanism to regulate the cross-border flow of capital. Used extensively by postwar governments in Europe and Japan, capital controls allowed governments to protect domestic capitalists and better guide the rebuilding of their war-devastated economies free of the fear that U.S. capitalists would dominate the new economies.

Some of the more common regulations include:

Restricting Currency Conversions: Capitalists cannot move their money freely between countries unless they can easily convert unlimited quantities of capital from one currency into another. Restricting or slowing currency conversions can effectively prevent foreigners from buying domestic assets or from taking too much of their profits from such investments out of the country. And it can prevent domestic capitalists from moving their wealth abroad. Establishing currency convertibility has been a policy priority of major Western institutions such as the International Monetary Fund, and of economists such as Jeffrey Sachs, Harvard's consultant to the Polish government. Sachs has pressed the Polish government to allow the Polish zloty to be freely convertible with foreign currencies as a precondition for the full entry of foreign capital into Poland.

Limiting Income Repatriation: The return of investors' foreign-earned profits to their home country is called income repatriation. Restricting the amount an investor can repatriate at any given time encourages foreign investors to reinvest their profits in the country the profits were made. It also allows a government to reduce, at least in the short term, pressures on the country's foreign exchange by companies taking profits out of the host country.

Banning or Reviewing Foreign Direct Investment: To limit direct foreign ownership of domestic property, a government can set as preconditions for such investment so-called performance guarantees — minimum employment or wage levels, adequate reinvestment of profits, mandatory domestic purchasing of supplies, extensive reparations in the event the investor closes the property, etc. As long as an agency exists with the power to deny investment, such guarantees can limit the negative impact of capital mobility.

Mandating Foreign Exchange Licenses: Short of full restrictions on currency conversion, governments can slow the flow of capital across their borders by insisting that investors apply for a license to exchange currency. This can restrict currency speculation and can also allow a government to speed the transactions it thinks important and slow or halt those it deems harmful.

Restricting Bank Accounts: Governments can restrict the amount of money they allow foreigners to hold in domestic bank accounts and limit the amount citizens can hold in foreign accounts. Because these assets are very mobile, such regulations can reduce capital flight and speculation.

of capital flight is now just as real in Flint, Michigan, as it is in Morelos, Mexico.

Fleck Manufacturing Inc., for example, a Canadian auto parts supplier with a plant in Ontario, recently purchased a factory in Nogales, Mexico. It then offered its Ontario workers a raise of just 22 cents an hour, warning that if they struck for more Fleck would close the plant. The workers balked, and Fleck shut the plant.

RETRIEVING THE REINS

In the face of capitalists' increasing freedom and power, ordinary people need to retrieve the reins. One way to do this is to reinstitute capital controls. The two things those without wealth possess that the wealthy need are labor and a market for their products. By restricting or putting conditions on capitalists' access to both, people can curb some of the negative effects of mobile capital.

Capital controls don't eliminate the flow of capital between countries, only reduce their negative effects. To curb currency speculation by financial capitalists, for example, governments can impose large transaction fees. To diminish the problem of runaway factories, governments can insist on performance requirements: agreed-upon employment levels, domestic content targets, advance notification of plant closings, mandatory corporate funding for retraining or relocating workers. Unless a company, foreign or domestic, agreed to such requirements, it could not operate in the United States. This would reduce the mobility of firms.

It would also give governments greater autonomy. In the early postwar period, countries with controls were able to lower interest rates and pursue high-employment and high-growth policies. One recent study of industrialized capitalist countries in the 1960s and 1970s found that the greater the controls, the more governments were able to pursue autonomous policies.

With capital so mobile and politically powerful, however, capital controls are difficult to implement effectively. They have to be enacted on a large enough scale to avoid the very capital flight the measures seek to prevent. An aggressive plant closing law on the state level, for example, could drive businesses out of the state, while similar national legislation would prevent businesses from playing states off against one another. In Europe, progressive groups are now pushing for an EEC-wide social charter to prevent such corporate whipsawing.

For those working for TNCs, of course, the most important strategy to limit capital's mobility is to improve international cooperation among unions. Workers in different countries working for the same company can exchange information on the state of the company's operations, finances, pay, benefits, and labor standards. And they can engage in sympathy actions to support one another. Some U.S. and European unions already have an extensive electronic mail network to facilitate this kind of solidarity work.

To deal with capital flight to Third World countries, labor groups have pushed the U.S. government to enforce the fair labor standards provision in federal trade legislation. Similarly, the AFL-CIO is organizing to push for health and safety standards for U.S. corporations operating so-called *maquiladora* factories across the Mexican border. There is also a drive to include in upcoming trade negotiations with Mexico policies on a social charter, a coherent economic development program, social investment, and immigration. In addition, unions such as the Amalgamated Clothing and Textile Workers organize international exchange visits for their members to raise awareness and solidarity.

Whether it be labor actions or government measures, citizens will have to take direct action to respond to the increasing freedom now enjoyed by the wealthy. The free flow of capital across national boundaries is not technologically inevitable. It springs from the domination of government policy by transnational business interests. To limit the destructive effects of capital flight on workers, communities, taxpayers, and government institutions, citizens will have to exercise control over the prerogatives of capitalists.

Resources: Gerald Epstein and Juliet Schor, "Structural Determinants and Economic Effects of Capital Controls in the OECD," in *Financial Openness and National Autonomy*, Tariq Banuri and Juliet Schor, editors; Gerald Epstein, "Mortgaging America," *World Policy Journal*, Winter 1990-91; Robert Reich, "Who Is Us?," *Harvard Business Review*, January-February 1990.

THE QUALITY MOVEMENT

IS IT DEFECTIVE?

BY DAVID LEVINE

At Ford, "Quality is Job 1." IBM managers wrote a book about their quality movement and sponsored a PBS television series. *Business Week* published a special issue on "The Quality Imperative." Quality gurus such as Edward Deming, J.M. Juran, Phil Crosby, and Kaoru Ishikawa lecture and consult around the globe.

Under pressure from Japanese competitors whose defect rates may be a tenth of theirs, hundreds of the U.S.'s largest companies are adopting quality programs. The programs at firms as different as Hewlett Packard, Ford, and Motorola have led to dramatic increases in quality and productivity.

Managers, consultants, and unions have variously described the quality movement as:

• a set of techniques to reduce the defect rates in manufactured products;

• a way of simultaneously increasing customer and worker satisfaction, while increasing profits; or

• a management speed-up that *makes* workers work harder, but is unlikely to improve the quality of U.S. products.

In the United States the management speed-up description has more truth than the others at present. But, if U.S. management can change its behavior sufficiently, the movement could succeed here as it has in Japan.

WHAT IS THE QUALITY MOVEMENT?

In the early 1950's the American Deming lectured in Japan on how to use statistical methods for quality control. Kaoru Ishikawa and other engineers and managers quickly coupled Deming's statistical tools with changes in Japanese workers' roles. These included training workers in problem-solving techniques and giving them leeway to design and implement solutions. The quality movement emphasized reducing waste, which includes defective parts, time spent on inspections, and high levels of inventory. Quality practices worked well in Japan due to compatible labor relations. Many large Japanese corporations, for example, avoid layoffs, giving workers confidence that if they improve efficiency they will not lose their jobs.

Management's "empowerment" of production employees has been equally important to quality's success. Upper management gives production workers more responsibility and authority, while reducing the number of managers and inspectors. Workers play a large role in designing how products are made, and in many cases are allowed to redesign their own jobs. This improves morale and productivity, and frees up engineers' time, greatly increasing the speed of developing new products. That speed makes Japanese companies formidable competitors in computer-controlled machine tools and other rapidly-innovative industries.

But Japan's quality movement has problems and contradictions. One concerns who shall participate in quality-improvement activities. Ishikawa stresses that workers will be more creative if they participate voluntarily, without "coercion from above." Yet he also argues that "If there are six persons in one workplace ... Participation by all six is imperative."

In most large Japanese companies the second principle is dominant. Participation in quality activities is formally voluntary, but employees (and their bosses) are given low performance ratings if they do not participate, and meetings usually take place on workers' own time.

The quality movement has other major drawbacks for Japanese workers. Quality's focus on eliminating all waste has contributed to high levels of job stress. Some Japanese wives have sued companies for the "death from overwork" of their husbands.

Japanese companies rarely extend the benefits of high levels of training and job security to women and older employees (over 55). Few workers in small companies get these benefits either.

HOW DOES QUALITY WORK?

The quality movement — at its best — helps companies produce products that have few defects and match customers' desires. A company can organize work in many ways to satisfy these goals at a reasonable cost.

At laboratories and special restaurants, food engineers employed by McDonald's, Inc., experiment. They alter recipes and try new combinations of flavorings. The engineers carefully track customers' responses as they vary salt, temperature, seconds of frying, and other variations, to determine the "one best way" to cook a hamburger.

In contrast, McDonald's hamburger flippers do not experiment. They follow the recipes and processes that the engineers design. The workers cannot alter their recipes to match local tastes or which fresh produce is available. Their job is routine, and quite boring.

Like assembly lines or data processing offices around the globe, McDonald's expects defects. Managers and quality inspectors try to catch most of these defects before they reach the customers. Since no inspector is perfect, McDonald's employs a world-wide corps of inspectors of inspectors, and inspectors of inspectors' inspectors.

The quality movement, at its best, combines the creativity of home cooking, the scientific problem solving of industrial engineers, and the efficiency of McDonald's workers. One quality tool is statistical process control (SPC).

Suppose a spaghetti sauce that I make is so popular I open a restaurant. The cooks want each batch of sauce to have optimal consistency. We track complaints, and our waiters regularly ask the customers what they like.

We notice that customers complain most frequently about the sauce being too thick. To solve this problem, we use the quality movement's Plan-Do-Check-Act cycle. During the Plan phase, we fill out control charts (the basic SPC tool) over the next few weeks to track the consistency of the sauce. About 10% of the batches turn out overly thick. We discuss possible causes and decide that having the heat too high is the most likely suspect.

Then we Do the recommended action: We lower the heat, and Check what happens. In this case, our control charts show that lower heat avoids the thickening, but increases the cooking time too much.

During the Act phase, we start the cycle over, adding more liquid when the sauce is too thick. When we evaluate this new method, we decide it solves the problem, and we modify the standard recipe.

BACK TO THE U.S.A.

After a series of setbacks in the 1980's, Cummins Engine Co. adopted quality techniques. Cummins' now finds production defects in 1% of its engines rather than the 10% of earlier years, and warranty costs have fallen 20% since 1989.

Motorola suffered through several bad years at the hands of Japanese competitors. Since devoting itself to quality in the mid-1980's, the company has slashed defects from 6,000 to 40 per million.

The U.S.'s top three automakers have cut their defect rates from 7 per car in 1981 to 1.5 today, close to the 1.1 rate in Japanese cars. Ford was the first U.S. automaker to focus on quality, bringing in Deming in 1981. Ford used one technique, "design for manufacturing," and reduced the number of parts in its V-8 engine by 25%.

Workers can appreciate quality practices for several reasons. Most like to do a good job and to satisfy customers, with whom they identify. When practiced correctly, workers learn new skills and more autonomy. They can perform their own quality control, influence their immediate work environment, and make decisions about how to increase quality. Employee satisfaction and productivity increase, leading to lower turnover and higher take-home pay.

Quality requires managers who reward experimentation and recognize that most experiments do not work. Employees must feel confident that bosses will view their mistakes as sources of learning, not examples of failure. Even *Business Week* argues that empowering workers is crucial to success, "because it's the employees themselves who generally find the best solution."

But such empowerment violates long-standing American management practices, such as not listening to workers or giving them a role in decisionmaking. As a result, in most companies the quality movement is likely to go the way of Zero Defects, quality circles, quality of work life, and other short-lived management fads.

A study of 584 companies reported in the *Wall Street Journal* found that "among most U.S. companies, virtually no quality-boosting practices have reached ... meaningful levels." Bill Sheeran, a vice president at General Electric's appliance operations, has said that quality circles failed because companies "didn't empower employees to carry through with it." And quality management has failed at a number of U.S. auto plants, such as General Motors' plant in Van Nuys, California.

In many factories, managers have burdened workers with the added task of filling in SPC charts that track machine performance, without rewarding workers for their efforts. In one auto parts plant, for example, only engineers were trained to analyze data from the charts, and they rarely did. The workers found that even if they entered numbers at random, no one complained. When SPC occurs without empowerment, it is little more than a speed-up.

Without the cooperation of the employees, SPC loses its potential for improving quality. But managers are more likely to punish American workers than reward them for trying to increase quality. Management treats each report of a quality problem as an admission of failure, or a criticism of management. Thus, employees are often afraid to share their ideas. One think-tank, the American Quality Foundation, found that "70% of American workers are afraid to speak up with suggestions or to ask for clarification." These fears are particularly acute for the four-fifths of American workers who are not in unions and so have no protection against unjust dismissals.

Everyone is in favor of quality. If corporations would empower workers and share with them the benefits of higher productivity, quality practices could increase the competitiveness of American enterprises without lowering the living standards of workers. But due to the intransigence of management, the movement has had only modest effects at most American factories and offices. Until American managers take the desires of workers and customers seriously, quality will remain an elusive goal.

Resources: David I. Levine, "Japan's Other Export," *Dollars & Sense*, Sept., 1990; Juran, J.M., ed., *Juran's Quality Handbook*, 4th edition, 1988; *Business Week*, 10/25/92; *Wall Street Journal* 5/14/92.

CHAPTER 4
Fiscal Policy

November/December 1993

THE CLINTON BUDGET

THE SAME OLD SNAKE OIL

BY JOHN MILLER

ed? And how will the federal budget affect us and the economy?

THE DEFICIT GETS TOP BILLING

On the campaign trail Clinton devoted relatively little attention to the deficit. His economic blueprint, *Putting People First*, promised to put people to work by investing more "while cutting the deficit in half." These investments, not the deficit reduction, were to "create millions of high-wage jobs and help America compete in the global economy."

By the summer of 1993, things had changed. In August, during a televised speech from the Oval Office, President Clinton listed the top four reasons to back his budget. Number one was "it would cut the budget deficit sharply" — by nearly $500 billion in five years. New government investment didn't make the list.

It's the economy, stupid. That message won Clinton the presidency. But something got lost between Little Rock and the White House. The message of the Clinton budget, both in its initial version and as passed by Congress, reads "It's the deficit, stupid." And that ain't the same thing.

True enough, under George Herbert Walker Bush deficit reduction would have been more painful for more people. Bush's 1990 tax increases fell less on the well-to-do than will Clinton's. And a Bush administration would have cut social spending more and defense spending less. These are not small differences.

But no matter what it accomplishes on the deficit front, Clinton's program is unlikely to get the economy going or to create jobs. That's tragic. During the current recovery, the economy has created fewer jobs than during any other recovery since World War II.

This will also be a political tragedy for Bill Clinton. Without the "jobs, jobs, jobs" he promised to create with his laser beam on the economy, Clinton will be packing up his message boards, whatever they read in 1996, and heading back to Little Rock.

What went wrong? Did Congress, under pressure from corporate and other special interests, decimate what had begun as a good plan? Or is this the budget Clinton want-

Why the change? Clinton says the projected deficit was higher "than we thought it would be." But it's doubtful that these numbers were a surprise. Others chalk up the change to politics — political manipulation, gamble, or necessity, depending upon their point of view. A more intriguing answer is economic hubris. The Clinton advisors truly think they can reduce the deficit and at the same time, or at least during the same presidency, create eight million additional new jobs.

To most economists, this makes little sense. Herb Stein, chair of Richard Nixon's Council of Economic Advisors, calls the argument that reducing the deficit will create jobs "counter-the-textbook." Most textbooks still follow the theories of John Maynard Keynes that emphasized spending as the key to reviving an ailing economy. Shrinking the deficit reduces spending. Cutting government spending takes money out of the economy. Government employees lose their jobs, and companies that supply the government with everything from missiles to schoolbooks lay off workers when the government buys less of their products. The same holds for higher taxes. People have less money to spend and their consumption falls. Less spending, public or private, slows economic growth and means fewer new jobs.

Just about every economist not on the administration's payroll believes the Clinton budget package, which cuts $255 billion from spending and adds $241 billion in taxes over five years, will contract the economy. On the left, the Economic Policy Institute (EPI) estimates that the tax hike and spending cuts will reduce demand by about $80 billion next year and cause a $394 billion drop in gross domestic product over five years. On the right, Michael Boskin, chair of Bush's Council of Economic Advisors, estimates that Clinton's budget will "take about a point off the growth rate and reduce base-line job growth by perhaps 3/4 of a million" over the next two or three years (see "Shrinking the Debt," page 59).

THE OLD SNAKE OIL

What makes Clinton's economic advisors think their budget will not hurt the economy? Deficit reduction is supposed to lower interest rates and encourage investment. Selective tax breaks and pro-business spending, including public investment, would call forth more private investment than traditional "tax and spend" policies.

By the time Clinton's budget made it through Congress, however, it amounted to, as a *Wall Street Journal* headline put it, "A bet on interest rates." The bet is twofold: first, that the deficit reduction plan will keep interest rates low or drop them further; and second, that lower rates will override the economic drag from the budget.

The first part of the bet is likely to come true. Interest rates will probably remain low, although not drop further. This September the yield on 30-year U.S. Treasury bonds fell below 6% for the first time since 1972. Laura Tyson, the head of Clinton's Council of Economic Advisors, attributes these lower interest rates to "anticipation of the Clinton deficit reduction plan." But that's not clear. Interest rates in all major industrial countries have fallen for more than a year as those economies have slowed. Without coordinated international action, U.S. rates are unlikely to drop in response to further deficit reduction. Nor is there much hope that a Federal Reserve Board headed by Alan Greenspan will push rates yet lower. Forever vigilant against the possible return of inflation, Greenspan, in his midyear report to Congress, warned that the Fed was leaning toward higher rates, not lower ones.

The second half of the bet is more dubious. Low interest rates alone are unlikely to stimulate job-creating investment in today's slack economy. Interest rates are only one of many factors that influence corporate investment. They reduce the cost of acquiring capital. A corporation, however, must also consider whether the demand for its product is growing and if its cash flow, chiefly from past profits, can pay back loans used to finance investments. In a recent study, Dean Baker, an economist at the Economic Policy Institute, reports that, "Virtually all econometric studies show cash flow and sales growth to be far more important than interest rates in promoting investment" (see "Boosting Investment," page 36).

Neither are in good shape today. At home, stubbornly high unemployment, stagnating real wages, and consumer debt burdens conspire to dampen consumer demand and slow sales growth. In addition, a weak global economy rules out an export boom capable of picking up the slack in domestic demand. On top of this, corporate debt levels, while lower than a few years ago, remain high and still constrain cash flow.

Whatever effect lower interest rates have on investment the response will not be immediate, nor will it be strong. Corporations usually take up to two years to implement the bulk of their new investment. A recent study by Barry Bosworth, an economist at the Brookings Institute, found that investment increases only 0.06% for each 1% drop in interest rates. According to Bosworth's estimates, the fall in long-term interest rates since Clinton took office will generate less than $15 billion of yearly spending in terms of investment. This is far less than the nearly $100 billion in annual spending that will be lost due to the deficit reduction included in Clinton's plan.

INDUSTRIAL POLICY TO THE RESCUE

For new Democrats, industrial policy can make up for the shortcomings of traditional macroeconomic policy. Industrial policy is a summary term for pro-business public spending, tax incentives, and regulatory practices intended to maintain the competitiveness of U.S. industries.

Three top Clinton economic advisors, Secretary of Labor Robert Reich, special advisor on health care Ira Magaziner, and Laura Tyson advocate just such an industrial policy. Even these true believers have backed off the proposition that government can pick winners — industries destined to be successful international competitors. Still, they remain convinced that active government policy must go beyond the aggregate Keynesian policy of two decades ago.

Unfortunately, the Omnibus Budget Reconciliation Act of 1993 that emerged from Congress contained very few industrial policy measures. That budget differs substantially from what Clinton promised on the campaign trail. Much of the government investment — in physical infrastructure, civilian research and development, education and training (including children's programs), and tax incentives for private investment — did not make it through Congress.

Gone from the Clinton program is his economic stimulus spending package. One half of its $16 billion, to be spent in fiscal year 1993 (FY93) and FY94, would have funded infrastructure spending, such as highways and mass transit, and education and training programs.

Also gone is the investment tax credit, meant to induce corporations to buy new machinery and equipment. This 7% tax credit for investment above a company's average during recent years would have cost $21 billion in lost tax revenues over five years. Congress and most business organizations opposed this tax break. Business said the Clinton proposal was too small to make much difference in their investment plans. Congress was reluctant to reopen this tax loophole that it had closed in the 1986 tax reform.

The budget battle also cut into the remaining investment programs. Education and job training were hardest hit. Student financial assistance, the Job Training Partnership Act, and Head Start, all received about a third of the increases that Clinton had proposed.

Todd Schafer, another economist at the Economic Policy Institute, points out that the Clinton budget, corrected for inflation, contains no more investment spending than the last Bush budget (see figure). Still, some programs did better than others. Children's programs, despite the watered-down increase for Head Start, fared the best. Physical capital investments also improved. But research and development outlays remain just about unchanged, and education and training investments will suffer a large decline, when adjusted for inflation.

The problems with Clinton's industrial policy go beyond an uncooperative Congress. The rhetorical claims of industrial policy advocates are exaggerated, perhaps as exaggerated as those of Ronald Reagan's supply-side economists. Even if Clinton's proposed budget had gone through Congress without a single change, there are several reasons why its industrial policies could not have offset the contractionary effect of higher taxes and less spending.

The spending figures are too small to pump up a $6 trillion dollar economy. Clinton's proposed $155 billion of spending on infrastructure, education and training, and civilian research and development (R&D), including the stimulus package, would have raised public investment by a sizable amount (about 9% before inflation) to just under 2.4% of Gross Domestic Product. But even at that level, Clinton's program is a far cry from his campaign promise of "the most dramatic economic growth program since World War II." Another $40 billion is necessary to reach the postwar high for public investment relative to the size of the economy.

This lack of public investment haunts U.S. cities. Roads, harbors, bridges, and schools decay at the same time that inner city residents can find neither entry-level jobs nor the training necessary for other jobs. Clinton's proposal — housing expenditures of $6 billion over the next 4 years and another $3.5 billion of tax incentives and direct grants for enterprise zones — falls far short of what is necessary to revive our ailing urban economies. After the Los Angeles uprising, the U.S. Conference of Mayors proposed spending $35 billion to rebuild the cities. Their report, *Ready to Go*, identified more than 7,200 public-works projects that are on hold across the country because cities lack funds. Those projects would create 418,000 jobs.

Moreover, public investment's impact comes not only from the immediate Keynesian effect of increasing spending, but also through long-term increases in productivity. Higher productivity bolsters private profits, calls forth more private investment, and juices up economic growth. But this takes time. It may take a decade for infrastructure spending to have its full impact on business decisions to modernize their plants and equipment. Training programs work more quickly, but still require lead time and jobs for trainees. Investing in better education and immunization for children could profoundly affect the productivity of U.S. industry, but only once today's children reach adulthood.

Finally, these proposals miss the causes of slower productivity growth in the U.S. economy. Public investment and further job training alone will not restore the international competitiveness of U.S. industry. David Gordon, an economist and former advisor to Jesse Jackson's presidential campaign, argues that U.S. employers have harmed productivity by relying too heavily on browbeating workers rather than promoting cooperation with them (see "Generating Affluence," page 33). U.S. corporations employ more than twice as many administrators and managers as German and Japanese corporations. Clinton's program calls neither for the genuine empowerment of workers nor for the reform of top-heavy corporate bureaucracies.

CLINTON'S ADVISORS TRULY THINK THEY CAN REDUCE THE DEFICIT AND AT THE SAME TIME CREATE EIGHT MILLION NEW JOBS.

The investment tax credit, another staple of Clinton industrial policy, is also off the mark. The credit does nothing to alter the underlying profitability of investment, but rather offers a temporary tax advantage. Even Jerry Jasinowski, president of the National Association of Manufacturers, argued that, "it was a bad idea that will simply shift investment from the future forward."

HALF TRUTHS ABOUT SPENDING

The Clinton budget also fails to address the inequities of the 1980s that Clinton deplored during his campaign so effectively. On the up side, increased funding expands the food stamp program to cover more working poor who use cars to get to work and those with high housing costs. New spending for the Family Preservation Program helps families who are at risk of becoming homeless. Besides these programs, a substantial increase in the earned income tax credit enlarges this tax cut for poor families with children and an employed adult, and for the first time provides a small benefit to childless families.

But to reduce the deficit, entitlement spending goes down $88 billion over five years. The bulk of that, $55.8 billion, cuts payments to doctors, hospitals, and other providers under Medicare, medical care for the elderly. While these cuts won't directly affect consumers of medical care, some providers may pass those costs not covered by Medicare onto patients in the form of higher fees. Medicaid, medical care for the poor, is cut by $7 billion. The budget makes it more difficult for older people to qualify for Medicaid coverage of nursing home costs.

Clinton's budget also cuts other discretionary social spending. Congress and the President agreed to extend the spending "caps" of the Budget Enforcement Act of 1990 for another five years. Freezing all discretionary spending (defense and non-defense) at 1993 levels cancels out $102 billion of scheduled spending increases.

Laura Tyson assured a radio audience that "defense spending is coming down dramatically" in the Clinton budget. But drama is in the eye of the beholder. The Clinton budget reduces defense spending $7 billion beyond the cuts proposed by Bush in FY94 and by $36 billion beyond the Bush proposal for FY98. While these are large cuts, the alternative budget of the Congressional Black Caucus would have taken more than twice those amounts out of defense spending. That proposal is more in line with proposals from other progressive groups — such as the National Commission on Economic Conversion and Disarmament — to cut the defense budget in half.

PROGRESSIVE TAX CHANGES

President Clinton claimed that his tax proposals would "increase taxes largely on those most able to pay and cost working families less than a dime a day in new taxes." He told the truth, if a carefully crafted one.

The bulk of the new tax revenues comes from higher individual income taxes for the well-to-do. The top tax

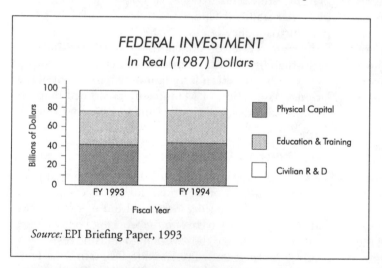

FEDERAL INVESTMENT
In Real (1987) Dollars

Billions of Dollars

- Physical Capital
- Education & Training
- Civilian R & D

FY 1993   FY 1994

Fiscal Year

Source: EPI Briefing Paper, 1993

bracket moves up from 31% to 36% and an added 10% surtax on those earning more than $250,000 brings their marginal tax rate to 39.6%. In addition, the budget repeals the cap on earnings (now $136,000) that are subject to the Medicare payroll tax.

David Gordon points out that the 1988 Jesse Jackson Campaign called for a top income tax bracket almost identical (less than one percentage point higher) to the one Clinton and Congress actually passed into law. But despite this significant improvement in its progressivity, the top U.S income tax bracket remains well below the average top rate, 47%, charged by the 86 countries with an income tax.

Most workers and their families will pay only a new energy tax. This moderate 4.3% levy on gasoline and diesel fuel will increase the price of gas and other commodities that will become more expensive to ship. For most workers, the direct cost of the tax will be between $30 and $50 a year — or about a dime a day. In addition, more than 10 million low and moderate income working families with children will receive a tax cut due to the expansion of the earned income tax credit.

For one out of eight retired workers and their families the tax package will cost much more than a dime a day. Couples who have more than $44,000 in annual earnings and property income, but are also collecting Social Security benefits, will now pay taxes on 85% of their benefits rather than on just half of them.

For business, the Clinton tax changes are a mixed bag. The corporate income tax, the tax on corporate profits, goes up one percentage point. Corporations also lose deductions for club dues, lobbying costs, and some travel. Business meals are now only 50% deductible (instead of 80%). At the same time, tax incentives for investment, including the deductibility of passive real estate losses, turn a third of these revenues back over to selected corporations.

In sum, the Clinton tax package is the most progressive in decades. According to the Congressional Budget Office, families with incomes above $200,000 will bear more than four-fifths of the burden of these new taxes. Only about one-tenth of the tax burden will fall on those with incomes under $100,000, with families earning less than $30,000 getting a tax cut.

Still, Clinton will not soak the rich. The tax increase for the super-rich, the wealthiest 1% of the population, whose average incomes are $800,000, will average only $53,600. This does not come close to taking back the $160,000 per family these wealthiest taxpayers will save this year alone from the supply-side tax giveaways of the 1980s.

All told, the federal government's economic program is a curious mix of conservative economics and more progressive proposals transformed into mainstream policies. In Clinton's hands, tax reform, public investment, and job training have become tools to support private investment. Moreover, Clinton will only use these tools to the extent that doing so is consistent with reducing the budget deficit. Too bad. As it stands now, the federal budget will prolong economic stagnation, not restore growth. An economic plan that had instead used those tools in the right way could have put people first in a growing economy.

Resources: "Rapid Deficit Reduction: The Fast Path to Slow Growth," Dean Baker, and "Still Neglecting Public Investment: The FY94 Budget Outlook," Todd Schafer, both are Economic Policy Institute Briefing Papers, 1993; *The Economic and Budget Outlook: An Update,* Congressional Budget Office, 1993.

POP AUSTERITY

CLINTON TALKS POPULISM BUT HIS PROGRAM THRILLS WALL STREET

BY BRYAN SNYDER

The first Democratic administration in Washington since 1980 entered office with a desire to achieve two contradictory goals. The first — stimulating the economy and restoring funding for social programs — requires greater federal spending. Without major tax increases for corporations and the wealthy, achieving this goal will cause the federal deficit to rise, at least initially. But Bill Clinton's second goal is to reduce the deficit, which can only be accomplished by cutting spending and increasing taxes.

With unemployment still hovering around 7% and real wages well below their levels of 20 years ago, the Democratic Party's natural constituencies — workers, their families, and the poor — desperately need the stimulus. But those to whom both the government and private industry are indebted and cannot operate without — financial capitalists such as bankers — strongly prefer a federal focus on deficit reduction, although this strategy will inevitably yield economic stagnation. Mindful of the political and economic histories of Jimmy Carter and Ronald Reagan, Clinton has chosen to side with the financiers.

PUMP PRIMING WITH A THIMBLE

When consumers are not buying enough and firms are not producing enough to yield full employment, one remedy is for government to stimulate increased spending on goods and services. Such "aggregate demand" for goods and services can be generated by direct government spending, or by cutting taxes so that households and businesses have more money to spend. Both policies must be financed by greater government debt. Clinton's proposals, in either their original or revised forms, would do the opposite on both counts.

Clinton initially proposed to increase federal spending by $30 billion during the next year. In response to objections from deficit hawks, the President reduced this to $16 billion in the legislation he submitted to Congress — far too little to significantly increase demand and create jobs. So, while the defeat of his short-term economic stimulus program by a Republican filibuster made for great political theater, it was of little consequence to working people.

Even $30 billion is less than one-half of one percent (0.5%) of the U.S. gross domestic product (GDP). One mainstream economist, James Tobin of Yale University, estimates that the economic "multiplier," which translates an increase in government spending into a rise in GDP, is between 1.5 and 2.0. Thus, a $30 billion (0.5% of GDP) stimulus could raise GDP by 0.75% to 1.0%. But our GDP is currently 5% to 6% below what it would be if all businesses were operating at capacity, says Tobin, so that Clinton's proposal is a small fraction of what is needed to move the economy to its full potential output.

The Japanese government's economic recovery program gives some indication of the size of the stimulus package that would be required to pull the American economy out of recession. In 1990, Japan's economy began to slip into recession. Rather than rejoice in the anti-inflationary benefits of high unemployment and falling industrial output, Japan increased government spending by 10.7 trillion yen ($89 billion) in 1992 and 13.2 trillion yen ($116 billion) in 1993. Matching the 1992 Japanese program would cost the United States $135 billion. This is about five times what Clinton's original plan called for.

How Clinton planned to spend the money is also a cause for concern. Through the neglect of the past 12 years, America now needs up to five trillion dollars to replace and repair its infrastructure, such as roads, bridges, and housing, says Professor Seymour Melman. Whereas the Japanese plan included $72 billion in 1992 for public works spending, there is little in Clinton's plan to address this pressing need.

The stimulus package, moreover, fails to assist conversion from military to civilian production. It will cost as much, if not more, to wean the economy off of reliance on military spending as it did to prepare for Armageddon. Firms that want to convert from weapons to civilian production will face a competitive marketplace for the first time — and one in which most companies are having trouble selling their products. Grumman, for example, makes both military aircraft and stretch buses. It could switch to just buses, but in today's fiscal climate what state and local governments would buy them? Clinton proposes nothing of substance to address this problem.

DAMOCLES SWORDS

And that's the good news. Clinton's short-term plans are inadequate, but his long-term plans are likely to drag us further into stagnation. Clinton has made reducing the annual federal deficit and paying debt service on the existing debt his top priorities. Over the years 1994-1998 Clinton proposes to cut federal spending by a cumulative total of $144 billion, while increasing taxes by $328 billion. Combined, this would mean withdrawing $473 billion in spending, an average of $95 billion per year, from the U.S. economy during that period.

Clinton proposes to reduce the federal deficit primarily through increasing taxes on individuals and corporations. But such tax hikes will exacerbate the debt problems of consumers and businesses, both of whom borrowed at unprecedented levels in the 1980s. Households' debts (including home mortgages) were 94% of their after-tax incomes in 1988, versus 71% in 1975. Such high levels of private borrowing shift capital from productive uses to debt service. This corrodes a nation's ability to increase productivity, and reduces the profitability of manufacturers. Bankruptcies, "downsizing," and stagnation result.

Progressive people should, however, be concerned about the U.S. government's growing deficit. One reason is that it helps to widen the gap between rich and poor in this country. Paying debt service shifts income to those wealthy individuals and institutions who purchase U.S. bonds in large quantities, and away from the vast majority of Americans who pay the interest on the debt through increased taxes. One source estimates that the wealthiest 10% of Americans receive 55% of federal interest payments (see "Debt & Distribution," *Dollars & Sense*, June 1992).

CLINTON'S SHORT-TERM PLANS ARE INADEQUATE, BUT HIS LONG-TERM PLANS ARE LIKELY TO DRAG US FURTHER INTO STAGNATION.

Clinton faces a difficult choice. He cannot simultaneously service the debt and stimulate the economy. Lately, the mainstream press have assumed that the deficit must take precedence. For example, the *New York Times* story on Japan's stimulus program ran under the headline "Tokyo-Style Plan Too Costly for U.S.; Economic Stimulus Package Precluded by Deficit."

Attempting to reduce the deficit at this time, moreover, will result in greater unemployment and falling output, thereby worsening Clinton's budget difficulties. Recessions reduce government revenues, as both workers and businesses earn less and pay less taxes. Mandatory government spending rises to pay for unemployment compensation, food stamps, and other social welfare programs. Thus, in the short term the President may not even succeed in reducing the annual deficit.

Clinton, and his advisers such as Labor Secretary Robert Reich, hope that productivity, and therefore output, can be increased in the long run through greater investment in public and private capital. But the term "productivity" is normally used to mean output per hour of labor time. In order to achieve more output, and lower costs per unit of output, business owners replace labor with high-efficiency machinery — which may yield unemployment. This is precisely what has happened in manufacturing in recent decades — as productivity has risen layoffs continue apace.

INTERESTED PARTIES

Austerity policies severely harm workers and their families. Unemployment brutalizes those who lose their jobs, and terrorizes all other workers, whose fear of being without work leads them to demand less of employers in terms of wages, benefits, and working conditions. Unionized labor is forced into concessions and give-backs.

Their employers, "industrial capitalists," gain to a degree from recessions, as their bargaining power grows relative to workers, leading to lower labor costs. But their profits are vulnerable to decreases in the demand for products and services. With fewer people working, and lower incomes, inventories rise and businesses reduce output in an attempt to stem losses. When stagnation becomes bad enough, industrial capitalists and working Americans have a mutual interest in a meaningful stimulus package.

But there is a group that gains greatly from austerity — "finance capitalists" — who derive their income from owning money and lending it to companies, families, and the government. For financiers, the prime enemy is inflation, not unemployment or stagnation. In fact, a fair amount of unemployment suits them just fine, since this helps to control inflation, by reducing wage increases. Because deficit reduction brings with it a slower economy, Wall Street reacted joyously to Clinton's focus on debt service.

While for industrial capitalists the prime issue is selling their output, for finance capitalists their main concern is maintaining the value of their assets, such as corporate and government bonds. At maturity, bonds pay a fixed rate of interest on their original sales price. Inflation erodes the real value of this interest, causing the market prices of bonds to fall, and financiers to lose money.

As James Tobin puts it, "there is no getting around the fact that the kind of economy those mythical mandarins [the Fed and bond investors] prefer is one that will make President Clinton run for re-election in 1996 not as the 'failed governor of a small state' but as the failed president of a great nation."

Bill Clinton made a clear choice for austerity. He firmly embraced Wall Street by immediately appointing Robert Rubin, of the brokerage firm Goldman Sachs, to the new White House Economic Security Council, and Robert Altman, of the Blackstone Group (an investment and securities firm), as Deputy Treasury Secretary. This may mark a new generation of Wall Street insiders, though their excessive zeal for debt service portends little change from the previous generations of "monetarists," those who believe that controlling the money supply and inflation should be the government's primary goal.

WHEN WALL STREET FELL ON JIMMY

Why has Clinton structured an economic policy that throws the federal government's weight so squarely behind the interests of Wall Street? The precedent of the last Democratic president and the fiscal beating he suffered at the hands of "the street" provides insights to the current president's actions. The sanctity and solvency of the monetary system is paramount to the government. If financiers refuse to lend money in times of economic uncertainty, they can throw the economy more quickly and surely into crisis than can the actions of industrial firms.

When Jimmy Carter was elected president in 1976, he promised relief from the persistent recession and rising inflation that had crippled Gerald Ford's administration. Carter attempted to balance the interests of industrial capital, and through it labor, with the demands of Wall Street. This balancing act lasted two years until rising inflation and uncertainty inflamed an already jittery capital market. Wall Street became increasingly reluctant to service the economy's finance and credit needs. This led to a painful bout of "stagflation" — simultaneously high rates of inflation and unemployment.

The chaos of stagflation and financiers' refusal to lend money forced Carter to stop accommodating the interests of industry and labor, and meet the needs of Wall Street instead. In October of 1979, Carter unleashed the Federal Reserve Bank's Chairman, Paul Volcker, allowing him to slam the economy into an even deeper recession by restricting money supply growth. This was the opening bell of the Fed's decade-long imposition of "monetarist" policy — in which inflation, not interest rates or unemployment, was its primary concern.

Restricting the money supply reduces the funds available to banks. With less money to lend relative to the demand for loans by businesses and households, banks are able to raise their interest rates. During 1980 these rates shot up to record levels (the prime interest rate, which is the rate available to major corporate borrowers, averaged 15.3%), and unemployment soon followed, as the economy was monetarily strangled.

Volcker and the Fed intended this monetarist shock treatment to create a recession deep enough to wring infla-

tion out of the economy. But it could not have happened at a more politically inopportune time. Jimmy was shown the door in the 1980 election.

High interest rates continued for several more years, while the recession worsened, with unemployment close to 10% in 1982 and 1983. But by 1984, with workers bargaining power in full retreat and inflation in remission, the economy began to recover just in time for Ronald Reagan's reelection bid.

Throughout the 1980s the Federal Reserve consistently applied monetarist policies. The result was a sharp drop in inflation and the promise of stable prices over time. This made lenders happy. Inflation greatly increases the risks involved in lending, because it means that lenders' money is worth less when the loans are repaid.

> WE CAN VIEW CLINTON'S CHOICE OF PRIORITIES AS A CLEAR RESPONSE TO RECENT U.S. POLITICAL AND ECONOMIC HISTORY.

Thus, Wall Street deeply appreciated the Fed's ability to keep inflation tightly under control during the presidencies of Reagan and George Bush. We can view Bill Clinton's choice of priorities as a clear response to recent U.S. political and economic history. Clinton the president, as was true for Clinton the candidate, wants to please everyone. While his heart may lie with the "little people" he loves to talk about, Clinton's head is firmly in line with those whose capital keeps the government and industry running.

It is unfortunate for working people that politics thrives on deception. In the last presidential campaign Clinton treated us to the rhetoric of "growing the economy," "industrial policy," and job creation. For populist politicians it is vital to maintain the appearance of tirelessly struggling for the interests of the "working folks" who elected them. As the progressivity of his electoral platform evaporates under the heat of the powers that be, one can expect greater haggling over what is essentially pocket change in the federal budget. Debates will rage as Washington compromises and underfunds programs that are necessary to reverse economic stagnation.

DEFICITS AND OUR CHILDREN

BY MARTIN H. WOLFSON

The fear that large federal deficits will put a burden on future generations has motivated much recent debate over economic policy. Most conspicuously, Ross Perot made headlines during the 1992 presidential campaign by suggesting that, like responsible parents, the government should not run up large bills and leave them for the next generation to pay.

In recent years, the federal government has indeed run large deficits, as tax revenue has been much less than spending. In order to finance the deficit, the government has had to borrow. Perot reasons that if the government issues an IOU (such as a Treasury bond) that is due in 30 years, our children and grandchildren will face the burden of repayment and thus the prospect of higher taxes. In addition, he argues that our children will be responsible for all the debt remaining from past budget deficits (the existing national debt), plus all the accumulated interest.

His solution is deceptively simple: don't borrow so much now. Just like a family that has borrowed too much, the government should try to cut spending and raise revenues. But Perot and other proponents of deficit cutting fail to ask one crucial question — how has the borrowed money been spent?

If, for instance, parents borrow money to finance a lavish vacation and leave the bill to their children, then Perot's analysis makes sense. But what if parents borrow money to pay for a training program or a college education for their child? Presumably this will enable the child to get a better job with a higher income in the future, so the debt can easily be repaid and the child can enjoy a higher standard of living. In this case, the decision to borrow seems wise.

Likewise, if the government borrows to finance better education and training for our children, then the borrowing makes sense. What we have left them is not a burden, but an opportunity for a better life.

The problem with the budget deficits of the past decade is that the government has not devoted the borrowed funds to such productive purposes. The large deficits created under Reagan financed a rapid increase in military spending and tax cuts for the wealthy. Neither of these policy choices helped our workforce become better trained or more productive or enabled our children to have higher incomes in the future (despite the claims of supply-side economists).

The policies of increasing government spending and reducing taxes — in other words, giving people more money to spend — might at least have helped to stimulate the economy, as Keynesian economists have long recommended. But the way the deficits of the 1980s were created limited their stimulative impact. Although producing bombs and luxury goods did provide some people with jobs and income, the benefits were limited and poorly distributed. As in the case of the lavish vacation, once the bombs were stockpiled (or exploded) and the luxury goods consumed, there was nothing left for the future but the bill.

Reorienting the federal budget to promote a higher standard of living means shifting its composition toward more productive purposes. These include not just education and training, but also improving our physical infrastructure (such as roads, bridges, and communication facilities) and making our workforce more productive. Creating a more productive workforce means allowing workers to fully use their talents: establishing incentives for participation and decision-making on the job, programs to eliminate illiteracy and ill health, and strategies to ease the transition between jobs and to reduce unemployment.

The deficit legislation enacted in 1993 took half a step toward a more sensible budget policy. It reduced military spending and made the tax burden more equitable. But it stopped short of using these budget savings to expand the federal government's role in promoting public investment and productivity. It failed to do so because the overriding objective was to reduce the size of the deficit rather than reorient the composition of government spending.

THE "CROWDING OUT" ARGUMENT

A second "burden-on-future-generations" argument has fueled the obsession with deficit reduction. The *crowding out* argument runs like this: 1) Large deficits lead to a huge government demand for credit, which puts pressure on a limited supply of savings and thus forces up the price of borrowing (the interest rate). 2) Higher interest rates discourage business from borrowing to finance new investment such as factories, office buildings, and computers. 3) With less space and equipment, workers will be less productive, so future generations will suffer from a lower standard of living. 4) Cutting the deficit will result in lower interest rates and avoid the crowding out of business investment.

There are problems with each of these assumptions. First, there is little evidence that large budget deficits cause high interest rates. The highest interest rates in the postwar period in the United States occurred between 1980 and 1982, before the large budget deficits created by the Reagan revolution began to appear in 1983. A more powerful force pushing up interest rates from 1980 to 1982 was the tight monetary policy of the Federal Reserve. And since 1982 interest rates have gradually fallen, even as our budget deficits have increased.

Second, it is doubtful that government borrowing crowded business out of credit markets in the 1980s. Although real interest rates (interest rates adjusted to take inflation into account) remained relatively high during the 1980s, business borrowing exploded. Unfortunately, most of that new borrowing served unproductive purposes: mergers and acquisitions, leveraged buyouts, hostile takeovers, and other forms of corporate restructuring.

Third, business investment, though important, is not the only (or perhaps even the main) factor responsible for increasing the productivity of U.S. workers. Public investment in infrastructure and people, from roads and bridges to health care and education, also makes our workforce more productive.

Finally, the link between lower deficits and lower interest rates is not as direct as popularly imagined. Long-term interest rates did fall in 1993 as Congress passed a $500 billion deficit reduction measure. But the rates did not necessarily decline because participants in credit markets anticipated less crowding out of private business. A more plausible explanation has to do with the expected effect of deficit reduction on the inflation rate. Reducing government spending and increasing taxes leave people with less money to spend. Consequently, with less ability to sell their goods, businesses produce less, lay off workers, and are less likely to raise prices. The prospect for lower inflation means that lenders will not see the purchasing power of their money erode, and they are therefore more willing to lend at lower interest rates.

What, then, should be done about the budget deficit? There are really three basic choices. We can continue the policies of the past: borrow to finance unproductive government spending and cut taxes for the wealthy. This policy did indeed put a burden on future generations, and generated antagonism from taxpayers toward government spending. Alternatively, we can react against the policies of the past by making deficit reduction our overriding economic priority, as the Clinton Administration has done. This path slows economic growth and condemns millions to unemployment. People who don't have jobs don't pay taxes, and require more unemployment, welfare, and other benefits. A sluggish economy, in other words, leads to fewer tax revenues and higher government spending, and therefore a greater budget deficit.

IT MAKES SENSE FOR THE GOVERNMENT TO BORROW TO FINANCE BETTER EDUCATION AND TRAINING FOR OUR CHILDREN.

But there is a third policy choice: reorienting government spending and tax policies toward more productive purposes. In the long run this shift should provide the incomes to reduce the debt. It should also stimulate the economy, put people back to work, and allow us to get closer to the goal of full employment at decent wages. Finally, it should enable us to focus on what Robert Eisner, past president of the American Economics Association, has called our "real deficits": workers permanently displaced from closed down factories, poverty, homelessness, inadequate health care, the conditions of the inner cities, and malnutrition among our children. Addressing these problems would help us provide a better life for our children and grandchildren. Neglecting them and focusing single-mindedly on deficit reduction would in fact leave future generations with a crushing burden.

DEFICIT DELIRIUM

THE BOGUS DEBATE OVER BALANCING THE BUDGET

BY MAX SAWICKY

Last June President Bush, the Republicans, some southern Democrats, and a band of deluded liberals tried to sanctify Reaganomics. They sought to pass a Constitutional amendment forcing the federal government to "balance" its budget.

The proposal failed when a vote in the House of Representatives did not get a two-thirds majority. House Democratic leaders and Senator Robert Byrd of West Virginia led the Congressional opposition, but activist organizations such as Common Cause, the American Association of Retired Persons, and the labor movement were the real forces which mobilized to stop the amendment.

The federal deficit, when calculated according to the government's standard definition, grew rapidly during the Reagan years and has remained high during Bush's term. Conservatives, liberals and progressives have all expressed fears that the annual deficit, and the accumulated federal debt, harm the economy by raising interest rates and depressing private investment. Progressives have also been concerned that the debt burden shifts income toward the rich.

But the real economic burden of the deficit on the economy is not significant at present. Even in the event of higher deficits, their negative economic impacts are likely to be small. They can even be positive if the federal government uses deficits to finance productive investments.

The intense focus on the deficit by the President, Congress, and the public has disastrous consequences, however. It helps those seeking to limit domestic public spending and taxes, and severely hampers the federal government's efforts to increase employment and finance public investment. A balanced budget amendment would exacerbate these problems, making it difficult to borrow money, improve the equity of the tax system, or increase revenues.

THE DEFICIT IS NOT AS BIG AS YOU THINK IT IS

Many analysts argue that deficits hurt the economy because government borrowing reduces the funds available for business to borrow and invest. Most economists view such investment as a key to growth in the economy and in wages. Each year, moreover, the national debt grows by the amount of that year's deficit. The bigger the debt, the more the government must spend per year in interest payments.

The Congressional Budget Office (CBO) estimates the 1992 deficit at $368 billion. But Robert Eisner, professor of economics at Northwestern University, argues that under a more meaningful definition of the deficit, its size is not significant. We could call this the "Economically Relevant Deficit" (ERD). The ERD excludes temporary expenses and income and adjusts for borrowing that does not add to the national debt's real burden on the economy. These adjustments are discussed below.

The ERD excludes three factors which affect the deficit at present but should not in the future. First, during recessions government spending on public assistance and unemployment compensation increases and tax revenue falls, resulting in higher deficits. If 7% unemployment becomes a constant feature of the U.S. economy, then unemployment is the problem, not the resulting deficits.

Second is spending on the savings and loan bailout. Two to three years from now, this spending is supposed to turn from a net loss to a net gain, as the government stops buying weak or failing banks and increases its sales of their assets to private investors. If this does not happen, Bush Administration officials will be guilty of major mismanagement. Here, too, the deficit is not the problem.

Third, payments from foreign countries to help pay for the war against Iraq have reduced the deficit. When these payments end, the deficit will increase.

The recession accounts for about $100 billion of the deficit. Excess spending on savings and loan bailouts, combined with receipts for the Gulf War, is another $60 billion. Without these three temporary items, the ERD for 1992 would be about $210 billion.

Federal, state, and local borrowing all affect the private sector's access to capital. Although some states have been in dire straits, for most of the past 12 years state and local governments as a whole have been in surplus, including $30 billion in 1991 (the last year for which data is available). Thus, if we consider the entire public sector, rather than the federal government alone, the ERD is reduced to $180 billion.

We should also subtract from the deficit borrowing that finances public investment. When a business firm borrows to purchase plant and equipment, its expenses can easily outstrip its revenues that year. But the firm is not bankrupt if higher profits in the future are sufficient to pay back the loans. Therefore, we should deduct from the deficit public investment financed by federal, state, and local governments. Borrowing a billion dollars to fund public capital, such as a new mass transit system, bridges, education, and basic scientific knowledge does not increase the burden of the debt.

But existing public capital such as roads and sewage systems are constantly wearing out. We must count such depreciation as dis-investment, which increases the ERD. New public investment minus depreciation totalled $70 billion in 1991, reports Eisner. Using this estimate (1992 figures are not yet available), we can reduce the 1992 ERD to $110 billion.

Finally, we should adjust the deficit to account for changes in the real value of the national debt. Just as with private mortgages, each year inflation reduces the real burden of any fixed debt. For every billion of national debt, 3% inflation cuts the government's liability by $30 million. With a national debt of $2,687 billion as of December 1991, inflation reduces its value by about $85 billion. In Eisner's view we should treat this as income to the federal government, reducing the ERD to only $25 billion.

Thus, the Economically Relevant Deficit is close to zero! The deficit debate of the past twelve years is completely out of proportion to the actual size of the ERD.

Do Lower Deficits Help the Economy?

Now let's ignore the calculations above and consider the economic impacts of whatever deficits do exist. Conventional wisdom asserts that lower deficits lead to lower interest rates, greater business investment, higher productivity and more economic growth. But neither theory nor evidence necessarily supports this claim.

First, a lower government deficit may not reduce interest rates:

• If the federal government borrows less, state and local governments may borrow more (or save less) to make up for the shortfall in federal spending.

• If the federal Treasury Department borrows less by selling fewer bonds to the public, the Federal Reserve could use this opportunity to further reduce inflation by slowing growth in the money supply. The Fed does this by selling some of its own bonds to private savers. Reducing growth in the money supply can eliminate part or all of the interest rate reduction.

In addition, if reduced public deficits do lead to lower interest rates and more private borrowing, some loans would go to finance home ownership. Since business borrowing would not increase as much, neither would productivity and economic growth.

The concern about interest rates rests on the belief that businesses will increase their investments if their cost of borrowing is reduced. But expected consumer spending is a much more important consideration for businesses than interest rates. If a firm does not expect to be able to sell its goods, it will not invest, no matter how low the cost of borrowing.

Theory aside, the relationship between government deficits and interest rates has been difficult to document. During most of the 1980s the deficit skyrocketed but interest rates did not. Studies by avid partisans of deficit reduction at the CBO and the Brookings Institution have failed to find strong evidence linking the deficit and interest rates.

Suppose businesses do borrow more when the federal government borrows less. No guarantee exists that they will use the funds to buy new plant and equipment. Businesses were awash in borrowed funds in the 1980s but used the money to finance mergers and acquisitions. Even if businesses do invest more in plant and equipment, the gains in productivity and economic growth may be less than from added public investment.

Finally, economic growth does not necessarily create prosperity for most of us. During the last two decades, growth in productivity and gross national product have increased while real wages have fallen and family incomes have stagnated.

A BALANCED BUDGET AMENDMENT WOULD MAKE IT DIFFICULT TO BORROW MONEY, IMPROVE THE EQUITY OF THE TAX SYSTEM, OR INCREASE REVENUES.

HERE'S THE BEAUTY OF MY DEFICIT REDUCTION PLAN—

IT KEEPS INTEREST RATES LOW, SO COMPANIES CAN BORROW...

...SO THEY CAN MAKE MORE GOODS THAT THEY CAN SELL...

...TO ALL THE PEOPLE THEY'VE LAID OFF

WASSERMAN ©'93 BOSTON GLOBE DIST. BY L.A. TIMES SYND

INCOME REDISTRIBUTION AND THE NATIONAL DEBT

Many progressives are concerned about the deficit's redistributive effects. They argue that since the tax system has become less fair, while interest payments on the national debt have increased, deficits redistribute money from lower-income taxpayers to upper-income holders of public debt.

But anyone who can buy a government bond can also buy stocks or corporate bonds. If the rich bought fewer Treasury bonds they might make, at worst, slightly less money from other investments.

The more important equity issue is the impact on younger generations. If government had borrowed in order to fund public capital, rather than military spending and tax breaks for the wealthy, the debt burden would be greatly reduced. Instead, the fiscal policy of the 1980s has depleted the capital of both the public and private sectors, dimming the prospects of future workers.

POLITICIANS AND THEIR SUPPORTERS USE DEFICIT REDUCTION AS A GUISE TO REDISTRIBUTE INCOME TOWARD THE RICH.

As the baby boomers retire, payroll taxes to finance Social Security and Medicare will rise, weighing more heavily on workers. Taxes of all types to pay for the needs of the aged will also increase. Unless our economic policies change soon, the future will be a bitter struggle among rich retirees, other retirees, and future workers over who pays for public services.

DEFICIT REDUCTION IS A RIGHT-WING ISSUE

Since 1978, the obsession with the federal deficit has dominated domestic policy. Even the Carter Administration sacrificed plans for welfare reform due to fears of increased federal spending.

The Reagan Administration pumped up the deficit to an unprecedented level. Reagan also played a key role in discrediting the public sector and creating an atmosphere in which proposals of new taxes for worthy purposes were made politically impossible.

Given the long history of Republican opposition to public borrowing, could the deficit have been just a terrible mistake? The evidence suggests otherwise: the deficit was a deliberate creation of conservatives to cripple the public sector, making either redistribution or improvements in domestic programs almost impossible.

In his book, *The Triumph of Politics*, Reagan's Budget Director David Stockman takes responsibility for colossal blunders in estimating future levels of taxes, spending, and economic growth. But the truth is more damning. Senator Daniel Moynihan has written that Stockman told him the deficits were a deliberate device to shrink the government.

Many others, including Stuart Butler of the right-wing Heritage Foundation, have acknowledged this crime.

Republicans created the deficit debate because doing so serves their wealthy constituents. But it's no favor to the rest of us. Critics of the deficit are compelled to propose tax increases and spending cuts which will be costly to many people. Yet deficit reduction has few visible benefits to the public. Reducing the deficit wins politicians many enemies and few friends. This has been the dilemma of the Democrats from 1984 on.

The goal of Reaganomics was not deficit reduction, but lower public spending for domestic, non-military purposes. From this standpoint, the Gramm-Rudman deficit-reduction laws, and the budget deal of 1990, have worked quite well. Domestic public spending by the Federal government has stagnated since 1981. Entire programs, such as the Comprehensive Employment Training Act (CETA) and revenue sharing, were killed.

Both presidential candidates have endorsed reductions in capital gains taxes and the corporate income tax. At the same time, elite editorialists and commentators speak of the need to "control" entitlements, meaning Social Security, Medicare, Medicaid, unemployment compensation, and public assistance. Once again politicians and their supporters will use deficit reduction as a guise to redistribute income toward the rich.

WHAT IS TO BE DONE

The federal government needs to borrow money for two principal purposes: attaining full employment and financing public investment. Any balanced budget amendment makes these responsibilities more difficult to fulfill.

Increased government spending and tax cuts are two primary methods for stimulating the economy during recessions and depressions. Pursuit of either option requires deficits.

Even with full employment, public borrowing to finance public investment would still be beneficial. Such investment provides transportation systems, educated citizens, and other benefits that last for many years, so financing them through debt is sensible.

The federal budget should have two pieces — operating expenditures and capital investment. The government should finance the capital portion with borrowing. It should pay for debt service and other spending on programs providing benefits in the present with taxes, user fees, and other revenues.

Now is the time for progressives to emphasize that public borrowing for constructive purposes benefits all of us. Additional resources can be obtained by capturing the peace dividend and restoring taxes on the rich. And we must ensure that this money is used to meet basic human needs and to begin the rebuilding of America.

Resources: Robert Eisner, *How Real is the Federal Deficit*; George Iden and John Sturrock, *Deficits and Interest Rates: Theoretical Issues and Empirical Evidence*, Staff Working Papers, Congressional Budget Office, January 1989.

November/December 1993

SHRINKING THE DEBT
(AND THE ECONOMY)

The demon of the debt has been looming large in 1993 popular discourse. Deficit reduction, as Federal Reserve Board Chairman Alan Greenspan has said, "is by far the most potent stimulus that I can imagine." Like few other notions, the idea that reducing the debt will jump-start the economy has crossed party lines.

Economists of all stripes are also in agreement about it — but according to them, reducing the debt will contract, not expand, the economy, at least in the near future.

The liberal establishment's short-term prognosis for the economy under rapid deficit reduction is bleak. Robert Reischauer, the director of the Congressional Budget Office (CBO), estimates that eliminating the deficit over a five- to ten-year period would slow growth by about 0.5% and rob the economy of 500,000 new jobs each year.

Two private forecasting companies, DRI/McGraw Hill and the WEFA group, recently reached similarly disheartening conclusions (see table). Both firms conduct research for corporate clients who would tend to favor the view that a large deficit "crowds out" private investment and is bad for business. Nevertheless, even DRI found that moving to a balanced budget by 2001 would lead to an average reduction in growth of 0.4% per year and about 450,000 fewer jobs per year than in the baseline scenario.* Moreover, the University of Michigan's estimate took into account the potential economic benefits of Clinton's now-defunct stimulus package and still pre-

dicted a fall in gross domestic product of about 0.3% by 1995 (with 250,000 fewer jobs). A model developed by Ray Fair, a Yale professor and author of the 1984 economic theory text *Specification, Estimation, and Analysis of Macroeconometric Models*, put the loss of growth at 0.6% per year, matching the estimate by the Economic Policy Institute (EPI), a progressive Washington, D.C. think tank.

Many political proponents of deficit reduction claim that it is essential to lowering interest rates, counteracting the debt's "crowding-out" effect and encouraging firms to invest and create new jobs. But as Dean Baker of EPI points out, the interest rate is only one factor of many that firms consider when undertaking investment (see "The Clinton Budget," in

this issue). "The impact of rapid deficit reduction is obviously negative," says Baker. "The fact that investment is only loosely linked to deficit reduction and that the short-term effect of deficit reduction is contractionary is recognized by virtually all economists and incorporated into most serious macroeconomic forecasts."

— *Betsy Reed*

Resource: Dean Baker, "Rapid Deficit Reduction: The Fast Path to Slow Growth," Economic Policy Institute Briefing Paper, August 1993.

*Each model worked from the CBO's projected baseline scenario, which put the economy's potential rate of growth at 2.1% per year in the September 1993 *Economic and Budget Outlook*.

FORECASTS OF THE IMPACT OF THE DEFICIT REDUCTION

Model	Number of Years in Plan	Amount of Annual Deficit Reduction in Final Year (in billions)	Average Change per Year in GDP Growth from Baseline	Total Change Job Growth from Baseline (in millions)
DRI	4.0	$160	−0.4%	−1.8
WEFA	3.5	281	−2.0	−3.4
CBO	5.0	320	−0.5	−2.5
Michigan	2.0	56	−0.3	−0.25
Fair	3.0	140	−0.6	−1.4
EPI	3.0	140	−0.6	−1.4

Source: Congressional Budget Office 1993, pp.79-80; DRI/McGraw Hill 1993; The WEFA Group 1992; RSQE 1993; Fair 1993. Compiled by Dean Baker for EPI.

SOAKING THE POOR

STATE AND LOCAL TAXES ARE THE UNFAIREST OF ALL

As the recession spreads throughout the country, over half the states face budget shortfalls. Cities and towns aren't faring much better, with business failures and falling property values cutting into property-tax revenues. Many legislators are responding with tax hikes. But according to a recent study, state and local taxes are the unfairest of all, and it doesn't have to be this way.

The study, issued in April by Citizens for Tax Justice (CTJ), calls for state and local organizing around a basic economic question: Who pays how much and for what? According to CTJ's "A Far Cry from Fair," in 48 states and the District of Columbia, state and local taxes are regressive — relative to income, the rich pay less, the poor pay more. Besides being unjust, this bad bargain also empties state coffers and diminishes services for everyone because those with money are let off the hook.

While the federal government relies on the personal income tax for 72% of its tax revenues, state and local governments get only 26% from income taxes. Instead, they depend more heavily on sales and excise taxes, which generally take a bigger bite out of the poor than the rich. And cities and towns rely overwhelmingly on property taxes, which are also regressive.

In its study, CTJ estimates the state and local taxes on married couples with two children for different income brackets.

• The richest 1% — average 1991 family income $875,000 — pay 7.6% of their income in state and local taxes. The middle 20%, earning $39,100, pay 10%. The poorest 20%, earning $12,700, pay 13.8%.

• The District of Columbia and 46 states tax the middle fifth higher than the top 1%. Only California, Delaware, Maine, and Vermont make rich families pay more than middle-class families.

• The highest tax rate a rich family pays anywhere in the country is 11.3%, which is what the wealthiest New York families (average income: $2.3 million) pay. Low-income families pay a higher rate than that in 38 states.

• In every state but New York, the poor pay a higher tax rate than the middle class.

THE ABILITY TO PAY

Public officials, parroting business lobbyists, defend low taxes on businesses and the wealthy as prerequisites to attracting investment dollars and jobs. But taxing the poor instead of the rich is not only insensitive, it's just plain foolish because it denies states the wherewithal to pay for the schools, roads, and other public services a viable economy needs. "Soaking the poor simply doesn't raise much money, since the poor, by definition, don't have much," CTJ writes.

Different taxes affect people differently. So what makes a particular levy fair? According to CTJ, ever since the federal government levied a temporary income tax during the

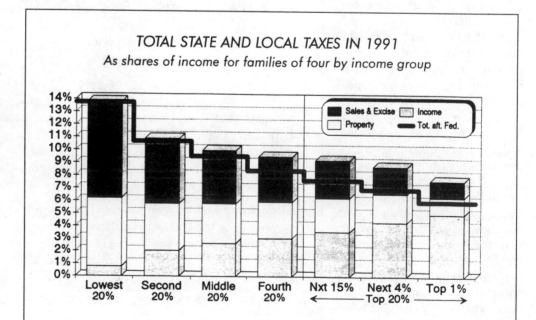

TOTAL STATE AND LOCAL TAXES IN 1991
As shares of income for families of four by income group

Civil War, the measure of fairness in the United States has been ability to pay. This principle underlies federal income taxes, which are termed progressive because tax rates rise as income rises.

Because they rely less on progressive income taxes, states and localities raise revenue more unfairly. According to CTJ, only the tax systems in Vermont and Delaware are even slightly progressive. Tax rates for low-income families are at least twice those for the rich in CTJ's "Terrible Ten" — Nevada, Texas, Florida, Washington, South Dakota, Tennessee, Wyoming, New Hampshire, Pennsylvania, and Illinois (see table). The ratio is worse than five to one in Nevada, Texas, Florida, and Washington. In these states, the middle fifth is hard hit, too, with rates up to three times greater than those for the richest 1%.

South Dakota, Nevada, Tennessee, and Washington add insult to injury. Between 1985 and 1991, these four, plus Connecticut, West Virginia, and Alaska, cut taxes on the rich and raised everyone else's. While upping taxes 18% on the bottom fifth, Connecticut relaxed taxes on the rich by 12%. Florida and Illinois were a bit more gracious: they left the rich alone — but raised taxes significantly for everyone else.

In all these states, public officials brag about low taxes. However, says CTJ, "This raises a fundamental question: 'low tax' for whom?" Consider the state of Washington. With no income tax, it is nevertheless "the highest-tax state in the entire country for poor people." Washington's poor pay over 17% of their income in state and local taxes. The rich pay 3.4%.

WHO'S THE FAIREST OF THEM ALL?

Now that we can talk taxes, let's talk about the right ones. President Bush's read-my-lips pledge meant no new taxes *on the rich*, but what is a fair tax? A good definition is a tax paid by those most able to afford it. A tax is termed progressive if you pay a higher percentage of your income the richer you are. With a regressive tax, the wealthy pay a smaller percentage of their income. Keep that in mind as you hear these different taxes batted around in the coming debates.

Income taxes are among the fairest options. Thirty-seven states use progressive tax rates that increase with income. Unfortunately, many are not structured to take full advantage of taxing the highest incomes the most heavily. Three states have flat rates. Exemptions for low-income people help make income taxes more progressive.

Sales taxes across the board tend to be regressive because poor people spend more of their income than the wealthy and save less. Forty-five states have sales taxes, which are usually their major single revenue source. Most states exempt basic necessities like food and fuel, reducing the regressive impact. Almost all states tax only goods, but the trend is to extend the base to some services. This can be progressive if businesses and richer people are the main consumers of the services.

Excise taxes apply to specific items—gasoline, cigarettes, alcohol. Every state levies excise taxes. These tend to be very regressive, since consumption of these goods (except for alcohol) varies little with income. However, excise taxes on those luxuries that only the rich can afford are progressive.

User fees are those pesky payments to register your car and hunting rifle, hang out a professional shingle, get the garbage picked up. Most are regressive. States and localities have increasingly turned to these "revenue raisers" that technically aren't taxes ("quack quack"). Communities have levied them in lieu of unpopular property taxes, while many states like them because they are often hidden or don't need legislative approval.

Property taxes, which are always local, are generally regressive. At the low-income end, landlords pass them on to renters, and low-income homeowners can't easily exchange homes for other forms of wealth. But property taxes can be made more progressive. After all, rich folks own lots of property and hence pay more taxes. Adding a "circuit breaker," which automatically limits tax payments if they exceed a certain percentage of a renter's or home- owner's income, can reduce the regressive impact. In addition, real-estate speculation can be controlled by charging high rates on property held for short periods of time.

Corporate income taxes are a bone of contention, since no one is sure who pays them in the end—the corporation or its customers. To the extent that corporations can pass on the tax to workers and consumers, they will. The more owners bear the burden, the more progressive the tax is. In any case, progressives have sharpened tax debates by publicizing corporate tax evasion.

WHAT'S FAIR, AND WHAT'S NOT

The eight worst states in the "Terrible Ten" share a common feature: along with Alaska, they lack a tax on personal income. Instead, like most state and local governments, they rely for revenues on sales and excise taxes, both of which are very regressive.

Sales taxes are regressive because low-income families, out of necessity, spend a higher fraction of their income than the rich. Excise taxes are levied on particular goods, especially gasoline, tobacco, and alcohol. While environmental and health factors may justify these taxes, low-income families spend a larger share of their income on them also. Together, sales and excise taxes nationwide take 7.6% of low-income families' earnings, 4.2% from those in the middle, and 1.3% from those at the top.

CTJ's report also looks at property taxes, the pillar of local finances. They're regressive as well. Though the tax is levied on property owners, who tend to be middle-income or wealthy, they then pass on much of the tax to tenants in the form of rent increases. Some estimate that renters end up absorbing 75% of the property taxes on rental properties. CTJ used a more conservative estimate of 50% for its study, but still found that low-income families spend 5.4% of their earnings on property taxes, while the rich spend only 1.3%. Middle-income families pay more than twice as large a share as do the rich in property taxes.

"The personal income tax," says CTJ, "is the linchpin of any tax system that is serious about distributing tax burdens according to people's ability to pay." Thus, Vermont, with the most progressive rates, has a graduated income tax. Its effective rate ranges from -1.9% for the poorest fifth (a refundable tax credit) to 6.1% for the top 1%.

Still, having a personal income tax does not necessarily make a state's tax system fair. Illinois and Pennsylvania have an income tax but overall hit their poor almost three times as heavily as the rich. That's because the income-tax rates are very low and are not graduated — tax rates do not rise with income.

SOAK THE RICH

CTJ connects this dismal state of affairs to some recent history. Since 1977, while most Americans struggled to stay abreast of inflation, the rich got richer. Federal tax cuts, overwhelmingly beneficial to the wealthy, allowed the federal government to shuffle responsibility for many broad-based domestic programs off to the states. Their reliance on more regressive tax systems has disproportionately burdened the poor and middle class.

To reverse the taxing trend, CTJ wants to "make it plain to state lawmakers that middle- and lower-income taxpayers should no longer be the first targets of proposals to raise taxes — or to cut services." And given CTJ's hard data, clear recommendations emerge on the elements of fairer local and state taxes. Sales taxes should be as low as possible and softened by exempting food, utilities, and other necessities. Credits for low-income families would also help offset the regressive impact of sales and excise taxes.

Graduated personal income taxes are crucial. The good news from the CTJ study is that state income taxes have become a bit more progressive since 1985 as states followed the federal lead and closed some loopholes for the rich and raised personal exemptions. However, given the low real tax rates on the rich, graduated personal income taxes could contribute far more to a fair tax structure that generates the revenue the states sorely need.

Resource: "A Far Cry From Fair" is available from Citizens for Tax Justice, 1311 L St., NW, Washington, DC 20005. All charts and graphs are from "A Far Cry From Fair." CTJ is a non-profit coalition of labor, public-interest, and citizens groups working for fairer federal, state, and local taxes.

"THE TERRIBLE TEN"
States with the highest taxes on poor and middle-income families compared to taxes on the richest one percent

State	Tax Rates on:			Poor/ Rich	Middle/ Rich	Income tax?
	Poor	Middle	Rich			
Nevada	10.0%	5.7%	1.8%	556%	314%	No
Texas	17.1	8.4	3.1	553	273	No
Florida	13.8	7.6	2.7	518	283	No
Washington	17.4	9.5	3.4	509	278	No
South Dakota	16.2	8.7	3.5	465	249	No
Tennessee	15.2	7.7	3.6	418	211	No*
Wyoming	9.0	5.3	2.4	372	218	No
New Hampshire	12.7	7.6	3.8	329	198	No*
Pennsylvania	15.9	9.8	5.5	287	176	Flat
Illinois	16.5	10.8	6.0	273	179	Flat

* Only interest and dividends taxed

CHAPTER 5

Banks and Monetary Policy

March/April 1994

BANKS IN CONTROL

HOW THE FED FRUSTRATES FISCAL POLICY

BY DOUG ORR

Why should someone involved in environmental issues, or education reform efforts, or efforts to house the homeless care about monetary policy? In fact, why should anyone on the left, other than a few academics, care about monetary policy? After all, it only affects the financial markets, right? *Wrong.* Monetary policy is holding all other social policies hostage. Whenever any policy change is proposed, be it health care, housing, or transportation, the first question politicians ask is "What will the bond market think about this?"

"The bond market" is a euphemism for the financial sector of the U.S. economy and the Federal Reserve (Fed), which regulates that sector. The Fed controls monetary policy, and has been using its power to help the banking industry, while thwarting government attempts to stimulate the economy. Congress has before it two bills aimed at ending this situation — but, unfortunately, they have little chance of passing.

Since 1979, the Fed has had an unprecedented degree of independence from government control. This independence has put it in a position to veto any progressive fiscal policy that the Congress might propose. To understand how this situation developed, we must understand the function of banks, the structure of the Fed, and the role of monetary policy.

BANKS AND INSTABILITY

Government regulates the banking industry because private sector, profit-driven banking is inherently unstable. Banks do more than just store money — they help create it (see "What Is Money?" page 67). For every dollar deposited in a commercial bank, three cents is set aside as "reserves" to "cover" that deposit, and the remaining 97 cents is loaned out. It is through loans that banks create new money and generate profits. The drive to maximize profits often leads banks to become overextended: making too many loans and holding too few reserves. This drive for profits can undermine a bank's stability.

If depositors think the bank is holding too few reserves, or is making overly speculative loans, they might try to withdraw their money as cash. Large numbers of depositors withdrawing cash from a bank at the same time is called a "run on the bank." Since banks only hold 3% of their deposit liabilities as cash, even a moderate-sized "run" would be enough to drain the bank of all of its cash. If a bank has no cash, it is insolvent and is forced to close. At that point, all remaining deposits in the bank cease to exist, and depositors lose their money.

The failure of a bank affects more than just that bank's depositors. One bank's excesses tend to shake people's faith in other banks. If the run spreads, "bank panics" can occur. During the 1800's, such panics erupted every 10 to 15 years, bankrupting between 10% and 25% of the banks in the United States and creating a recession each time.

THE CREATION OF THE FED

The Panic of 1907 bankrupted some of the largest banks and led to demands for bank reforms that would stabilize the system. Reform proposals ranged from doing almost nothing to nationalizing the entire banking industry. As a compromise, the Federal Reserve was created in 1913. The U.S. government saw the Fed as a way for bankers to regulate themselves, and structured the Federal Reserve System so that it would be responsive to its main constituencies: banks and other financial-sector businesses. These constituencies are now euphemistically called "the bond market." While ideally it should serve the interests of the general public when it conducts monetary policy, in reality the Fed balances two, occasionally conflicting, goals: maintaining the stability of the banking system and maximizing bank profits. Over time, Congress and the President have varied the degree of independence that they have given to the Fed to choose between these goals.

ONE INDUSTRY ALWAYS LOSES FROM UNEXPECTEDLY HIGH INFLATION — BANKING.

Initially, the Fed enjoyed a high degree of independence. However, it did not fully understand how to wield its new tools. Thus, it was more successful in aiding bank profits than in stabilizing the system. During the 1920s, the Fed allowed member banks to engage in highly speculative activities, including using depositors' money to play the stock market. While many banks were very profitable, speculative excesses caused almost 20% of the banks in existence in 1920 to fail during the following decade. With the onset of the Great Depression, between 1929 and 1933, more than 9,000 banks, 38% of the total, failed.

Since the Fed had not achieved its first goal, in 1935 Congress responded with laws that put many new regulations on banks, and reduced the Fed's independence. Congress accomplished the latter goal by restricting the power of the 12 regional Fed banks, and centralizing authority in Washington.

Fed Independence Lost

Under the new regulations, commercial banks were restricted to taking deposits and making commercial loans. Thus, the only opportunity for making a profit was to maintain a "spread" between the interest rate paid on deposits and that charged on loans. Loans are made for relatively long terms, while checking deposits are not. If the short-term interest rate on deposits varies widely, the spread will grow and shrink, which makes bank profits unstable. In order to stabilize bank profits, during the 30 years after 1935 the Treasury mandated that the Fed keep this rate approximately constant.

Under this arrangement, Congress indirectly controlled monetary policy. If Congress wanted to stimulate the economy it could increase government spending or cut taxes. Both led to an increase in spending and the demand for money (see box, page 65). To keep interest rates, which are the price of money, from rising, the Fed had to increase the supply of money. Thus, the Fed "accomodated" fiscal policy decisions made by Congress and the President.

During most of this period, growth was moderate and prices were stable. The Fed went along because this arrangement did not interfere with bank profits. Starting in the mid-1960s, however, stimulative fiscal policy started to push up the inflation rate, which did threaten bank profits. A confrontation over Fed independence ensued, and grew in intensity throughout the 1970s.

Inflation's Impact

Contrary to the view commonly propagated by the media, inflation does not affect everyone equally. In fact, there are clear winners and losers. Inflation is an increase in the average price level, but some prices rise faster than average and some rise slower. If you are selling something whose price is rising faster than average, you win, otherwise, you lose. Inflation redistributes income, but in an arbitrary manner. The winners one year may be next year's losers. This uncertainty makes inflation unpopular, even to the winners. But one industry always loses from unexpectedly high inflation, and that industry is banking.

Banks make loans today that will be repaid, with interest, in the future. If inflation reduces the value of those future payments, banks' profits will fall. So bankers are interested in the "real interest rate," that is, the actual interest rate on the loan minus the rate of inflation. If the interest rate on commercial bank loans is 7% and the rate of inflation is 3%, the real rate of interest is 4%. In the early post-war period, real interest rates were stable at about 2%.

From 1965 on, unexpected increases in inflation reduced real interest rates. This cheap credit was a boon to homebuyers, farmers and manufacturers, but it greatly reduced bank profits. Banks wanted inflation cut. The Keynesian view of monetary policy offered a simple but unpopular solution: raise interest rates enough to cause a recession. High unemployment and falling incomes would take the steam out of inflation.

But putting people out of work to help bankers would be a hard sell. The Fed needed a different story to justify shifting its policy from stabilizing interest rates to fighting inflation. That story was monetarism, a theory that claims that changes in the money supply affect prices, but nothing else in the economy (see box, page 66).

The Monetarist Experiment

On October 6, 1979, Fed Chairman Paul Volcker, using monetarist theory as a justification, announced that the Fed would no longer try to keep interest rates at targeted levels. He argued that the Fed should concentrate on controlling inflation, and to do so he would now focus on limiting the money supply growth rate. As neither Congress nor the U.S. President attempted to overrule Volcker, this change ushered in an era of unprecedented independence for Fed monetary policy.

During the next three years, the Fed reduced the growth rate of the money supply. But this experiment did not yield

WHAT IS THE FEDERAL RESERVE?

The Fed is a federally chartered corporation, owned by its member banks. The directors of the corporation, called governors, are appointed by the president of the United States, and confirmed by Congress, for 14 year terms. Unlike other public officials, there are no provisions for recalling a governor if his or her policies run counter to those of the elected government.

There are twelve regional federal reserve banks. The presidents of these banks are elected by the member banks in each region. The seven national governors, along with five of these presidents, constitute the Fed's Open Market Committee, FOMC, which determines the direction of monetary policy. Thus, government appointees hold a slim majority in policy making, but these appointees do not have to answer to the government. Ultimately, Congressional influence comes only from the threat of restructuring the Fed.

The Fed has several tools to conduct monetary policy. To maintain stability, it can set the percentage of banks' assets that must be held in cash (the "reserve requirement"), and can act as a "lender of last resort," loaning emergency reserves to banks that are in danger of failing.

To assist bank profits, the Fed has control over bank lending policies, bank reserves, and the money supply. Banks make profits by lending money. If the Fed expands reserves in the banking system, banks can make more loans, create new money, and increase the size of the money supply. If the Fed reduces reserves in the system, banks can make fewer loans and the money supply is reduced. The FOMC makes and implements, in absolute secrecy, decisions to change the banking system's reserves.

the results predicted by the monetarists. Instead of a swift reduction in the inflation rate, the most immediate outcome was a rapid rise in real interest rates and the start of the worst recession since the Great Depression.

As the Keynesian view predicted, the recession occurred because high interest rates slowed economic growth and increased unemployment. In 1979, the unemployment rate was 5.8%. By 1982 it had reached 10.7%, the first double-digit rate since the Depression. With fewer people working and buying products, the inflation rate, which had been 8.7% in 1979, finally started to slow in 1981 and was approaching 4% by the end of 1982. Tight-money policies by the Fed kept nominal interest rates from falling as fast as inflation. This raised real interest rates (nominal rates minus inflation) on commercial loans from 0.5% in 1979 to 10% in 1982, five times the post-war average.

The Fed's fight against inflation had a severe impact on the entire economy. All businesses, especially farming and manufacturing firms, run on credit. The rise in interest rates, combined with lower prices, squeezed the profits of farmers and manufacturers.

Both these industries rely heavily on exports, and so were also hurt by the negative effect of high interest rates on the competitiveness of U.S. exports. U.S. real interest rates were the highest in the world, thereby attracting financial investment from abroad. In order for foreigners to invest here they first had to buy dollars. This demand for dollars drove up their value in international markets. While a "strong" dollar means imports are relatively cheap, it also means that U.S. exports are expensive. Foreigners could not afford to buy our "costly" agricultural and manufactured exports. As a result, during this period, bankruptcy rates in these two industries were massive, higher than during the 1930s.

Despite its high cost to the rest of the economy, the monetarist experiment did not benefit many banks. Initially, high real interest rates appeared to help bank profits. Regulations capped the interest rates banks could pay on deposits, but rates charged on loans were not regulated. This increased the profit on loans. Many investors, however, started moving their deposits to less-regulated financial intermediaries, such as mutual funds, that could pay higher rates on deposits. In addition, the recession forced many borrowers to declare bankruptcy and default on their loans. Both these factors pushed banks toward insolvency.

REVERSING COURSE

It was bank losses, rather than the pain in the rest of the economy, that led Volcker to announce in September 1982 that he was abandoning monetarism. His new policy aimed to provide enough reserves to keep most banks solvent and to allow a slow recovery from the recession. Unemployment remained high for the next five years, so inflation continued to slow. Real interest rates stayed near 8% through 1986, so interest-sensitive industries, such as farming and manufacturing, did not take part in the recovery.

KEYNESIAN AND MONETARIST VIEWS OF MONETARY POLICY

Keynesian

Keynesians view the interest rate as the price of money, which, like all prices, is determined by supply and demand. The Fed controls the supply and the public controls the demand. If the economy is expanding, people and businesses need more money to buy products and services. Such an increase in the demand for money will drive up its price — the interest rate. Likewise, a decrease in the demand for money will drive interest rates down. In economic jargon, interest rates are set in the "monetary sector."

According to the Keynesian view, money also affects the "real" economy. If interest rates are high, investment and consumption spending will be reduced and economic growth will slow. This leads to excess unemployment. If interest rates are low, increased spending will lead to growth in output and employment. However, if demand for output exceeds the capacity of the economy to produce it, inflation speeds up. Thus, Keynesians see inflation as driven by the "real sector."

Monetarist

The centerpiece of monetarist theory is the "equation of exchange," $MV = PQ$, where M = money supply, V = velocity (the speed at which money is exchanged, or the number of times each dollar is used in a year), P = prices, and Q = quantity of goods. This equation simply states the truism that the total dollar value of all purchases (P times Q) is equal to the total dollars used to make these purchases (M times V). If we buy $4 trillion of goods and services in a year and the money supply is $1 trillion, then each dollar must have been used four times.

To convert this equation into a theory, the monetarists make two assumptions. The first is that the economy will always be operating at full employment, so physical output, Q, is constant. The second is that velocity, V, is constant. Under these assumptions, a change in the supply of money, M, cannot affect output or velocity, so it must change prices, P, and only prices. So, counter to the Keynesian view, monetarists see inflation as a direct result of changes in the money supply (the "monetary sector"). They also believe that real interest rates are set in the "real sector" and, in the long-run, there is almost no link between the monetary sector and the "real" economy. This theory yields a simple policy recommendation: the Fed should fight inflation. Any other problems in the economy are someone else's fault and responsibility.

Volcker made his allegiance to the banking industry clear during a meeting, in February 1985, with a delegation of state legislators and farmers who were demanding easier money and lower interest rates. He told them, "Look, your constituents are unhappy, mine aren't."

Yet by 1985, the crisis in the savings and loan industry (see "No Expense Too Great: A history of the savings & loan bailout," *Real World Banking*, 1993), was spreading into commercial banking. To provide cash ("liquidity") to banks, Volcker allowed the money supply to grow by 12% during 1985 and by 17% in 1986. Monetarists raised the spectre of a return to double-digit inflation. Instead, inflation continued to slow, demonstrating that a simple link between the money supply and inflation does not exist.

THE VETO

Despite the failure and subsequent abandonment of monetarist policies, the Fed still uses monetarist theory to justify its continued focus on fighting inflation. The Fed's 1979 shift away from accommodating fiscal policy was based on the myth that monetary policy only affects inflation. This shift allowed the Fed to more narrowly serve the interests of its constituency. Today, nominal interest rates have fallen but because inflation is so low, real interest rates remain high. Currently real interest rates on commercial loans are about 5% — 2.5 times the post-World War II average. Real interest rates remain high because the "bond market" worries about any possible increase in future inflation.

Fighting inflation benefits "the bond market." However, despite the near-depression that monetarism caused in the 1980s, the Fed continues to claim that fighting inflation serves the interests of the entire country. The public's widespread belief in this thesis denies Congress the support it needs to force the Fed back to accommodating fiscal policy.

If Congress decides to spend more for environmental cleanup, housing the homeless, education, or compensating the victims of illegal radiation testing, "the bond market" will raise the spectre of renewed inflation. In fact, if Congress passes any program to stimulate the economy and reduce unemployment, the bond market will raise this same spectre. In response to its constituency, the Fed is likely to tighten the money supply in order to "control inflation." This policy will raise interest rates, slow the economy, and prevent the government stimulus from taking effect. Since Congress is aware of this probable outcome, and knows it will incorrectly be blamed for it, Congress is unlikely to propose the stimulus package at all. This is how the bond market holds Congressional policy hostage.

As long as Congress and the President allow the Federal Reserve to follow an inflation-fighting policy, the Fed can maintain a veto threat over the elected government. Two bills currently before Congress are designed to increase electoral control over Fed decision-making, by requiring that all members of the Fed's critical decision-making body (the Federal Open Market Committee — see box) be appointees of the U.S. President. But since neither bill would allow the President to give orders to his appointees, or to remove them from office, the Fed would remain largely outside democratic control.

Resources: Secrets of the Temple: How the Federal Reserve Runs the Country, William Greider, 1987; "Congress Threatens the Fed," Thomas Havrilevsky et al, *Challenge*, March-April 1993; *Real World Banking*, Dollars & Sense, 1993.

November/December 1993

WHAT IS MONEY?

BY DOUG ORR

We all use money everyday. Yet many people do not know what money actually is. There are many myths about money, including the idea that the government "prints" all of it and that it has some intrinsic value. But actually, money is less a matter of value, and more a matter of faith.

Money is sometimes called the universal commodity, because it can be traded for all other commodities. But for this to happen, everyone in society must believe that money will be accepted. If people stop believing that it will be accepted, the existing money ceases to be money. Recently in Poland, people stopped accepting the zloty, and used vodka as money instead.

In addition to facilitating exchanges, money allows us to "store" value from one point in time to another. If you sell your car today for $4,000, you probably won't buy that amount of other products today. Rather, you store the value as money, probably in a bank, until you want to use it.

The "things" that get used as money have changed over time, and "modern" people often chuckle when they hear about some of them. The Romans used salt (from which we get the word "salary"), South Sea Islanders used shark's teeth, and several societies actually used cows. The "Three Wise Men" brought gold, frankincense and myrrh, each of which was money in different regions at the time.

If money does not exist, or is in short supply, it will be created. In POW camps, where guards specifically outlaw its existence, prisoners use cigarettes instead. In the American colonies, the British attempted to limit the supply of British pounds, because they knew that by limiting the supply of money, they could hamper the development of independent markets in the colonies. Today, the United States uses a similar policy, through the International Monetary Fund, in dealing with Latin America.

To overcome this problem, the colonists began to use tobacco leaves as money. This helped the colonies to develop, but it also allowed the holders of large plots of land to grow their own money! When the colonies gained independence, the new government decreed gold to be money, rather than tobacco, much to the dismay of Southern plantation owners. Now, rather than growing money, farmers had to find or buy it.

To aid the use of gold as money, banks would test its purity, put it in storage, and give the depositor paper certificates of ownership. These certificates, "paper money," could then be used in place of the gold itself. Since any bank could store gold and issue certificates, by the beginning of the Civil War, over 7000 different types of "paper money" were in circulation in the United States, none of it printed by the government.

While paper money is easier to use than gold, it is still risky to carry around large amounts of cash. It is safer to store the paper in a bank and simply sign over its ownership to make a purchase. We sign-over the ownership of our money by writing a check. Checking account money became popular when the government outlawed the printing of paper money by private banks in 1864.

HOW BANKS CREATE MONEY

Banks are central to understanding money, because in addition to storing it, they help to create it. Bankers realize that not everyone will withdraw their money at the same time, so they loan out much of the money that has been deposited. It is from the interest on these loans that banks get their profits, and through these loans the banking system creates new money.

If you deposit $100 cash in your checking account at Chase Manhattan Bank, you still have $100 in money to use, because checks are also accepted as money. Chase must set aside some of this cash as "reserves," in case you or other depositors decide to withdraw money as cash. Current regulations issued by the Federal Reserve Bank (the Fed) require banks to set aside three cents out of each dollar. So Chase can make a loan of $97, based on your deposit. Chase does not make loans by handing out cash but instead by putting $97 in the checking account of the person, say Emily, taking out the loan. So from your initial deposit of $100 in cash, the economy now has $197 in checking account money.

The borrower, Emily, pays $97 for some product or service by check, and the seller, say Ace Computers, deposits the money in its checking account. The total amount of checking account money is still $197, but its location and ownership have changed. If Ace Computer's account is at Citibank, $97 in cash is transferred from Chase to Citibank. This leaves just $3 in cash reserves at Chase to cover your original deposit. However, Citibank now has $97 in "new" cash on hand, so it sets aside three cents on the dollar ($2.91) and loans out the rest, $94.09, as new checking account money. Through this process, every dollar of "reserves" yields many dollars in total money.

If you think this is just a shell game and there is only $100 in "real" money, you still don't understand money. Anything that is accepted as payment for a transaction is "real" money. Cash is no more real than checking account money. In fact, most car rental companies will not accept cash as payment for a car, so for them, cash is not money!

Today, there is $292 billion of U.S. currency, i.e. "paper money," in existence. However, somewhere between 50% to 70% of it is held outside the United States by foreign banks and individuals. The vast majority of all money actually in use in the United States is not cash, but rather checking account money. This type of money, $726 billion, was created by private banks, and was not "printed" by anyone. In fact, this money exists only as electronic "bits" in banks' computers. [The less "modern" South Sea Islanders could have quite a chuckle about that!]

The amount of money that banks can create is limited by the total amount of reserves, and by the fraction of each deposit that must be held as reserves. Prior to 1914, bankers themselves decided what fraction of deposits to hold as reserves. Since then, this fraction has been set by the main banking regulator, the Fed [see "Banks in Control," page 63, for a detailed look at the Fed].

Until 1934, gold was held as reserves, but the supply of gold was unstable, growing rapidly during the California and Alaska "gold rushes," and very slowly at other times. As a result, at times more money was created than the economy needed, and at other times not enough money could be created. Starting in 1934, the U.S. government decided that gold would no longer be used as reserves. Cash, now printed by the Fed, could no longer be redeemed for gold, and cash itself became the reserve asset.

Banks, fearing robberies, do not hold all of their cash reserves in their own vaults. Rather, they store it in an account at a regional Fed bank. These accounts count as reserves. What banks do hold in their vaults is their other assets, such as Treasury bonds and corporate bonds.

THE FED AND BANK RESERVES

The only role of the government in creating money is through the Fed. If the Fed wants to expand the money supply, it must increase bank reserves. To do this, the Fed buys Treasury bonds from a bank, and pays with a check drawn on the Fed itself. By depositing the check in its reserve account at the Fed, the bank now has more reserves, so the bank can now make more loans and create new checking account money.

By controlling the amount of reserves, the Fed attempts to control the size of the money supply. But as recent history has shown, this control is limited. During the recent recession, the Fed created reserves, but many banks were afraid to make loans, so little new money was created. During the late 1970s, the Fed tried to limit the amount of money banks could create by reducing reserves, but banks simply created new forms of money, just like the POW camp prisoners. In 1979, there was only one form of checking account money. Today, there are many, with odd names such as NOW's, ATS's, repos, and money market deposit accounts.

These amorphous forms of money function only because we believe they will function, which is why the continued stability of the banking system is so critical. Banks do not have cash reserves to cover all checking account money. If, through a replay of the savings & loan debacle, we lose faith in the commercial banking system and all try to take out our "money" as cash, the banks will become insolvent (fail), and the money they have created will simply disappear. This would create a real crisis, since no market economy can function without its money.

> MONEY IS LESS A MATTER OF VALUE, AND MORE A MATTER OF FAITH

September 1991

HARD TIMES FOR BANKERS

INNOVATION, POOR JUDGMENT, AND DEREGULATION BRING DOWN THE BANKS

BY JOHN MILLER

Bankers are a breed apart. Unlike the financial cowboys, outright crooks, and takeover artists behind the financial excesses of the 1980s, bankers are stodgy, stiff, invariably conservative dressers, and prudent investors. Hell, bankers, especially Yankee bankers, are downright tight-fisted.

Bankers were surely immune to the eighties fever and the feeling that the good times would roll on forever. They must have looked past the short-term profit taking and seen the financial disaster awaiting the gamblers and risk takers.

Right?

Wrong.

For a decade and a half, bankers have feverishly crammed their portfolios with risky loans to Third World debtors, commercial property developers, and financial raiders. That reckless lending, plus increased competition from other financial institutions for what was traditionally only banks' business, combined to bring down a record number of banks across the nation in recent years.

Over 1,000 banks have failed since 1985. That's more bank failures than occurred between 1934, the year the Roosevelt administration established the Federal Deposit Insurance Corporation (FDIC), and 1985. Still another 1,000 "troubled" banks are tottering and likely to fail.

Losses to date have all but exhausted the FDIC insurance fund. At the end of 1990, the fund held $8.4 billion, or less than 40 cents for every $100 of insured deposits in the United States—an all-time low far below the $1.25 level regulators consider safe. Even FDIC boss William Seidman admits that, unless the fund is replenished, it will become insolvent sometime in 1992, if not before.

The banking industry's problems go well beyond the unprecedented number of bank failures. Profitability in banking has declined steadily for two decades. So has banks' share of the financial business of the United States.

Even if the economy continues its recovery from the 1991 recession, banks will continue to falter. *Business Week*, in a special report on "The Future of Banking," maintains that "the banking industry, at least as we know it, is dying."

The problems of the banking industry are, unfortunately, our problems. As each new bank fails, the probability rises that taxpayers will be called on to at least partially bail out the FDIC.

More importantly, the declining power of banks has left a financial vacuum in the economy. Commercial banks are the "department stores of finance." They make a wide variety of loans to consumers and businesses and offer savings and checking accounts insured by the FDIC for up to $100,000. In return for their public charter and the federal bank deposit insurance program, banks are expected to meet the credit needs of their local communities, including low- and moderate-income neighborhoods. They are the only financial institutions obligated by law to do this. Without active local banks, neighborhood housing and businesses suffer, and residents do not have easy access to checking services.

On the national level, the decline of U.S. banks has coincided with the rise of other financial institutions less tied to their communities and more focused on short-term speculation and financial investment. Hyman Minsky, a leading financial theorist, calls today's economy "money market capitalism"—capitalism financed by mutual funds, pension funds, and insurance companies. This turn towards short-term profits and financial investments, in evidence throughout the economy, has pulled investments away from new businesses, harming the real economy that produces goods and services. Successful banking reform must strengthen banks' role in community development. That means more public control of the banking industry.

BAD DAYS AT THE BANK

How did banks get into trouble? Stagflation and rising interest rates, financial innovations such as mutual and money-market funds, and deregulation have left commercial banks with a dwindling share of U.S. financial business, especially their core business—commercial and industrial loans.

In the mid- and late-1970s, stagflation, a combination of slow economic growth and high inflation, and the Volcker Federal Reserve Board's decision to monitor the money supply, rather than interest rates, drove market interest rates to double-digit levels. This was well above the maximum rate banks were allowed by law to pay on deposits. Even government securities such as Treasury bonds, an extremely conservative investment, offered rates of return well above the regulated interest rates banks were limited to paying.

At the same time, advanced technology also empowered competitors to banks. New information and computer systems allowed other financial corporations, such as Fidelity Investments and T. Rowe Price, to create attractive personal investment alternatives. Money-market mutual funds (which invest in short-term bonds and stocks and offer checking services), and stock and bond mutual funds (which sell shares in large stock funds) blossomed. Depositors followed the higher returns and deserted banks. In response, Congress struck down the cap on bank interest rates in the early 1980s, freeing banks to set the interest rates they pay their depositors. Almost immediately, banks began paying depositors more on all types of accounts, decreasing their profit margins.

Because of their lower overhead, and not having to pay FDIC insurance premiums, money-market mutual funds began to out-compete banks and replace them as sources of finance capital for large corporations. These funds made attractive short-term, large-denomination loans to creditworthy corporations by purchasing a corporation's "commercial paper" (large short-term bonds). These corporate loans grew rapidly. Between 1960 and 1990, the ratio of outstanding commercial paper to bank loans increased from less than 10% to better than 75%, as banks' share of short-term loans to corporations also dropped.

Financial innovations have also eaten into bank profits from their loan business, including consumer, mortgage, and business loans. Prior to the 1980s, banks and thrifts made almost all mortgage loans. In return for assuming the risk of holding these loans for many years, banks charged a margin that kept their profits high. But a new financial development, "securitization," lured non-bank companies, such as pension funds and insurance companies, into the business, breaking banks' control of the lending business.

Securitization, or bundling, places a mortgage into a pool with several thousand other mortgages, allowing banks and other lenders to sell shares of the cash flow from the pool. Today over one-third of all residential mortgages in the United States is bundled in this way. Not only did non-bank companies compete for consumer and mortgage loans, the increased competition lowered interest rates on loans, reducing the return that once accrued to banks for making long-term loans.

Finally, non-bank companies—such as General Electric, Sears Roebuck, and General Motors—began offering a wide range of bank-like services in the 1970s. The 1980s allowed these companies to capture an even larger share of the business.

All told, since 1970, bank profits have suffered a disastrous decline. Banks' return on assets are but one-eighth of what they were 20 years ago. In 1990, banks earned a 7.7% return on equity, compared with an almost 13% return earned by the 10 largest non-bank finance companies. Large banks, with more than $1 billion in assets, were even harder hit. These big troubles, not big plans, drove some of the largest banks to merge. Just this summer the megamerger of New York's Chemical Bank and Manufacturer's Hanover formed the second largest bank in the nation.

DESPERATELY SEEKING PROFITS

With the higher costs of obtaining deposits and stiffer competition within the loan business, bankers desperately began seeking new, more profitable, investments. Stagflation, however, had also brought slower growth and fewer investment opportunities.

Beginning in the mid-1970s, bankers ventured deeper into riskier territories—international lending, loans for corporate takeovers, and commercial real estate—and accepted a higher level of risks in their asset portfolios. As a result, cash and investment securities, mainly government, corporate, and foreign bonds, the most secure forms of

bank assets, decreased from 36% to 27% of total bank assets. Meanwhile, loans, a riskier category of assets, increased from 54% to 61%, an additional $700 billion in bank loans.

In the 1970s, bankers poured loans into Third World economies. Lured by the potential profits of variable interest rates that could be adjusted to inflation rates, comforted by the countries' alleged ability to repay loans by taxing their citizens, and lulled further by economic forecasts about potential oil revenues they had little ability to evaluate, bankers jumped to lend money to Mexico, Brazil, and other developing countries. After a decade of periodic defaults, U.S. banks had to repeatedly devalue these loans as assets and place the equivalent of 25% to 30% of them in special loan loss reserves.

Back in the United States, bankers participated in financing the leveraged buyouts and takeovers that reshuffled $1.3 trillion of corporate assets during the 1980s. While high-interest junk bonds financed many of these deals, banks also joined in lending liberally to overleveraged corporate raiders. Today 11 major U.S. banks have $3 billion or more in loans outstanding to companies that got into deep debt during the roaring eighties.

Real estate provided bankers another opportunity to prosper, and to fail, during the 1980s. In 1982, the Garn-St. Germain Act, embraced by both the Reagan White House and Congress, eliminated restrictions on the percentage of real estate loans in a bank's portfolio and allowed banks to loan to developers with little equity. Banks rushed in. During the 1980s, banks' construction loans and commercial mortgages nearly doubled as a percentage of bank assets. Bankers rode the boom for all it was worth, hoping to restore their lost profits. Fully 32% of all the existing office space in the nation was built in the 1980s.

During the building craze, bankers used questionable lending practices. In New Hampshire, for example, bankers pumped cash into fast-appreciating commercial real estate and resort projects, often lending 110% and 120% of the developers' needs. But the boom crashed. Rising office vacancies and falling property values stuck banks with more and more bad loans. Almost 10% of real estate loans are unlikely to be repaid. In the District of Columbia and Massachusetts, and for troubled banks like Citicorp, the largest real estate lender in the country, the percentage was almost twice that high.

NEW ENGLAND STORIES

Outside of Texas, nobody knows the banking story better than New Englanders. This January, Massachusetts residents experienced the first run on a large bank since the Great Depression. Depositors withdrew more than $1 billion from the Bank of New England (BNE) over one weekend immediately before an FDIC takeover. The takeover curbed the run on money, but did not stem growing concern over the health of New England's banking industry. According to Veribanc Inc., a bank rating company, New England houses 11 of the nation's 29 troubled banks that

pose the greatest threat to the bank insurance fund.

BNE was once a conservatively managed bank called New England Merchant National Bank. Under the leadership of Roderick MacDougall, the Boston-based bank grew into a premier lending institution with a portfolio long in commercial and industrial loans, the staple of old-line banking. In 1982, MacDougall sold the bank for an attractive sum to Connecticut Bank and Trust, a large retail lender, and retired to serve as Harvard University's treasurer.

Walter Connolly, a prototypical go-go banker of the roaring 1980s, headed the Connecticut bank. In 1983, he came to Boston to direct BNE, the holding company formed from the merger. He immediately began to expand the bank aggressively. Connolly told underlings "the market is share driven. Get the share and the profits will follow." He instructed managers to "grow it, grow it."

Grow it they did. In just three years BNE acquired 23 other banks to become the second largest bank in the region. BNE often paid top-dollar and questionable prices for its acquisitions. The largest, Conifer Group of Worcester, Mass., cost Connolly $656 million, nearly $100 million more than the next highest bid.

> THE DECLINE OF U.S. BANKS HAS COINCIDED WITH THE RISE OF OTHER FINANCIAL INSTITUTIONS LESS TIED TO THEIR COMMUNITIES AND MORE FOCUSED ON SHORT-TERM SPECULATION AND FINANCIAL INVESTMENT.

BNE binged on New England's superheated real estate market. According to the *Boston Globe*, "BNE never met a real estate deal it didn't like." At one point real estate accounted for 37% of BNE's loans—a higher concentration of money in real estate than any other bank in the country. When the New England real estate market collapsed in 1989, bad loans overwhelmed BNE.

At the time of its failure, BNE had $22 billion in assets, making it the fourth largest bank failure in U.S. history. Some 15% of its remaining assets were non-performing.

Following its "too big to fail doctrine," the FDIC protected every penny of every deposit in the bank, including uninsured deposits over $100,000 and deposits in BNE's foreign branches (virtually all in the Bahamas). The bailout will cost the insurance fund more than $2.5 billion.

It didn't have to cost this much. If the FDIC had honored only 45% of uninsured accounts, as it did with Freedom National Bank, one of the nation's largest black-owned banks, it could have reduced the cost of the bailout by hundreds of millions.

Tighter supervision by bank regulators would also have cut down the cost of the bailout. Representative Henry Gonzales, chair of the House Banking Committee, suggests bank regulators knew as early as 1988 that BNE's real estate loans were a possible "time bomb." Despite citing the bank in 1986 and 1987 for underwriting problems, insufficient loan-loss allowances, and poor asset quality, regulators never pressed BNE to take action or to limit the growth of its loans.

> A STABLE BANKING INDUSTRY AND A STABLE ECONOMY REQUIRE AN INDUSTRIAL POLICY IMMUNE TO THE SPECULATIVE FRENZIES OF THE 1980s.

Some New England bankers, however, did not succumb to the eighties fever, yet still prospered. Earlier this year, Woodbury C. Titcomb, chairman of Peoples Bancorp of Worcester, told the *Wall Street Journal* that "some incredibly foolish requests crossed my desk in the past few years." Unlike many of his competitors, he turned them down. He is now the head of a solidly profitable bank that almost doubled in size during the 1980s.

Unlike Walter Connolly, Woodie Titcomb was not about to invest recklessly merely because deregulation and a lack of supervision freed him to do so. An old-line banker, Titcomb was trained in the 1950s and early 1960s by bankers with vivid memories of the financial panics of the Depression. He worries "about the worst-case scenarios for the New England economy" and invests accordingly. "Woodie is conservative—a belt and suspenders man," according to Corine Turner, a director of Peoples Bancorp.

BUSHED BANK REFORM

But making all bankers as conservative a lender as Woodie Titcomb is not the answer to creating a more stable banking industry that tries to promote the long-term interests of the United States. Nor is the Bush administration's proposal.

The Bush administration prescribes further deregulation and freer financial markets as a cure-all for the ailing banking industry. The proposal currently before Congress would grant banks new powers to expand across state lines and to move into investment banking—selling securities, insurance, and mutual funds.

These reforms will not nurse the banking industry back to health. Leaving banking unregulated and subject to market forces has been a sure formula for financial panic. In fact, modern banking regulation came into being in the 1930s to curb the speculative excesses of earlier free-market banking. In addition, whenever banks have gotten into new areas, like commercial real estate in the 1980s, the results have been calamitous.

Ultimately, the Bush reforms will fail because they don't address the root causes of the banking crisis. Favorable economic conditions and successful regulation helped produce the stable banking of the postwar boom. Slower economic growth and higher inflation during the late 1970s and 1980s ate away at the profitability of banking as it ate away at the profitability of other industries. While a deteriorating economy and changing financial markets made the regulatory schemes imposed 50 years earlier work less well, the slow-to-adjust regulation did not compel bankers to make "bad loans." Nor will repealing "bad regulation laws," as the Bush administration suggests, turn go-go bankers like Walter Connolly into prudent investors like Woodie Titcomb. Rather, unregulated bankers will be able to make more bad loans and reckless investments than those made by bankers who were inhibited by government regulation.

Sound banking requires a sound economy. Only financial restructuring that creates an authentic public control over the banking industry will bring about both. That must begin with new regulations for banks: honest and public reporting of banking practices; more demanding capital requirements and limits on loans for all banks, and stricter public supervision of troubled banks' investment and dividend policies. It would also demand that banks respond to the needs of their local community, particularly the low-income housing market.

But most importantly, a stable banking industry and a stable economy require an industrial policy immune to the speculative frenzies of the 1980s. Progressive industrial policy would substitute democratic planning of investment for our current reliance on financial elites—like large bankers and Wall Street bond dealers—who have proven themselves to be unfit custodians of the long-term interests of the economy.

Resources: James Barth, R. Dan Brumbaugh, and Robert Litan, "Bank Failures are Sinking the FDIC," *Challenge,* March/April 1991; *Business Week,* "The Future of Banking," April 22, 1991; L.J. Davis, "The Problem with Banks? Bankers." *Harpers,* June 1991.

November 1992

TRANSFORMING THE FED

A PATH TO FINANCIAL STABILITY AND DEMOCRATIC SOCIALISM

BY ROBERT POLLIN

The U.S. financial system faces deep structural problems. Savings & loans and banks have failed in record numbers. Households, businesses, and the federal government are burdened by excessive debts. The economy favors short-term speculation over long-term investment. An unrepresentative and unresponsive elite has extensive control over the financial system. Moreover, the federal government is incapable of reversing these patterns through its existing tools, including fiscal, monetary, and financial regulatory policies.

I propose a dramatically different approach: transforming the Federal Reserve System (the "Fed") into a public investment bank. Such a bank would have substantial power to channel credit in ways that counter financial instability and support productive investment by private businesses. The Fed would use its powers to influence how and for what purposes banks, insurance companies, brokers, and other lenders loan money.

The U.S. government has used credit allocation policies, such as low-cost loans, loan guarantees, and home mortgage interest deductions, extensively and with success. Its primary accomplishment has been to create a home mortgage market that, for much of the period since World War II, provided non-wealthy households with unprecedented access to home ownership.

I propose increasing democratic control over the Federal Reserve's activities by decentralizing power to the 12 district Fed banks and instituting popular election of their boards of directors. This would create a mechanism for extending democracy throughout the financial system.

My proposal also offers a vehicle for progressives to address two separate but equally serious questions facing the U.S. economy:

• how to convert our industrial base out of military production and toward the development and adoption of environmentally benign production techniques; and

• how to increase opportunities for high wage, high productivity jobs in the United States. The U.S. needs such jobs to counteract the squeeze on wages from increasingly globalized labor and financial markets.

Transforming the Federal Reserve system into a public investment bank will help define an economic path toward democratic socialism in the United States.

My proposal has several strengths as a transitional program. It offers a mechanism for establishing democratic control over finance and investment — the area where capital's near-dictatorial power is most decisive. The program will also work within the United States' existing legal and institutional framework. We could implement parts of it immediately using existing federal agencies and with minimal demands on the federal budget.

At the same time, if an ascendant progressive movement put most of the program in place, this would represent a dramatic step toward creating a new economic system. Such a system would still give space to market interactions and the pursuit of greed, but would nevertheless strongly promote general well-being over business profits.

HOW THE FED FAILS

At present the Federal Reserve focuses its efforts on managing short-term fluctuations of the economy, primarily by influencing interest rates. When it reduces rates, it seeks to increase borrowing and spending, and thereby stimulate economic growth and job opportunities. When the Fed perceives that wages and prices are rising too fast (a view not necessarily shared by working people), it tries to slow down borrowing and spending by raising interest rates.

This approach has clearly failed to address the structural problems plaguing the financial system. The Fed did nothing, for example, to prevent the collapse of the savings and loan industry. It stood by while highly speculative mergers, buyouts, and takeovers overwhelmed financial markets in the 1980s. It has failed to address the growing crisis in the banking system, and the unprecedented levels of indebtedness and credit defaults of private corporations and households.

During the current recession the Fed has had minimal success even influencing the economy's short-term prospects. While it has cut interest rates many times over the past two years — to a point where short-term rates have reached their lowest level in 30 years — the recession has persisted and the prospects for recovery remain grim.

New Roles for the Fed

Under my proposal, the Federal Reserve would shift its focus from the short to the long term. It would provide more and cheaper credit to banks and other financiers who loan money to create productive assets and infrastructure — which promote high wage, high productivity jobs. The Fed would make credit more expensive for lenders that finance speculative activities such as the mergers, buyouts, and takeovers that dominated the 1980s.

The Fed would also give favorable credit terms to banks that finance decent affordable housing rather than luxury housing and speculative office buildings. It would make low-cost credit available for environmental research and development so the economy can begin the overdue transition to environmentally benign production. Cuts in military spending have idled many workers and productive resources, both of which could be put to work in such transformed industries.

Finally, the Fed would give preferential treatment to loans that finance investment in the United States rather than in foreign countries. This would help counter the trend of U.S. corporations to abandon the domestic economy in search of lower wages and taxes.

The first step in developing the Fed's new role would be for the public to determine which sectors of the economy should get preferential access to credit. One example, as I have suggested above, is industrial conversion from military production to investment in renewable energy and conservation.

Once the public establishes its investment goals, the Fed will have to develop new policy tools and use its existing tools in new ways to accomplish them. I propose that a transformed Federal Reserve use two major methods:

• set variable cash ("asset reserve") requirements for all lenders, based on the social value of the activities the lenders are financing; and

• increase discretionary lending activity by the 12 district Federal Reserve banks.

Varying Banks' Cash Requirements

The Fed currently requires that banks and other financial institutions keep a certain amount of their assets available in cash reserves. Banks, for example, must carry three cents in cash for every dollar they hold in checking accounts. A bank cannot make interest-bearing loans on such "reserves." I propose that the Fed make this percent significantly lower for loans that finance preferred activities than for less desirable investment areas. Let's say the public decides that banks should allocate 10% of all credit to research and development of new environmental technologies, such as non-polluting autos and organic farming. Then financial institutions that have made 10% of their loans in environmental technologies would not have to

hold any cash reserves against these loans. But if a bank made no loans in the environmental area, then it would have to hold 10% of its total assets in reserve. The profit motive would force banks to support environmental technologies without any direct expenditure from the federal budget.

All profit-driven firms will naturally want to avoid this reserve requirement. The Fed must therefore apply it uniformly to all businesses that profit through accepting deposits and making loans. These include banks, savings and loans, insurance companies, and investment brokerage houses. If the rules applied only to banks, for example, then banks could circumvent the rules by redefining themselves as another type of lending institution.

Loans to Banks That Do the Right Thing

The Federal Reserve has the authority now to favor some banks over others by making loans to them when they are short on cash. For the most part, however, the Fed has chosen not to exercise such discretionary power. Instead it aids all banks equally, through a complex mechanism known as open market operations, which increases total cash reserves in the banking system. The Fed could increase its discretionary lending to favored banks by changing its operating procedures without the federal government creating any new laws or institutions. Such discretionary lending would have several benefits.

First, to a much greater extent than at present, financial institutions would obtain reserves when they are lending for specific purposes. If a bank's priorities should move away from the established social priorities, the Fed could then either refuse to make more cash available to it, or charge a penalty interest rate, thereby discouraging the bank from making additional loans. The Fed, for example, could impose such obstacles on lenders that are financing mergers, takeovers, and buyouts.

In addition, the Fed could use this procedure to more effectively monitor and regulate financial institutions. Banks, in applying for loans, would have to submit to the Fed's scrutiny on a regular basis. The Fed could more closely link its regulation to banks' choices of which investments to finance.

Implementing this procedure will also increase the authority of the 12 district banks within the Federal Reserve system, since these banks approve the Fed's loans. Each district bank will have more authority to set lending rates and monitor bank compliance with regulations.

The district banks could then more effectively enforce measures such as the Community Reinvestment Act, which currently mandates that banks lend in their home communities. To date the Fed has had only limited success in requiring banks to increase their financing of local housing and small businesses. Banks that are committed to their communities and regions, such as the South Shore Bank in Chicago, could gain substantial support under this proposed procedure.

OTHER CREDIT ALLOCATION TOOLS

The Fed can use other tools to shift credit to preferred industries, such as loan guarantees, interest rate subsidies, and government loans. In the past the U.S. government has used these techniques with substantial success. They now primarily support credit for housing, agriculture, and education. Indeed, as of 1991, these programs subsidized roughly one-third of all loans in the United States.

Jesse Jackson's 1988 Presidential platform suggested an innovative way of extending such policies. He proposed that public pension funds channel a portion of their money into a loan guarantee program, with the funds used to finance investments in low cost housing, education, and infrastructure.

There are disadvantages, however, to the government using loan guarantee programs and similar approaches rather than the Fed's employing asset reserve requirements and discretionary lending. Most important is that the former are more expensive and more difficult to administer. Both loan guarantees and direct government loans require the government to pay off the loans when borrowers default. Direct loans also mean substantial administrative costs. Interest subsidies on loans are direct costs to government even when the loans are paid back.

In contrast, with variable asset reserve requirements and discretionary lending policies, the Fed lowers the cost of favored activities, and raises the cost of unfavored ones, without imposing any burden on the government's budget.

INCREASING PUBLIC CONTROL

The Federal Reserve acts in relative isolation from the political process at present. The U.S. president appoints seven members of the Fed's Board of Governors for 14 year terms, and they are almost always closely tied to banking and big business. The boards of directors of the 12 district banks appoint their presidents, and these boards are also composed of influential bankers and business people within each of the districts.

The changes I propose will mean a major increase in the central bank's role as an economic planning agency for the nation. Unless we dramatically improve democratic control by the public over the Fed, voters will correctly interpret such efforts as an illegitimate grasp for more power by business interests.

Democratization should proceed through redistributing power downward to the 12 district banks. When the Federal Reserve System was formed in 1913, the principle behind creating district banks along with the headquarters in Washington was to disperse the central bank's authority. This remains a valuable idea, but the U.S. government has never seriously attempted it. Right now the district banks are highly undemocratic and have virtually no power.

I propose reversing the equation — democratizing and empowering them. The district banks exercise power now only because five of the 12 bank presidents, along with the seven members of the Board of Governors, sit on the Federal Open Market Committee, which influences short-term interest rates by expanding or contracting the money supply. One way to increase the district banks' power is to create additional seats for them on the Open Market Committee.

A second method is to shift authority from the Washington headquarters to the districts. The Board of Governors would then be responsible for setting general guidelines, while the district banks would implement discretionary lending and enforcement of laws such as the Community Reinvestment Act.

The most direct way of democratizing the district banks would be to choose their boards in regular elections along with other local, regional, and state-wide officials. The boards would then choose the top levels of the banks' professional staffs and oversee the banks' day-to-day activities. Other approaches to democratization are also possible. Specifying the details of any proposal is less important than gaining acceptance for the basic idea of increasing democratic control over the Fed.

TRANSFORMING THE FEDERAL RESERVE SYSTEM INTO A PUBLIC INVESTMENT BANK WILL HELP DEFINE AN ECONOMIC PATH TOWARD DEMOCRATIC SOCIALISM IN THE UNITED STATES.

HISTORICAL PRECEDENTS

Since World War II other capitalist countries have extensively employed the types of credit allocation policies proposed here.

Indeed, according to a study sponsored by the Congressional Joint Economic Committee in the early 1970s, "Central banks in most countries designate certain sectors of the economy that are to receive favorable treatment from the central bank. This means either making loans in these favored sectors at below market rates of interest or making credit more available in these sectors than it would be if so-called market forces were allowed to operate."

Japan, France, and South Korea are the outstanding success stories, though since the early 1980s globalization and deregulation of financial markets have weakened each of their credit policies. When operating at full strength, the Japanese and South Korean programs primarily supported large-scale export industries, such as steel, automobiles, and consumer electronics. France targeted its policies more broadly to coordinate Marshall Plan aid for the development of modern industrial corporations.

We can learn useful lessons from these experiences, not least that credit allocation policies do work when they are implemented well. But substantial differences exist between experiences elsewhere and the need for a public investment bank in the United States.

In these countries a range of other institutions besides the central bank were involved in credit allocation policies. These included their treasury departments and explicit planning agencies, such as the powerful Ministry of International Trade and Industry (MITI) in Japan. In contrast, I propose to centralize the planning effort at the Federal Reserve.

We could create a new planning institution to complement the work of the central bank. But transforming the existing central banking system rather than creating a new institution minimizes both start-up problems and the growth of bureaucracies. Moreover, revamping the Fed in a period of pervasive financial problems has historical precedents. During the 1930s depression, for example, the federal government greatly increased the Fed's power to set interest rates and extend emergency credit.

A second and more fundamental difference between my proposal and the experiences in Japan, France, and South Korea is that their public investment institutions were accountable only to a business-oriented elite. This essentially dictatorial approach is antithetical to the goal of increasing democratic control of the financial system.

The challenge, then, is for the United States to implement effective credit allocation policies while broadening, not narrowing, democracy. Our success ultimately will depend on a vigorous political movement that can fuse two equally urgent, but potentially conflicting goals: economic democracy, and equitable and sustainable growth. If we can meet this challenge, it will represent a historic victory toward the construction of a democratic socialist future.

Resources: Robert Pollin, "Transforming the Federal Reserve into a Public Investment Bank: Why it is Necessary; How it Should Be Done," forthcoming in G. Epstein, G. Dymski and R. Pollin, eds. *Transforming the U.S. Financial System,* M.E. Sharpe (a project of the Monetary and Financial Restructuring Working Group of the Economic Policy Institute).

February 1993

SPRING CLEANING AT THE FDIC

BANKING CRISIS REDUX

BY JOHN MILLER

Happy New Year! The holiday season is now behind us. All that is left to do is to clean up and assess the financial damage.

That's exactly what the regulators at the Federal Deposit Insurance Corporation (FDIC), the fund that protects deposits in the nation's 12,000 commercial banks, are up to this new year. Bank regulators expect to close the doors of at least 46 banks in the next three months. By closing or merging these problem banks, the FDIC says regulators can put the banking industry back on solid footing and avoid a taxpayer bailout. The worst of the crisis, it says, is behind us.

Several independent bank experts are not so sure. As they see it, the banking industry's serious problems continue, and the cost of the cleanup looms far larger than

the FDIC lets on.

If the real estate market slumps further and interest rates rise, even more banks could fall. Roger J. Vaughan and Edward W. Hill, the banking economists who penned the controversial new report *Banking on the Brink,* estimate that, if the economy doesn't improve, perhaps 1,200 troubled banks will go belly-up or be forced into mergers in the next few years. These include several bank holding companies, each with more than $10 billion in assets (see glossary).

For the last three quarters, low interest rates have pumped up bank profits, which have hit record levels. But such rates won't last; and, in the meantime, these aberrant profits are hiding a host of problems. Banks are still saddled with fallout from their reckless lending, especially to commercial property developers. And a new breed of nonbank financial corporation is out-competing banks for depositors and borrowers. As these corporations have invaded banks' turf, they have intensified the debate over bank regulation. Should banks be more regulated, or less? The banking crisis provides an opportunity for the United States to re-think the role of banks in its economy. Whether the FDIC, the president, Congress, and the banking industry have the will to confront and reshape the troubled industry is questionable. If they do not, one of Vaughan

and Hill's predictions could come true —
a banking industry dominated by "a slowly rising tide of failures."

NOT EXACTLY A SURPRISE

During October's final presidential debate, billionaire presidential candidate Ross Perot warned of a "December Surprise" — a wave of bank bailouts regulators had postponed until after the election — that could cost taxpayers $100 billion. He asked the powers-that-be "to just tell us now," a reference to the 1988 bi-partisan silence by the Federal Savings and Loan Insurance Corporation (FSLIC), Congress, and the president in order to postpone S&L bailouts until after that election.

Did bank regulators purposely postpone closing troubled banks until after last year's election? The answer is unclear, though Perot's charge is not as far-fetched as some of his other conspiracy theories. From 1987 to 1991, regulators shut down an average of 175 banks a year. At the end of 1991, the FDIC projected that it would close another 200 banks with $50 billion of combined assets during 1992. By November 16th, however, the insurance fund had closed only 110 banks with $38 billion in combined assets (see chart, page 79). The FDIC claims lower interest rates boosted banks' profits and saved some banks.

Bank regulators may have delayed some bank closings, but this coming spring's wave of bank failures will be no surprise. It was planned. Through Congress's FDIC Improvement Act of 1991, the FDIC agreed to clamp down on banking practices by raising real estate lending standards, lowering executive pay, and reducing deposit insurance coverage. In exchange, the FDIC received a loan and line of credit to replenish its nearly depleted insurance fund. And starting December 19, 1992, a year after the law passed, the FDIC was to shut down within 90 days "critically undercapitalized" banks (see glossary). Previously, the FDIC only seized banks after they had technically failed. By the time of the presidential debates, the agency had already identified 46 critically undercapitalized banks with assets of $19 billion.

More important than whether the FDIC did delay bank closings is whether the agency can fund this year's bank bail-

GLOSSARY OF BANK TERMS

Bank failure: A bank fails when the state or federal agency that charters the bank decides to close it. This occurs when the agency judges the bank to be critically undercapitalized and cannot find anyone to buy its assets, even if the agency itself buys the bad loans.

When regulators close a failed bank, they do not necessarily use taxpayer money. Regulators close a bank in two ways. They purchase the institution's nonperforming loans (so that the bank can be sold to a healthier institution), or they liquidate the bank and pay off the depositors. In the latter case, regulators must use FDIC funds to make up the difference between the value of the bailed-out bank's assets and the total value of deposits.

Bank holding company: A corporation that owns or holds the stock of at least one commercial bank and either at least one other bank or at least one other non-bank company.

Critically undercapitalized bank: A critically undercapitalized bank is one whose owners' stock equity is less than 2% of the total value of its assets. A bank's assets include loans and other investments. Bank analysts' conventional wisdom holds that banks should be capitalized at a 6%-8% rate at least.

FDIC: Created by the Glass-Steagall Act amidst the financial collapse and bank runs of the Great Depression, the Federal Deposit Insurance Corporation (FDIC) insures deposits in commercial and savings banks. The federal government established the insurance to restore depositor confidence in the banking system. The fund is financed by a deposit premium charged to member banks.

In 1989, the FDIC took over the duties of the Federal Savings and Loan Insurance Fund (FSLIC). Since then, it has administered the Bank Insurance Fund, which insures deposits in savings and commercial banks, and the Savings Insurance Fund, which insures deposits in savings & loans. The FDIC is governed by a five-member board of directors, including the FDIC chairman, the comptroller, the director of the Office of Thrift Supervision, and two others appointed by the president.

Resolution Trust Corporation: Agency that oversees the cleanup of the savings & loan industry. This agency does not regulate or insure savings & loan deposits.

Source: Excerpted in part from *Banking on the Brink,* 1992.

outs, and those to come over the next few years, without additional taxpayer money. The over 1,000 bank failures since 1985 emptied the FDIC insurance fund by the end of 1991. Today, the FDIC has $6 billion in its insurance fund from premiums paid by banks, or less than 30 cents for every $100 of deposits it insures in the United States — far below the $1.25 level regulators consider safe. The FDIC also has left a $30 billion line of credit from the funds granted them by Congress in 1991.

According to its own estimates, in 1993 the FDIC will lock the doors of 100 to 125 banks at a cost of $13 billion. Though the insurance fund predicts it will close or merge fewer banks than it has over the last few years, these troubled banks hold larger assets and carry more bad debt. Looking further down the road, the FDIC believes it will

than the FDIC estimates. Edward Kane, a finance professor at Boston College, told *The New York Times*, "They [FDIC regulators] are giving a rosy projection, no matter how you cut it." Kane thinks the insurance fund will need nearly $70 billion, not $45 billion, to protect depositors at failing commercial banks in the next few years.

Vaughan and Hill generally agree. They believe that the cost of bailing out failed commercial banks will run between $45 billion and $59 billion. But it is "conceivable," they add, "that the cost of failures and arranged mergers could exceed $95.5 billion."

Should any giant bank holding companies fail, then all predictions are out the window. These banks hold over 18% of all FDIC-insured assets. According to some analysts, the FDIC would have to spend as much as $10 billion to cover the deposits at just one of these failed companies. In *Banking on the Brink*, Vaughan and Hill argue that the real core of the banking crisis lies in 14 of these 57 giants. If their portfolios were given honest market valuations, it is likely none would have had a positive net worth at the end of 1991. The bank managers do not consider their institutions insolvent, however. Although some troubled banks have been forced to downgrade the value of their assets, most still list at the original purchase price, not the lower current value, the properties they lent developers money to buy in the 1980s.

Citicorp, the nation's largest bank-holding company, is among the most troubled giants, as are Wells Fargo and Chase Manhattan. Citicorp's assets alone total $216 billion. To meet the recom-

---

TROUBLED GIANTS
10 problem bank holding companies with assests of at least $10 billion

Dollars in millions, December 1991

Holding Company	State	Assets	Equity Deficit[1]	
			Optimistic	Pessimistic
Citicorp	NY	$216,922	($15,008)	($19,485)
Chase Manhattan Corp.	NY	$98,197	($5,005)	($7,450)
Security Pacific Corp[2]	CA	$76,411	($3,906)	($7,159)
Wells Fargo & Company	CA	$53,547	($1,308)	($4,360)
Shawmut National Corp.	CT	$22,832	($917)	($1,846)
Midlantic Corp.	NJ	$17,461	($1,285)	($2,381)
MNC Financial, Inc.	MD	$18,170	($950)	($2,079)
Marine Midland Banks, Inc.	NY	$16,947	($866)	($1,322)
UJB Financial Corp.	NJ	$13,384	($394)	($1,057)
Michigan National Corp.	MI	$10,717	($188)	($838)
Problem Total	10	$544,587	($29,827)	($47,977)

[1] *equity deficit:* For undercapitalized banks, this is the amount of capital by which they fall short of the standard 8% equity-to-asset ratio. Each bank would need to raise this deficit in new capital to simply be considered safe.
[2] Since 1991 Security Pacific Corp. has merged with Bank of America.

Source: Roger J. Vaughan and Edward W. Hill, *Banking on the Brink*, 1992.

---

need $45 billion to cover bank closings through 1996. It says it can fund these without taxpayer assistance. If the economy doesn't fall back into recession, if interest rates stay low, and if real estate values prove to have already hit bottom, then perhaps only these banks will fail and the FDIC will muddle through with the insurance premiums it will collect in the next few years.

But these assumptions seem weak. Four years ago, the now bankrupt FSLIC consistently understated the costs of the S&L cleanup. Mainstream bank economists and bank rating services believe the bank failures will be more costly

mended 8% equity-to-asset ratio, it would need to raise between $15 and $19.5 billion (see table). Citicorp's collapse alone could overwhelm the banking insurance system. But government officials insist that the corporation, which has downgraded the value of its foreclosed and nonperforming real-estate assets to about 55 cents on the dollar, is on the mend. Perhaps.

HOW BAD IS IT??

Whether or not the banking crisis takes on S&L proportions depends on exactly how much trouble is brewing.

Taxpayers are already getting soaked for more than $300 billion over the next 30 years for the S&L bailout. The banking industry has not collapsed to date, as the S&L industry had by 1988 — although in some states, like Texas, many of the largest banks have failed.

Regulators were especially heartened by the record profits reported during the first three quarters of 1992. Lower interest rates have helped. Banks often pay depositors just 3% while lending at 7%, or even much higher on credit cards. The Citibank credit card, for example, charges nearly 20%.

Others view the 1992 profit reports differently. Kane, the Boston College banking expert, told the Senate Banking Committee that "favorable interest rate conditions are masking banks' current problems." Those problems — overvalued assets, lax accounting standards, and shrinking business — still exist.

"The economic conditions of crippled banks today parallel those of an AIDS victim who has been lucky enough to get over a bout of pneumonia," he continued. "Although each crippled bank has received a welcome gift of time, its condition remains terminal." Low interest rates will not continue indefinitely. "Commercial bankers may soon be caught in the same vise that squeezed thrift executives a decade ago," comment Vaughan and Hill about the possibility of rising interest rates. This possibility also worries the FDIC. Andrew Hove, acting chair of the FDIC, has stated that if interest rates rise he would "fully expect that failure rates [of banks would] accelerate significantly."

Higher interest rates are not banks' only worry. Many institutions still carry 1980s-era loans to Third World debtors and financial raiders who cannot pay the banks back on schedule, if at all. The collapse of the commercial real estate market has also sharply reduced the value of the industry's assets, and many of these developers are not making their loan payments, leaving banks to foreclose on much of this property. Commercial banks have $100 billion in such loans, mostly in real estate, on their books.

But many banks do not accurately assess their loans' new lower values. Lax accounting standards, says Kane, are like "the rigged scales dishonest butchers use to overcharge their clients." Vaughan and Hill's study found an "enormous discrepancy between conventional bookkeeping [in banking] and the real economy." Current accounting rules

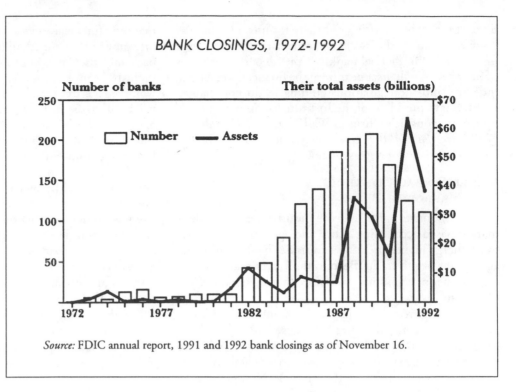

BANK CLOSINGS, 1972-1992

Number of banks — Their total assets (billions)

Source: FDIC annual report, 1991 and 1992 bank closings as of November 16.

permit banks to value assets at cost rather than market price — a time bomb in cases where the asset is an office building worth less than 50 cents on the dollar. Adopting market-based accounting, according to Vaughan and Hill, would reveal roughly 2,000 troubled banks with book value assets of more than a $1 trillion. Of those, 1,150 "are now insolvent — and would be shuttered if their books revealed the true value of their assets." Even the FDIC, despite its optimism, maintains a list of 1,044 troubled banks that require close scrutiny.

The industry's 1992 profits are undoubtedly a short-term gift from the banking god. Banks' profits have declined for two decades, as have their share of U.S. financial business. This loss of financial business is yet another problem confronting the industry. Non-bank financial corporations — such as Fidelity Investments and T. Rowe Price — have created attractive alternatives to depositing cash investments in banks, including money-market, stock, and bond mutual funds. And non-bank companies — such as General Electric, Sears Roebuck, and General Motors — now compete against commercial banks in the lending business. On top of this, more blue-chip corporations, for years the industry's best customers, now borrow directly from the securities markets by issuing commercial paper, rather than going through banks. In short, too many banks are competing for too little profitable business. Robert Litan, a banking expert at the Brookings Institute, estimates that commercial lending capacity is still a third too large for what is justified by the industry's core business.

The future of the banking industry is in question to some observers. Vaughan and Hill see a wave of bank failures — brought on by "real estate losses and the inevitable interest rate spikes waiting out there for unwary bankers" — overwhelming the industry. Some bank watchers even predict that commercial banks — the "department stores of finance" — will disappear from the financial scene if the industry, and the regulations guiding it, do not change. Karen Shaw, president of the Institute for Strategy Development, a consulting firm in Washington, D.C., told the *Wall Street Journal* that one policy question is "whether banks can make money as a bank."

WIDER SOCIAL CONTROL, NOT NARROWER BANKS

Most economists agree that the industry needs to adopt market-based accounting. They also agree that the FDIC must charge higher premiums to riskier banks, which the agency has begun to do. Beyond those proposals, a growing number of economists advocates narrowing the scope of deposit insurance.

Creating narrow or "safe" banks is one of the hottest ideas among economists, partly because Nobel prize-winning economist James Tobin has done much to publicize this alternative. He would give depositors a choice of types of banks in which to place their money. Narrower banks would offer a maximum amount of security but only a modest rate of return. The bank would invest solely in Treasury securities, an extremely safe investment, and the FDIC would fully insure depositors. Those seeking a higher return for their savings could place their money in unregulated and uninsured banks that are free to invest wherever they choose. Should these banks fail, the FDIC would not bail out the depositors — period.

Tobin's proposal has its problems. For one thing, it ignores the reason the federal government first instituted deposit insurance. The failure of an unsafe bank harms far more than its depositors. If a failure ignites a bank panic, it also puts at risk other uninsured sound banks, as well as the economy as a whole.

More important, the Tobin proposal would leave many local communities without access to financial services. Because of the Community Reinvestment Act (CRA), a 1977 federal law, banks are now obligated to serve their local communities. Many banks still ignore low-income, particularly minority, neighborhoods, but at least the CRA gives the neighborhoods a legal mechanism for demanding financial service. In recent years, many community groups have successfully used the law to bring banks back into their neighborhoods. But if safe banks invest exclusively in Treasury bills, what financial institution would make the loans to small businesses, low-income neighborhoods, and consumers? Uninsured banks would have no such obligation.

Reforming deposit insurance needn't mean limiting it. In fact, we could form a social compact with the entire financial industry: In return for receiving modified FDIC-like coverage, all financial institutions — from banks to insurance companies — would agree to accept more extensive government regulation and serve the needs of their local communities. Such regulation would force financial institutions to invest other people's money prudently and to serve currently under-served neighborhoods.

In a more fundamental way, narrow or safe banks are a wrongheaded response to today's banking problems. The fall of the banking industry demonstrates the need for *more* control over all financial institutions, not less. Currently, the federal government and many policy makers view bank regulation as a *quid pro quo* the public receives in return for backing up the FDIC insurance fund. But such regulation is a necessity for a stable economy.

Responsible regulation can actually benefit the economy, the banking industry, and depositors. For example, regulating banks to allow for a "fair return" on their investments, as we do with utilities, can reduce bank failures and avert costly taxpayer bailouts. And Congress could extend the CRA to stimulate investment in low-income communities. It could require all financial institutions, not just banks, to meet local credit needs for housing, small business, farms, and economic development before they acquire banks across state lines or combine with securities firms, as deregulation proponents would allow. Tighter regulations might even help stabilize banks' profits by directing them away from the speculative ventures that led to today's problems.

Resources: Roger J. Vaughan and Edward W. Hill, *Banking on the Brink*, 1992 (available from the Washington Post Company Briefing Books, 1150 15th Street, NW, Washington, DC 20071 (202) 334-4256); and various issues of *Dollars & Sense*, the *Wall Street Journal*, the *Boston Globe*, and *The New York Times*.

CHAPTER 6
Unemployment and Inflation

March 1993

THE ZERO-INFLATION PLOY

THE UNEMPLOYMENT-INFLATION TRADE-OFF

BY CATHERINE LYNDE

According to Barry Bluestone and Bennett Harrison in *The Deindustrialization of America*, each additional 1% of unemployment translates into an estimated additional 3,300 commitments to state prisons, 4,000 commitments to state mental hospitals, 920 suicides, and 37,000 deaths (20,000 of those from heart attacks). Unemployment also means lost production, lower levels of investment, lower productivity growth, and, over the long run, lower levels of output of goods and services. The cost in lost output of slowing inflation from 1981-86 alone has been estimated at $750 billion.

Indeed, the unemployment rates the Bush administration called the "successes of the 1980s" would have signalled recession in the 1950s and 1960s. The last time inflation was as low as 5% was in 1967, but only 3.7% of the labor force was officially out of a job — instead of the 5.4% unemployed in early 1990.

The chairperson of the Federal Reserve, the Reserve's Board of Governors, and all twelve presidents of its banks have a mission. They aim to eliminate inflation by 1995.

Since the early 1980s, the Federal Reserve, in collaboration with the Bush and Reagan administrations, has squeezed quite a bit of inflation out of the economy. The inflation rate, currently hovering around 4%, is lower than at any time from 1968 to 1985.

But as the postwar history of the U.S. economy indicates, the mission to eradicate inflation is a virtually impossible one. Since 1959, the inflation rate has not fallen below 1%. In fact, over the last 30 years, the annual inflation rate has averaged 5%, peaking in the late 1970s and reaching lows in the early 1960s and late 1980s.

No one, rich or poor, enjoys inflation. So zero-percent inflation would be a nice purchase — if it didn't come with such a high price tag. But it does. The Federal Reserve and the Reagan administration bought the lower rates of inflation of the 1980s with the deepest recession since the 1930s (1979-82). Almost 11 million people were unemployed during those years, and since then unemployment rates have hung between 5% and 10%.

The experience of the last several years has once again established that the trade-off between inflation and unemployment still exists, despite the supply-sider claims of the 1970s and 1980s. The record demonstrates that the only way policy-makers in this country can bring down inflation is by pushing up unemployment, and that the only way they can lower unemployment is by pushing up inflation. In the late 1980s, the inflation rate crept up — rising by over a third from 1986 until the latest recession began in 1989. If the Fed governors are serious in their Don Quixote-like quest for zero inflation, millions more Americans may lose their jobs.

THE TRADE-OFF

Some members of the Federal Reserve are serious about meeting their goal. Robert Perry, president of the San Francisco Federal Reserve, claimed before the 1989-91 recession that zero inflation might require "a long period of slow growth ... but a recession won't be necessary." What Perry didn't choose to explain is that even a slowdown in

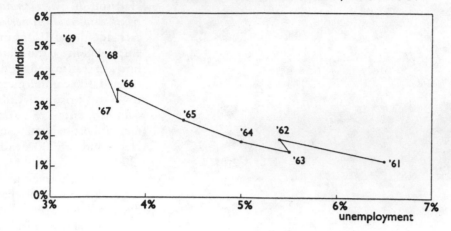

FIGURE 1: INFLATION AND UNEMPLOYMENT, 1961-1969

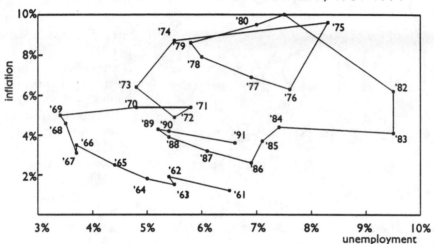

FIGURE 2: INFLATION VS. UNEMPLOYMENT, 1961-1991

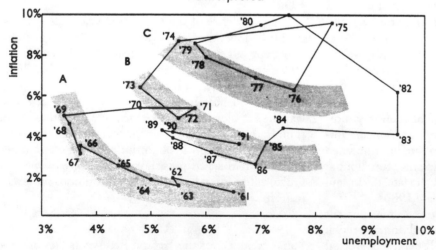

FIGURE 3: INFLATION VS. UNEMPLOYMENT, 1961-1991,
Reinterpreted

Note: In all three graphs the rate of inflation is the percentage change in the GNP deflator, an alternative to the better-known consumer price index (CPI). Economists often use the GNP deflator because it includes all prices — those paid by business and government as well as consumers. Using the CPI wouldn't change any of the main points of our analysis.

output growth drives up unemployment rates.

Why is the link between inflation and unemployment so strong? Because when people lose their jobs, they have less money to spend. During a recession, consumer spending usually drops off. Businesses, faced with declining sales, find it a bad time to raise prices, and the rate of inflation falls. At the same time, when millions of people are competing for a few jobs, employed workers find their bargaining position weakened. This further depresses the rate of inflation because workers are less likely to demand or receive large wage hikes or other concessions.

Conversely, as the economy recovers, unemployment declines and consumer spending increases. Rising sales make it easier for businesses to raise prices. Also, workers' bargaining position improves, and labor is better able to win wage gains. Thus, prosperity and lower rates of unemployment add to inflation, while recession and higher rates of unemployment subtract from it.

THE PHILLIPS CURVE

During the 1960s, a graph of the inflation-unemployment trade-off became enshrined in the literature of economics as the "Phillips Curve" (named after the British economist who did statistical work on the issue). The experience of the United States in that period can be illustrated rather neatly by such a curve, as in Figure 1, which shows the levels of inflation and unemployment during each year of that decade.

In 1961 — the dot on the graph furthest to the right — the official unemployment rate was 6.5%, while prices were rising at an annual rate of 1.2%. By 1969 unemployment had dropped to 3.4% and the rate of inflation had jumped to 5.0%. The trade-off is expressed in the shape of the curve: As the points for the later years move toward the left (toward lower unemployment), they also move upwards (toward higher inflation).

Beginning in the 1970s, "stagflation" (the combination of high unemployment and high inflation) became the word of the day. Economists and policy-makers began denying the existence of the trade-off. After all, both unemployment and inflation rose dramatically during that decade, as can be seen in Figure 2. Among those rejecting the trade-off were those who believed that it was the "natural rate" of unemployment that was rising. They defined the natural rate as the lowest attainable unemployment rate compatible with a stable rate of inflation. Any attempts to lower the rate further, claimed natural-rate proponents, would only set off rounds of accelerating wage and price increases. Interestingly, those who disapprove of an active government policy to reduce unemployment conveniently argue that this natural rate has risen from 2-3% in the 1960s to 5-6% in the 1970s to only slightly below the average unemployment rate in the 1980s, 7.2%.

Supply siders also rejected the unemployment-inflation trade-off. Their theory, which found favor during the Reagan administration, held that tax cuts, especially for business and the rich, would bring down both unemployment and inflation. They argued that lower taxes would lead to a miraculous outpouring of work, savings, investment, and consequently, economic growth. The supply of goods and services would rise so rapidly that prices would stop going up.

As we now know, supply-side economics did not deliver as promised. In fact, a closer look at the same data suggests that while the simple, stable Phillips curve of the 1960s no longer exists, the unemployment-inflation trade-off is alive and well. Figure 3 indicates that one way to make sense out of the apparent chaos of Figure 2 is to reinterpret it as consisting of three different Phillips curves. Curve A in Figure 3 applies to the 1960s, Curve B the late 1980s, and Curve C the late 1970s.

In essence, government policy-makers face the same basic dilemma they always have. When they adjust aggregate demand through government spending, tax changes, and monetary policies to bring down either inflation or unemployment, they inevitably drive the other one up.

What Goes Up . . .

While this trade-off is a fact of life in most capitalist economies, it doesn't explain everything that happens to inflation and unemployment from year to year. Other factors have an important impact on inflation and help explain the shifts in the Phillips curve over time. For example, the price of oil influences inflation. When the price of imported oil jumped in 1973-74, and again in 1979-80, it pushed up other prices throughout the U.S. economy. Thus for any given unemployment rate, the oil price shocks pushed up the corresponding inflation rate. Rising oil prices also slowed output of goods and services in the economy, pushing up unemployment.

Moreover, any given inflation rate tends to persist, because people and businesses normally expect past rates of inflation to continue into the future. Between 1969 and 1979, as actual inflation increased, workers and businesses began to incorporate expectations of higher and higher inflation into their behavior. The Phillips curve consequently shifted upward (from Curve A to Curve C in Figure 3). More unionized workers bargained successfully for automatic cost-of-living provisions (COLA) in their contracts. COLA provisions protected workers' real wage levels, but they also helped perpetuate inflation by putting upward pressure on prices. For their part, businesses also planned for a certain level of inflation and continued to raise prices even during periods of rising unemployment and sluggish growth.

. . . May Not Come Down

The experience of the 1970s and early 1980s indicates that a lengthy and severe recession with large numbers of people losing their jobs is required to lower inflation substantially. Thus, the mild recession in the early 1970s, when the unemployment rate reached only 5.8%, had a barely noticeable impact on inflation. By contrast, the deep recession of 1973-74, when unemployment climbed to 8.3%, significantly slowed price increases in 1976.

But it wasn't until the 1980s that a recession was allowed to become severe enough to largely eliminate the inflation built into the economy during previous expansions. Relatively low inflation and high unemployment in the mid-1980s had lowered people's expectations of inflation. From 1986-91, inflation rates were equivalent to those of the mid-1960s. As we can see in Figure 3, the unemployment-inflation trade-off of the last few years is closer to that of the early 1960s (Curve A) than to the early 1980s (Curve C).

There are differences between the 1960s and the last few years. The cost of the recently lowered inflation rate has been generally higher unemployment rates in the 1980s and early 1990s than in the 1960s, causing hardship and suffering for millions of people.

The Reagan administration policies that raised unemployment and kept it high during the 1980s are the primary but not the sole reason for the drop in inflation. Several

ZERO-PERCENT INFLATION WOULD BE A NICE PURCHASE — IF IT DIDN'T COME WITH SUCH A HIGH PRICE TAG.

other important factors have contributed to a downward shift in the Phillips curve, most significantly falling oil prices. The most dramatic oil price declines occurred in early 1986, but oil prices had been slowly moving downward relative to other prices since the end of the 1970s. They rose only slightly in the last half of the 1980s. If this trend continues, oil prices will not add to the pressure shifting the Phillips curve back out.

Also, through early 1985, policies followed by the Reagan administration, particularly tight monetary policy combined with large government deficits, made the value of the dollar very high compared to the currencies of other countries. This in turn meant that imported goods were relatively cheap. (When a dollar can buy 150 Japanese yen, for example, the price of a two-million yen Toyota is $13,333; but when the value of the dollar goes up to 250 yen, the Toyota costs only $8,000.) Cheap imports helped dampen inflation by making it more difficult for domestic producers of competing goods to raise their prices.

After 1985, the value of the dollar began falling and by the end of the decade had returned to the levels of the early 1980s. This drove up the inflation rate for both domestic and imported goods. Imported consumer goods became more expensive, and the higher prices of imported inputs drove up the prices of domestically produced goods.

The rate of inflation picked up in the late 1980s (mov-ing toward the left along Curve B). But that period is not simply the story of the early 1980s in reverse. The falling dollar has not led to an equivalent rise in import prices. Importers have held prices down in an effort to remain competitive in the U.S. market. Should they continue to do this, a declining dollar will not be especially inflationary.

Another reason is that people and businesses expect much lower inflation now than they did previously — the 1982 recession effectively wrung expectations out of the economy. As a result, price increases do not necessarily cause an upward spiral of further price increases. Businesses aren't expecting spiralling inflation, so they won't raise their selling prices now in anticipation of future inflation.

The continued budget deficits of the Bush administration and the looser monetary policy of the Federal Reserve Bank in the late 1980s also added to inflationary pressure. As the inflation rate climbed steadily approaching the 1990s, however, the Federal Reserve began to tighten credit.

The 1989-91 recession, generated in part by the tightening of credit, shows that the trade-off between inflation and unemployment still exists. However, the terms of the trade-off appear to have deteriorated in this recession; rising unemployment rates did not produce as much of a fall in inflation as they had in previous recessions.

As Gerald Corrigan, president of the New York Fed, said, "I am very hard pressed to recall a single case where a significant reduction in inflation was accomplished in a major industrial country without relatively large costs." These costs include massive unemployment — the 1989-91 recession was the most severe in 60 years, with almost two million people losing their jobs. It is people, and their communities, who pay.

Resources: Economic Report of the President, 1990; Wall Street Journal, 10/2/89, 2/7/90.

> IF THE FED GOVERNORS ARE SERIOUS IN THEIR DON QUIXOTE-LIKE QUEST FOR ZERO INFLATION, MILLIONS MORE AMERICANS MAY LOSE THEIR JOBS.

November 1992

THE NEW UNEMPLOYMENT

Over the past two years, a tidal wave of pink slips and dismal economic data has battered American workers. Perhaps none of the data better explain the deep despair of workers than those on "the new unemployment" — permanent job loss:

• According to the newsletter *Workplace Trends*, U.S. corporations are permanently reducing their work force this year at a rate of 1,500 per day (that would mean 550,000 for all of 1992). From January through July, permanent cuts ran 2.3% ahead of last year's very rapid pace.

• The Bureau of Labor Statistics (BLS) estimates that during the first two years of the recent recession (July 1990-June 1992), 85% of the job losers were "displaced workers" — their jobs are gone forever. Only 15% had been "laid off" with reason to believe they'd be rehired when business conditions improve.

• The BLS also reported that during the five-year period 1987-1991, about 5.6 million workers over the age of 20 permanently lost jobs they had held for at least three years. That figure is 12% higher than the corresponding one for the 1979-1983 five-year recessionary period.

• Lawrence Mishel of the Economic Policy Institute estimates that if lost permanent jobs held *less* than three years are added to the Bureau's 1987-1991 count, the total is a whopping 12.3 million.

To put the 1990-1992 figures on permanent job loss in perspective, the BLS compared them with those in the four previous recessions [1969-1970, 1973-1975, 1980 (January to July), and 1981-1982]. It found that over the course of those earlier downturns. one half to two-thirds, or an average of 56% of job losers were permanently displaced — nearly 30% lower than in the current recession (see chart).

Not surprisingly, the BLS data also confirm that workers in manufacturing suffered the most dramatic shift to permanent job loss during the current recession. While in the first year of other recent recessions about half of the manufacturing losses were permanent, in the 1990-1992 period about 85% were.

For workers outside manufacturing, the figures on permanent job loss are equally devastating. Roughly 85% of those who have lost their jobs during the current recession have no hope of being rehired. Typically, the figure is around 75%.

What accounts for these massive permanent job losses and for the continuing gloomy forecasts? One key reason for the huge permanent job losses in the private sector is the single-minded determination of many U.S. corporations to maintain their short-term profit margins in the face of growing international competition and recession-ridden consumers at home and abroad. Unwilling to invest for the long term in worker retraining and productivity-enhancing equipment (or unable to do so because of huge debts), corporate America has been slashing its domestic work force and shifting more and more of its operations to low-wage countries.

Defense cuts also are a major cause. *Business Week* recently reported that in just eight months (December 1991-August 1992), six key defense-related industries (producing ships, aircraft, missiles, ordnance, communication gear, and navigation equipment) lost 100,000 jobs. Those losses — almost all of them permanent — constitute two-thirds of the total decline in manufacturing employment in the eight-month period.

In sum, without governmental support for large-scale programs to convert military industries to civilian production and to retrain workers for the jobs thus created, prospects for the hundreds of thousands of displaced American workers will remain grim.

Resources: U.S. Department of Labor, Bureau of Labor Statistics, *Issues in Labor Statistics: Recent Job Losers Less Likely to Expect Recall*, July 1992. "No Help Wanted: Ongoing Layoffs Are Hobbling the Recovery," *Business Week*, September 21, 1992. Gene Koretz, "The White Collar Jobless Could Really Rock the Vote," *Business Week*, September 28, 1992.

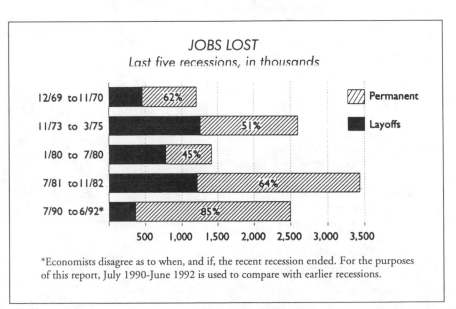

JOBS LOST
Last five recessions, in thousands

*Economists disagree as to when, and if, the recent recession ended. For the purposes of this report, July 1990-June 1992 is used to compare with earlier recessions.

July/August 1991

THE REAL UNEMPLOYMENT RATE

As the recession takes its toll across the country, the national unemployment rate is ticking upward, reaching 7.1% in the first quarter of this year. (The seasonally-adjusted rate was 6.5%.) As high as that seems, the rate would jump to nearly 12% if the Bureau of Labor Statistics, the government agency that tracks unemployment, counted everyone who wanted to work but couldn't.

The BLS calculates unemployment rates from a monthly random telephone sampling of about 60,000 households. BLS surveyors ask all members of the household over the age of 16 a series of questions about their work activities, then classify the respondents as employed, unemployed, or out of the labor force.

The BLS counts you as employed if you work full or part time for pay, work 15 hours or more without pay in a family business, or are on unpaid leave because of illness, a labor dispute, bad weather, or personal reasons. You are considered unemployed if you were jobless during the survey week, were available for work, and had made specific efforts to find work sometime during the past month — answering want ads, contacting an employment agency, etc. The BLS categorizes students, retirees, people at home because of long-term ill health or disabilities, homemakers, and those who have given up looking for work as out of the labor force.

The BLS undercounts the unemployed in a number of ways, understating the economic distress of millions of people. The most glaring exclusion is the category of "discouraged workers," those who say they want work but are not looking because they believe no jobs are available. In the first quarter of this year, the BLS counted one million discouraged workers.

Adding them to the official unemployment figure lifts the first-quarter total from 8.8 to 9.8 million. To arrive at the real unemployment rate, though, we should include other categories of workers as well. Another 5.9 million workers told the BLS they were working part time but wanted full-time work and couldn't find it. We can incorporate these workers into the unemployment count by assuming they work on average half time and counting half of them as unemployed. This brings underemployment into our unemployment total.

We should also add the 2.2 million people who told the BLS they wanted jobs but couldn't work because home responsibilities or other reasons kept them out of the labor force. These include one million women who desired but could not seek paid work because of home responsibilities, most commonly, caring for dependents. If adequate dependent care were available, these women (and probably some of the 20 million homemakers who said they did not want a job now) would need jobs too.

Adding these to the discouraged workers, involuntary part-timers, and those the BLS lists as unemployed, the number of unemployed people rises to 15 million, six million more than the official number. This "real unemployment rate" better measures our economy's ability to provide paid work to all those willing to do it. With every eighth person — and every fifth Black person — unemployed or underemployed, the economy is failing far more people than official statistics suggest.

Source: Bureau of Labor Statistics.

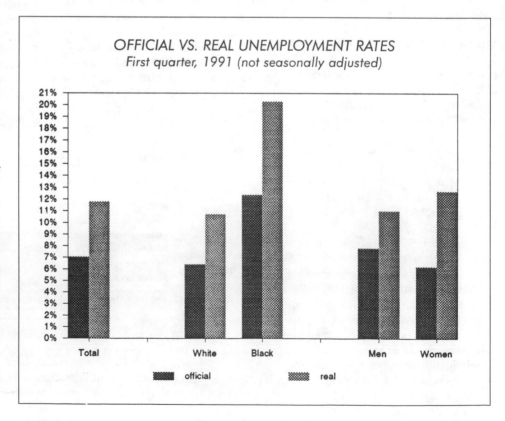

OFFICIAL VS. REAL UNEMPLOYMENT RATES
First quarter, 1991 (not seasonally adjusted)

Categories: Total, White, Black, Men, Women — bars for official and real.

January/February 1994

POLICIES FOR PEACE

EASING THE TRANSITION TO NEW INDUSTRIES

BY CATHERINE HILL AND ANN MARKUSEN

Do you remember the peace dividend we all thought was waiting for us at the end of the cold war? Did your check get lost in the mail? There are two reasons why you haven't heard much about the dividend lately. First, although military cutbacks so far have been substantial, most of the reductions are yet to come. And even the 18% reductions from 1991 to 1997 promised by Clinton are measured against the all-time high of the mid-1980s Reagan-Bush military buildup. These cuts would only return us to the still-high levels of military spending of the late 1970s.

Second, to date most of the military's surplus comes to us not in cash but in kind. Lower military spending creates unemployed workers and empty facilities, whether or not the government makes funds available for investments in other job-creating activities. Clinton's budget will, for the foreseeable future, devote much of the peace dividend to reducing the federal deficit. But the dividend could instead fund some of our most pressing civilian needs. Conversion policies based on a more aggressive social agenda could put our people and resources back to work.

Defense-dependent companies are losing contracts daily, and over one hundred major military bases are shutting down. Without serious conversion plans, defense cuts will translate into massive layoffs. Employment in military industries and in the armed services could plunge from today's six million to three-and-a-half million by the year 2001, an average job loss of 250,000 a year.

Blue-collar defense workers have long been subject to feast-or-famine cycles in defense work. Sometimes layoffs persist for years before a new weapons system comes on line. This time, assuming the military budget stays at a lower level, many more layoffs will be permanent. And since civilian industries are racked by deindustrialization, few new jobs will be available to laid-off machinists, welders, and metalworkers. Most scientists and engineers will eventually find other work, albeit at lower pay or skill levels. But many blue-collar workers will succumb to involuntary retirement or be forced to take low-wage service jobs.

Perhaps most devastating will be the lost opportunities for young Americans, particularly African Americans. For many of them the armed services offered a means to obtain technical training and financial aid for higher education, and a channel to career options not available in the more discriminatory private market.

SURVIVAL OF THE FITTEST?

Many neoclassical economists recommend that defense contractors and their workforces be left to sink or swim in the changing market. Why should taxpayers continue to shore up companies that were nurtured on a steady diet of public contracts, after the need for their products and services has vanished? Because these firms have so often been caught overcharging the government, engaging in bribery, and lobbying for an aggressive U.S. military posture, this argument has great appeal.

But matters are not that simple. The investment of trillions in the Cold War buildup has created an array of aerospace, communications, and electronics (ACE) industries which now embody much of our leading-edge technological capability. These industries have posted the nation's highest rates of manufacturing output growth in the last two decades, and they account for the lion's share of net industrial trade receipts. They employ disproportionately large shares of the nation's scientists and engineers. Even sectors such as computing and semiconductors, which have developed extensive commercial markets, still rely heavily on military contracts for basic research and innovation funding.

Without strenuous and innovative shepherding by government, substantial cuts in defense spending will exacerbate stagnation in the American economy. We must have a vision of which economic sectors have good growth prospects, and an agenda for investigating new technologies. Otherwise the abrupt scrapping of physical plants and workforces, carefully constructed over more than four decades, will deepen the crisis already evident in those civilian industries which have depended on sales to the military, including steel, auto, machinery, electronics, and apparel. This would be ironic, since it was public support for the ACE complex at the expense of civilian industries that hastened the latter's downward slide.

WEAK BUSINESS RESPONSES

Conversion is defined as the reorganization of military-related facilities and human resources for production of non-military goods and services. Efforts by companies themselves to convert have had mixed results. It is undeniable that the Pentagon's lack of concern with costs led to inefficiency in firms that rely on military sales, making it difficult for them to compete in civilian markets. But a conclusion that such companies are too specialized and/or spoiled to succeed in new endeavors may not be justified.

Pessimistic assessments of defense contractors' ability to convert are based on the record of losers, not winners. Those that failed to shift complain loudly about their plight, while those that successfully converted are no longer among the ranks of defense contractors. Many companies converted their facilities and redirected their labor forces into civilian work with little fanfare. Others reused former military facilities.

AT&T's Bell Labs left the military contracting business years ago without incident. Harley-Davidson now makes precision equipment at the old York Naval Ordnance Plant in Pennsylvania, employing 1,600 people, which more than replaces the 1,092 civilian jobs associated with the Navy's former production of ammunition and ordnance at the plant.

Frisby Airborne Hydraulics reduced its defense dependency in the late 1980s from 90% to 20%, through a restructuring of management to involve workers more directly in production decisions. Greg Frisby, owner of the Long Island firm, attributes much of the success of his company's conversion effort to cooperative relations between workers and management. But due to cost pressures, even this enlightened businessman decided not to open a second plant in Long Island.

After the Vietnam War, efforts by companies to enter civilian markets — such as Grumman's attempt to build buses, and Boeing-Vertol, Ingalls, Allied-Signal, and Rohr's entries into the mass transit market — met with numerous problems. For example, Boeing-Vertol produced trolley cars before completing testing of prototypes and incurred large financial losses correcting its mistakes. But the firm learned from this experience and performed better in its next contracts with San Francisco and Chicago.

Military contractor responses to Pentagon cuts in the late 1980s have been discouraging. Many defense firms chose to write off large losses resulting from their inability to exploit commercial applications. Many companies that tried to diversify into civilian industries failed to compete with existing firms, whose cost consciousness and marketing expertise gave them a considerable lead. Firms that we interviewed conceded that without new government initiatives in civilian sectors, or better transition assistance, layoffs and plant closings will be the most likely response to military cutbacks.

COMMUNITIES ORGANIZE

In addition to efforts by individual companies, states and local communities have struggled to protect jobs by diversifying their economies. Such diversification strategies are similar to those undertaken by localities facing economic decline due to deindustrialization or other causes. Agencies or community groups take inventories of local resources, identify potential activities and employers, and offer technical assistance and subsidies to existing or new enterprises. Many have received planning grants and guidance from the Department of Defense's Office of Economic Adjustment.

Local economic development efforts have their strengths and weaknesses. On the one hand, tools at the disposal of state and local government are quite limited. Because their tax bases are strained during periods of economic distress, they must rely on exhortation, tax abatements, and federal grants. Nevertheless, in the past decade many have responded to intensified deindustrialization and cuts in federal funding with remarkable innovation. Examples include business incubators, which provide start-up firms with low-cost rent and services; revolving loan funds, which offer publicly-subsidized loans to businesses that accomplish specific public goals; new efforts at worker training and ownership; and export promotion programs.

Even when company diversification and community economic redevelopment are successful, however, not all former defense workers find themselves satisfactorily employed. Diversified companies often hire new types of workers in new locations. Community economic recovery efforts may attract new businesses which need fewer or different workers.

CONVERSION POLICY

The goal of government conversion policy is to minimize employment losses in communities and individual plants, while moving resources as quickly as possible into activities that build infant industries and enhance our quality of life. Unfortunately, in some cases, such as the Pentagon's reluctant order for more Seawolf submarines, Congress and the President have continued military production simply to keep workers at their jobs.

The Clinton administration has attempted to stem job losses through technology grants and worker and community adjustment assistance. Half of federal conversion dollars have been dedicated to "dual use initiatives" (projects whose research has both civilian and military applications) and high-technology investment programs, with assistance for military personnel, workers, and communities sharing the remaining half.

The pre-Gorbachev U.S. conversion movement envisioned site-based conversion with management and workers developing new civilian products using existing facilities and equipment. Such efforts are initially more expensive than leaving firms, workers, and communities to independently find paths to civilian work. But the investment could pay off by linking worker retraining, reinvestment in technology, and equipment purchases with local economic development assistance to businesses.

The Clinton administration should include such comprehensive site-based conversion in its programs. Currently, the Pentagon asks contractors to plan weapon systems many years in advance, but does not require firms or bases to develop alternative use plans to prepare them for eventual cuts. While defense firms will no doubt resist the participation of labor and community leaders in planning for the firms' futures, these local public-private ventures could be the beginning of a less antagonistic relationship between business and government in the United States.

Labor advocates, as well as some Congressional leaders, have proposed new efforts directed explicitly at military-industrial workers and former armed service personnel. Some proposals are analogous to existing Department of Labor programs, including the Trade Adjustment and Assistance program, which targets workers displaced by import competition, and the Title III program of the Job Training Partnership Act.

But our research finds that existing programs are hampered by their short term focus, delays, and minimal coverage. Counseling services are poor and often available only after layoffs are announced. Training is usually short-term, inappropriate for mid-career skilled workers, and provided by unregulated and often unsatisfactory private institutions.

As in all labor retraining efforts, the question of "training for what" looms large for participants, particularly for blue collar workers for whom few civilian opportunities exist. In addition, workers face lower pay scales and reduced benefits. That is why committing part of the peace dividend to new job creation is so essential.

All displaced workers face the same problem: learning new skills to match new occupations amid intensifying competition. Policies directed toward military-industrial workers could thus be blended with strategies for displaced workers from all sectors. Consolidating worker retraining and education programs could save administration and overhead costs, simplify the application process for individuals, and provide a more equitable distribution of resources for workers. Existing community and technical colleges could house worker retraining programs, with minor changes to their facilities and curriculum. The Department of Labor could coordinate new federal spending on student loan and financial aid programs targeted to displaced workers. But even if all of these changes were implemented, the absence of links between worker adjustment and job creation limits the power of such programs.

INDUSTRIAL STRATEGY FOR HUMAN NEEDS

In addition to supply-side adjustment programs, part of the peace dividend should be reinvested via a national industrial policy. The government should direct this policy toward real social needs, replacing the stimulus provided in the past by military spending. It should foster infant industries in areas such as environmental protection, energy, and cleaner and more efficient transportation systems. By engaging former defense workers and communities in these endeavors we would offset our dependence on existing military industries and reduce political resistance to military cuts.

Many of our nation's social priorities are good candidates for seeding such industries. First is the looming environmental crisis, which presents an opportunity for the United States to be a world leader. Investment in technologies and projects to diminish air pollution through new energy and transportation modes, cut down on hazardous waste production through new materials innovations, and enhance recycling would provide new markets for defense and civilian companies. Although new investments and refurbishing of skills would be necessary, the expertise embodied in existing military firms and facilities could be devoted to these types of projects.

Second is health care. Initiatives to prevent and cure major illnesses, such as cancer and AIDS, to improve nutrition and resilience to disease generally, and to explore selective technologies that promise to alleviate serious health problems would complement the existing medical system. Some elements of existing military-oriented research systems could be devoted to such efforts.

A third element of a post-cold war industrial policy is world development. This may seem a strange goal for an economy beleaguered by internal problems, reeling from a decades-long fall in real wages, and made anxious by the meteoric rise of newly-industrialized Asian countries. A major contributing factor to U.S. economic stagnation in the 1980s, however, was the slippage of promising economies in Latin America and Africa into low growth rates and greater poverty.

Providing foreign aid to help improve output, productivity, and incomes in Third World and former Soviet bloc countries would also stimulate the U.S. economy. The United States is still the world's premier exporter of capital goods and equipment for agriculture, industry, and the service sectors. Furthermore, developing countries should be rewarded for ending arms purchases, rather than egged on to buy them, as they are under the federal government's current push to export American-made weapons.

At the dawn of the next century, we could be enjoying a richer and more peaceful world. Or we could be tightening our belts to pay for expensive weapons needed to confront Third World nations whose people have been similarly impoverished for the aggrandizement of their military establishments. It is a stark choice and one which must be made now.

Resources: This article is based on the authors' report, "Converting the Cold War Economy: Investing In Industries, Workers, and Communities," Economic Policy Institute (EPI), 1992. This and other EPI studies can be ordered from Public Interest Publications, P.O. Box 229, Arlington, VA 22210, or call 1-800-537-9359; *Dismantling the Cold War Economy*, Ann Markusen and Joel Yudkin, 1992.

CHAPTER 7
International Trade and Investment

November 1991

THE NEW EVANGELISTS

PREACHING THE BUSINESS OF FREE TRADE

BY ARTHUR MacEWAN

Free trade! It's the cure-all for the 1990s. With all the zeal of Christian missionaries, the U.S. government has been preaching, advocating, and pushing around the globe for "free trade."

While a Mexico-U.S.-Canada free trade pact is the immediate aim of U.S. policy, George Bush has heralded a future free trade zone from the northern coast of Canada to the southern tip of Chile. For Eastern Europe, U.S. advisers prescribe unfettered capitalism and ridicule as unworkable any move toward a "third way." Wherever any modicum of economic success appears in the Third World, free traders extol it as one more example of their program's wonders.

Free traders also praise their gospel as the proper policy at home. The path to true salvation — or economic expansion, which, in this day and age, seems to be the same thing — lies in opening our markets to foreign goods. Get rid of trade barriers, and allow business to go where it wants and do what it wants. We will all get rich.

Yet the history of the United States and other advanced capitalist countries teaches us that virtually all advanced capitalist countries found economic success in protectionism, not in free trade. Likewise, heavy government intervention has characterized those cases of rapid and sustained economic growth in the Third World.

Free trade, does, however, have its uses. Highly developed nations can use free trade to extend their power and their control of the world's wealth, and business can use it as a weapon against labor. Most important, free trade can limit efforts to redistribute income more equally, undermine progressive social programs, and keep people from democratically controlling their economic lives.

A DAY IN THE PARK

At the beginning of the nineteenth century, Lowell, Massachusetts, became the premier site of the country's textile industry. Today, thanks to the Lowell National Historical Park, you can tour the huge mills, ride through the canals that redirected the Merrimack River's power to the mills, and learn the story of the textile workers, from the Yankee "mill girls" of the 1820s through the various waves of immigrant laborers who poured into the city over the next century.

During a day in the park, visitors get a graphic picture of the importance of nineteenth century industry to the later economic growth and prosperity of the United States. Lowell and the other mill towns of the era were centers of growth. They not only created a demand for Southern cotton, they also created a demand for new machinery, maintenance of old machinery, parts, dyes, skills, construction materials, construction machinery, more skills, equipment to move the raw materials and products, parts and maintenance for that equipment, and still more skills. The mill towns also created markets — concentrated groups of wage earners who needed to buy products to sustain themselves. As centers of economic activity, Lowell and similar mill towns contributed to U.S. economic growth far beyond the value of the textiles they produced.

The U.S. textile industry emerged decades after the industrial revolution had spawned Britain's powerful textile industry. Nonetheless, it survived and prospered. British linens inundated markets throughout the world in the early nineteenth century, as the British navy nurtured free trade and kept ports open for commerce. In the United States, however, hostilities leading up to the War of 1812 and then a substantial tariff made British textiles relatively expensive. These limitations on trade allowed the Lowell mills to prosper, acting as a catalyst for other industries and helping to create the skilled work force at the center of U.S. economic expansion.

Beyond textiles, however, tariffs did not play a great role in the United States during the early nineteenth century. Southern planters had considerable power, and while they were willing to make some compromises, they opposed protecting manufacturing in general because that protection forced up the price of the goods they purchased with their cotton revenues. The Civil War wiped out Southern opposition to protectionism, and from the 1860s through World War I, U.S. industry prospered behind considerable tariff barriers.

DIFFERENT COUNTRIES, SIMILAR STORIES

The story of the importance of protectionism in bringing economic growth has been repeated, with local variations, in almost all other advanced capitalist countries. During the late nineteenth century, Germany entered the major league of international economic powers with substantial protection and government support for its industries. Likewise, in nineteenth century France and Italy, national consolidation behind protectionist barriers was a key to economic development.

Only Britain — which entered the industrial era first — might be touted as an example of successful development without tariff protection. Yet, in addition to starting first, Britain built its industry through the expansion of its empire and the British navy, hardly prime ingredients in any recipe for free trade.

Japan provides a particularly important case of successful government protection and support for industrial development. In the post-World War II era, when the Japanese established the foundations for the modern "miracle," the government rejected free trade and extensive foreign investment and instead promoted its national firms.

In the 1950s, for example, the government protected the country's fledgling auto firms from foreign competition. At first, quotas limited imports to $500,000 (in current dollars) each year; in the 1960s, prohibitively high tariffs replaced the quotas. Furthermore, the Japanese allowed foreign investment only insofar as it contributed to developing domestic industry. The government encouraged Japanese companies to import foreign technology, but required them to produce 90% of parts domestically within five years.

The Japanese also protected their computer industry. In the early 1970s, as the industry was developing, companies and individuals could only purchase a foreign machine if a suitable Japanese model was not available. IBM was allowed to produce within the country, but only when it licensed basic patents to Japanese firms. And IBM computers produced in Japan were treated as foreign-made machines.

Today, while Japan towers as the world's most dynamic industrial and financial power, one looks in vain for the role free trade played in its success. The Japanese government provided an effective framework, support, and protection for the country's capitalist development.

Likewise, in the Third World, capitalism has generated high rates of economic growth where government involvement, and not free trade, played the central role. South Korea is the most striking case. "Korea is an example of a country that grew very fast and yet violated the canons of conventional economic wisdom," writes Alice Amsden, in *Asia's Next Giant: South Korea and Late Industrialization*, widely acclaimed as the most important recent book on the Korean economy. "In Korea, instead of the market mechanism allocating resources and guiding private entrepreneurship, the government made most of the pivotal investment decisions. Instead of firms operating in a competitive market structure, they each operated with an extraordinary degree of market control, protected from foreign competition."

With Mexico, three recent years of relatively moderate growth, about 3%-4% per year, have led the purveyors of free trade to claim it as one of their success stories. Yet Mexico has been opening its economy increasingly since the early 1980s, and most of the decade was an utter disaster. Even if the 1980s are written off as the cost of transition, the recent "success" does not compare well with what Mexico achieved in the era when its government intervened heavily in the economy and protected national industry. From 1940 to 1980, with policies of state-led economic development and extensive limits on imports, Mexican national output grew at the high rate of about 6% per year.

VIRTUALLY ALL ADVANCED CAPITALIST COUNTRIES FOUND ECONOMIC SUCCESS IN PROTECTIONISM, NOT IN FREE TRADE.

The recent Mexican experience does put to rest any ideas that free market policies will improve the living conditions for the masses of the people in the Third World. The Mexican government has paved the road for free trade policies by reducing or eliminating social welfare programs. In addition, between 1976 and 1990, the real minimum wage declined by 60%. Mexico's increasing orientation toward foreign trade has also destroyed the country's self-sufficiency in food, and the influx of foreign food grains has forced small farmers off the land and into the ranks of the urban unemployed.

The Uses of Free Trade

While free trade is not the best economic growth or development policy, the largest and most powerful firms in many countries find it highly profitable. As Britain led the cheers for free trade in the early nineteenth century, when its own industry was already firmly established, so the United States — or at least many firms based in the United States — finds it a profitable policy in the late twentieth century.

For U.S. firms, access to foreign markets is a high priority. Mexico may be relatively poor, but with a population of 85 million it provides a substantial market. Furthermore, Mexican labor is cheap; using modern production techniques, Mexican workers can be as productive as workers in the United States. For U.S. firms to obtain full access to the Mexican market, the United States must open its borders to Mexican goods. Also, if U.S. firms are to take full advantage of cheap foreign labor and sell the goods produced abroad to U.S. consumers, the United States must be open to imports.

On the other side of the border, wealthy Mexicans face a choice between advancing their interests through national development or advancing their interests through ties to U.S. firms and access to U.S. markets. For many years, they chose the former route. This led to some development of the Mexican economy but also — due to corruption and the massive power of the ruling party — created huge concentrations of wealth in the hands of a few small groups of firms and individuals. Eventually, these groups came into conflict with their own government over regulation and taxation. Having benefitted from government largess, they now see their fortunes in greater freedom from government control and, particularly, in greater access to foreign markets and partnerships with large foreign companies. National development is a secondary concern when more involvement with international commerce will produce greater riches quicker.

In addition, the old program of state-led development in Mexico ran into severe problems. These problems came to the surface in the 1980s with the international debt crisis. Owing huge amounts of money to foreign banks, the Mexican government was forced to respond to pressure from the International Monetary Fund, the U.S. government, and large international banks. That pressure meshed with the pressure coming from Mexico's own richest elites, and the result has been the move toward free trade and a greater opening of the Mexican economy to foreign investment.

Of course, in the United States, Mexico, and elsewhere, advocates of free trade claim that their policies are in everyone's interest. Free trade, they point out, will mean cheaper products for all. Consumers in the United States, who are mostly workers, will be richer because their wages will buy more. In both Mexico and the United States, they argue, rising trade will create more jobs. If some workers lose their jobs because cheaper imported goods are available, export industries will produce new ones.

Stated, as they usually are, as universal truths, these arguments are just plain silly. No one touring the Lowell National Historical Park could seriously argue that people in the United States would have been better off had there been no tariff on textiles. Yes, in 1820, they could have purchased textile goods more cheaply, but the cost would have been an industrially backward, impoverished nation. One could make the same point with the Japanese auto and computer industries, or indeed with numerous other examples from the last two centuries of capitalist development.

In the modern era, even though the United States already has a relatively developed economy with highly skilled workers, a freely open international economy does not serve the interests of U.S. workers, though it will benefit large firms. U.S. workers today are in competition with workers around the globe. Many different workers in many different places can produce the same goods and services. Thus, an international economy governed by the free trade agenda will bring down wages for U.S. workers.

The problem is not simply that of workers in a few industries — such as auto and steel — where import competition is the most obvious and immediate problem. A country's openness to the international economy affects the entire structure of earnings in that country. Free trade forces down the general level of wages across the board, even of those workers not directly affected by imports. The simple fact is that when companies can produce the same products in several different places, it is owners who gain because they can move their factories and funds around much more easily than workers can move themselves around. Capital is mobile, labor is much less mobile. Businesses, not workers, gain from having a larger territory in which to roam.

Control Over Our Economic Lives

But the difficulties with free trade do not end with wages. Free trade is a weapon in the hands of business when it opposes any progressive social programs. Efforts to place environmental restrictions on firms are met with the threat of moving production abroad. Higher taxes to improve the schools? Business threatens to go elsewhere. Better health and safety regulations? The same response.

Some might argue that the losses from free trade for people in the United States will be balanced by gains for most people in poor countries — lower wages in the United States, but higher wages in Mexico. Free trade, then, would bring about international equality. Not likely. In fact, as pointed out above, free trade reforms in Mexico have helped force down wages and reduce social welfare programs, processes rationalized by efforts to make Mexican goods competitive on international markets.

Gains for Mexican workers, like those for U.S. workers, depend on their power in relation to business. Free trade and the imperative of international "competitiveness" are just as much weapons in the hands of firms operating in Mexico as they are for firms operating in the United States.

The great mobility of capital is business' best trump card in dealing with labor and popular demands for social change — in the United States, Mexico, and elsewhere.

None of this means that people should demand that their economies operate as fortresses, protected from all foreign economic incursions. There are great gains that can be obtained from international economic relations — when a nation manages those relations in the interests of the great majority of the people. Protectionism often simply supports narrow vested interests, corrupt officials, and wealthy industrialists. In rejecting free trade, we should move beyond traditional protectionism.

Yet, at this time, rejecting free trade is an essential first step. Free trade places all the cards in the hands of business. More than ever, free trade would subject us to the "bottom line," or at least the bottom line as calculated by those who own and run large companies.

For any economy to operate in the interest of the great majority, people's conscious choices — about the environment, income distribution, safety, and health — must command the economy. The politics of democratic decision-making must control business. In today's world, politics operates primarily on a national level. To give up control over our national economy — as does any people that accepts free trade — is to give up control over our economic lives.

Resources: NACLA's Report on the Americas, Vol. XXIV, No. 6, May 1991, "The New Gospel: North American Free Trade"; Robert Pollin and Alexander Cockburn, "Capitalism and its Specters: The World, the Free Market and the Left," *The Nation*, February 25, 1991; P. Armstrong, A. Glyn, and J. Harrison, *Capitalism Since World War II*, 1984.

December 1992

HOW FREE TRADE FAILS

HOW GATT AND NAFTA HARM DEMOCRACY, ECOLOGY, AND THE THIRD WORLD

BY MARC BRESLOW

Thailand outlawed cigarette advertising. The European Community (E.C.) banned beef containing growth hormones. Mexico limits foreign investments in industries, such as oil, that it wants to control. The United States has strict limits on residues of the pesticide DDT in food. All sensible policies. But in the New World Order, international treaties will consider all of the above to be barriers to free trade and violations of international law.

George Bush is leading the effort in international negotiations, called GATT and NAFTA, to reduce barriers to trade and investment across national borders. Bush is using these proposed treaties to circumvent domestic opposition to his free-market policies, and to increase corporate dominance over the international economy.

While business profits may benefit handsomely from NAFTA and GATT, both threaten the living standards, health, environment, and democratic rights of people around the globe.

WHAT ARE GATT AND NAFTA?

GATT, the General Agreement on Tariffs and Trade, consists of worldwide negotiations involving 108 nations. As of this writing the GATT talks had stalled, in part due to objections from some members of the European Community to liberalizing agricultural trade.

Since 1948, national governments have negotiated GATT through a number of "rounds." Each round produces a new agreement. While earlier agreements concentrated on reducing tariffs, the current "Uruguay" round has focused on extending free trade principles to new areas such as agriculture, services, and intellectual property, and reducing "non-tariff" trade barriers. Such barriers have traditionally meant quotas and other numerical limits on imports and exports. But in this round they also include regulations to protect the environment, health and safety, and the rights of workers.

Currently, for example, many countries have strict limits on residues of toxic chemicals in food products. These nations typically ban importing such products if an exporting country has looser regulations. Exporters could use GATT to challenge such restrictive laws.

New GATT proposals would speed worldwide integration of national economies. Companies that hold strong competitive positions internationally, and can shift their operations around the globe with ease, would benefit most.

NAFTA is the North American Free Trade Agreement, which includes Canada, Mexico, and the United States. Last August the three nations' executive branches agreed on a NAFTA text, which each nation's legislature must now approve. In Mexico, President Carlos Salinas has sufficient political power to ensure passage, while in Canada the progressive New Democratic Party has promised to void the pact if they win the next election.

The treaty faces challenges in the U.S. Congress, many of whose members are concerned about its impact on domestic industries, workers, and the environment. Presidential candidate Bill Clinton has expressed similar reservations, but he has declared himself a "free trader," and would probably sign the agreement.

In contrast to GATT's global focus, NAFTA would integrate the three North American nations, creating a regional block with trade-regulation functions similar to the European Community. By favoring neighboring countries over other nations, such regional blocks conflict with GATT. NAFTA would require companies that want duty-free treatment to make products that have specific percentages of their content made in North America, putting producers and investors from elsewhere at a disadvantage.

Firms whose factories are primarily in the United States, Canada, and Mexico would benefit greatly from NAFTA. This includes U.S. automakers, who are shifting their assembly plants to Mexico but want protection against Japanese and other east Asian producers. The North American content requirement for autos will begin at 50%, rising to 62.5% after eight years.

By contrast, some companies, usually small firms, have factories only in the United States or Canada, and are unable or unwilling to move to Mexico. These include a segment of the textile and clothing industries, which fear that NAFTA will destroy their already shaky competitive positions.

Unions in Canada and the United States see NAFTA as an immediate threat to jobs and living standards for workers. Defeating the legislation is a priority for the AFL-CIO and the Canadian Labor Congress.

TRADE NEGOTIATIONS UNDERMINE DEMOCRACY

The United States and other governments have designed the GATT and NAFTA negotiations to minimize democratic input from their citizens. In May 1991, Congress agreed to a "fast track" method for considering GATT and NAFTA. The House and Senate must vote yes or no on the entire agreement within 60 days of the administration presenting it to Congress, and cannot propose amendments. Thus, because most members of Congress don't want to oppose free trade, Congress is unlikely to vote down the agreement, even if the GATT negotiators agree on rules that will weaken domestic regulatory policies.

Proposed GATT rules would take precedence over the laws of each participating country. Lori Wallach of Citizen Trade Watch argues that the draft text of GATT "was a declaration of war against popular sovereignty." Once the 108 participating governments agree to GATT rules, international regulatory bodies make decisions on specific trade disputes. Panels of bureaucrats, meeting in private and responsible only to their country's executive branch, wield immense power.

Each nation must abide by these decisions, or face the threat of retaliatory action. Moreover, GATT would require national governments to override any state or local laws that conflict with the proposed treaty.

While countries can choose to ignore GATT rulings, this is risky, especially for nations that depend heavily on trade and foreign investment. Retaliation by powerful trading partners, such as the United States, can cost them vital imports and revenues from exports.

GATT Director General Arthur Dunkel's proposal would provide stronger enforcement powers for GATT, through the creation of a new body, the Multilateral Trading Organization (MTO). The MTO could, for example, restrict a country's exports if it refused to abide by GATT rules.

A Rome-based agency called "Codex Alimentarius," for example, would oversee food safety. Government officials, accompanied by representatives of chemical and food companies, operate this agency in secret. Its current head is an appointee of the U.S. Department of Agriculture, which favors weaker regulation. One U.S. delegation to Codex included three corporate executives from Nestle; one each from Coca-Cola, Pepsi, Hershey, Ralston Purina, Kraft and CPC International; as well as representatives from several food-processor associations. Recently Codex set the maximum allowable residue levels for the pesticide DDT at a level many times higher than the U.S. standard.

WHO CONTROLS U.S. TRADE POLICY?

In recent years, with conservative ideologues controlling the U.S. presidency, Congress, which has mixed political allegiances, has restrained the policy shifts to the right. Congress has often hampered Reagan and Bush in their attempts to eliminate social programs, reduce the legal rights of organized labor, and water down regulations that protect health, worker safety, and the environment.

Bush is attempting to bypass the U.S. constitutional balance of power through GATT and NAFTA. Only the government's executive branch participates in these negotiations, often with corporate advisers actively involved. These representatives consistently advocate decisions that fit free-market ideology, even though they often conflict with existing U.S. laws.

Companies also exert influence through the Advisory Committee on Trade Policy and Negotiations (ACTPN), which has assisted the U.S. Trade Representative in the GATT and NAFTA negotiations. George Bush has evaded legal requirements that such federal advisory committees operate in public and have balanced memberships. The ACTPN has 44 members, of which 38 are corporations, four are trade associations, and only two are labor unions.

Consistent with such corporate dominance, Daniel Amstutz, former senior vice president of Cargill, the world's largest grain company, drafted the original U.S. proposal to GATT. Cargill has an enormous financial stake in reducing regulation of agricultural trade.

Mark Ritchie, director of the Institute for Agriculture and Trade Policy in Minneapolis, closely tracked the United States-Canada trade agreement of 1988. He argues that "both countries' negotiators pursued the interests of their respective transnational corporations instead of the interest of the general public."

"Harmonize" Down

To facilitate trade, the United States and other governments pushing GATT have focused on "harmonization," meaning that all countries participating in GATT should have similar regulations regarding the environmental, health and safety, and other domestic laws that affect imports and exports.

If harmonization raised regulatory standards to those of the most advanced (meaning in most cases the wealthiest) countries, it could improve these standards worldwide. But, largely because of the attitudes of the Bush Administration and transnational corporations, the negotiators are using GATT to reduce standards. GATT panels are ruling that the strict environmental, food safety, and worker protection laws in some European countries, Canada, and in the United States are trade violations.

GATT's subservience to the ravages of the market contrasts with the EC's attempt at economic integration in western Europe. The EC nations have held open negotiations, with democratic participation in each country, and have provisions for harmonization at higher rather than lower levels. These include redistributing resources to poorer countries and regions, and creating minimum workplace standards and benefits on an international level.

Trade, the Environment, and Human Health

Corporations and conservative governments are already using treaties from earlier GATT rounds to attack environmental protection and health and safety laws in one country after another.

In August 1991, a secret GATT dispute resolution panel declared illegal a U.S. ban on imports of tuna caught in a manner that kills large numbers of dolphins. The panel decided that no country can have laws to protect health or the environment if these laws extend beyond the nation's own borders and harm international trade. GATT also ruled that the nation creating a regulation had to show that its law was the "least trade restrictive means" to achieve a health or environmental goal.

According to Public Citizen's Congress Watch, this GATT ruling could threaten other important U.S. environmental laws and international environmental agreements. These include the Endangered Species Act, U.S. laws regulating pesticides and other toxic chemicals, the Montreal Protocol on the Ozone Layer, and the International Agreement for the Conservation of Fisheries.

The proposed GATT agreement would declare many national laws protecting human health to be violations of the agreement, unless all countries agree on the particular regulatory standards. Examples include the EC's ban on beef containing growth hormones, the U.S. prohibition of asbestos, and regulation of the tobacco industry.

As laws in the United States have restricted tobacco advertising and smoking in public places, the U.S. tobacco industry has concentrated on overseas expansion. To protect themselves from this onslaught, several nations have limited cigarette imports and banned advertising of tobacco products. In response, U.S.

PROPOSED GATT RULES WOULD TAKE PRECEDENCE OVER THE LAWS OF EACH PARTICIPATING COUNTRY.

Trade Representative Carla Hills has supported Philip Morris, R.J. Reynolds, and other cigarette firms, arguing that GATT prohibits such laws. GATT recently ruled against laws in Thailand, stating that "no country could use trade restrictions to enforce public health laws, unless the challenged country could show their policy was the least trade restrictive policy possible."

Expansion of "free" trade under NAFTA and GATT also threatens Third World workers with health hazards. One example is the Mexican *maquiladora* factories near the U.S. border. These plants now employ more than 500,000 workers and would expand if NAFTA passes. John O'Connor, chairperson of the National Toxics Campaign, says that their investigations along the border found "the highest levels of toxic exposure ever seen on earth...we have seen families drinking water from benzene barrels, children playing in toxic rivers."

Trade, Investment, and the Third World

Expanding GATT's jurisdiction, as the Dunkel draft proposes, particularly threatens developing nations. Many are struggling to expand their economies from dependence on agriculture and mining to manufactured products and services. The current GATT proposals, if passed, would threaten the rights of participating countries to restrict foreign investments, use "intellectual property" in developing their industries, and restrict food exports during shortages.

Developing countries often impose conditions on the investments of foreign corporations. They require companies to not just use cheap labor, but also contribute to the nation's development. They may mandate partial ownership by domestic investors, use of local materials, and training of local workers in technical skills. Both GATT and NAFTA would treat these measures as treaty violations.

Mexico's current ruling party strongly favors foreign investment. But investors' fears that a future government could restrict their operations, or even nationalize firms, limit capital flows into the country. NAFTA would, however, "put the rights of foreign investors into an international treaty that future Mexican governments would find it difficult or impossible to change," argue economists Jeff Faux and Thea Lee of the Economic Policy Institute, a progressive think tank.

Other GATT proposals would force all nations to allow free entry into their service sectors by foreign corporations. This threatens domestic control of the media, banking, insurance, and virtually all professional services. Under the proposed GATT rules, a country refusing to allow such entry "could be subjected to retaliation not only against its service enterprises but also in relation to its export products," says Martin Khor Kok Peng of the Third World Network, based in Malaysia.

In addition, the United States is demanding that all nations, rich and poor, agree to much stricter standards for patent protection. With corporations from the North owning 99% of patents in the world, these standards would force the Third World to pay billions of dollars more to transnational corporations in order to produce medicines and chemicals and to adopt advanced technologies. In India, for example, patent laws developed through 10 years of public debate and democratic processes would be challenged by GATT, says Vandana Shiva of the Third World Network. This is particularly unjust because corporations expect many of the new patents to be for products derived from genetic material found in tropical rainforests.

GATT would also undermine attempts by many countries to protect domestic agriculture and prevent dependence on food imports. One of the U.S. government's primary goals is to eliminate the subsidies and import and export controls used for this purpose throughout Europe, Latin America, and the United States. Some members of the EC, including France, heavily subsidize their own farmers, and so oppose freeing agricultural trade.

Agricultural trade is also an issue in NAFTA. For example, in Mexico the government sets price levels on corn high enough to allow several million peasant farmers to survive. It uses import controls to prevent cheap corn from the United States from undermining Mexico's minimum price. NAFTA would make such controls trade violations, forcing one million or more families off their land.

PROGRESSIVE ALTERNATIVES

Coalitions of labor, environmental, consumer, farm, and religious organizations oppose NAFTA and GATT and advocate alternatives. These include the Fair Trade Campaign, the Citizen Trade Watch Campaign, and Jobs with Justice. As of July, Democratic Congressmen Henry Waxman (Chair of the Subcommittee on Health and the Environment) and Richard Gephardt (the House Majority Leader), and 218 co-sponsors, had proposed House Concurrent Resolution 246, stating that Congress would reject any trade agreement that violates U.S. laws to protect the environment, health, labor rights, and consumer safety.

The Institute for Agriculture and Trade Policy is facilitating international discussions among progressives, designed to yield a positive vision for equitable trade. Kristin Dawkins of the Institute says such an approach should include negotiations that are regional rather than worldwide and that treat each industry separately. Trade agreements should link producers and consumers in managing supply and demand, permit no lowering of regulatory standards, and involve no preemption of national, state, and local laws, she says.

A progressive coalition, the Mobilization on Development, Trade, Labor and the Environment (MODTLE), has proposed an alternative to NAFTA. It includes enforcement of fair labor practices; upward harmonization of health and safety standards; corporate investment in social infrastructure, such as medical care and education; and environmental impact assessments.

"Free trade is not necessarily fair, indeed it is usually unfair...," argues Martin Khor Kok Peng. "When a strong party insists that a weaker party subject itself to the 'free flow of goods and services, trade and investment,' it does not take an expert to predict that the weak party may grow even weaker whilst the majority of benefits accrue to the strong."

In the New World Order of George Bush and his corporate backers, the United States will reinforce worldwide inequality through economic retaliation against any country that does not adhere to its preferred rules of the game. U.S. military might is, of course, also available to deal with threats to corporate dominance. Only organizing by workers, producers, consumers, environmentalists, and others within each country and on an international basis can turn "free" into "fair" trade.

Resources: "Everything You Always Wanted To Know About GATT, But Were Afraid To Ask," *Congress Watch*, Nov. 1991; Martin Khor Kok Peng, "The Future of North-South Relations: Conflict or Cooperation," Third World Network, 1992; "Exploiting both sides: U.S.-Mexico 'Free' Trade," AFL-CIO, Feb. 1991.

November 1992

HOW P.C. IS THE E.C.?

THE EUROPEAN COMMUNITY STRIVES TO FOSTER GROWTH WITH SOCIAL JUSTICE

BY MIKE COYNE & FRANCIS GREEN

For people in the Americas, 1992 marks the 500th anniversary of Christopher Columbus' invasion. Europeans, too, are noting this occasion, but with some irony. Five hundred years ago, Europeans turned toward the Americas; today, we are turning inward to a new, more unified Europe.

Since six countries founded the European Economic Community (E.C.) in 1958 (see box, page 99), Western Europe's economies have increasingly grown into a coherent whole. By the end of this year, Western European nations will have formed a "single market" by removing most of the remaining trade barriers among E.C. countries. Goods, labor, and capital will flow freely across national borders. Switzerland, Austria, and the Scandinavian countries, long holdouts from the E.C., will join the "European Economic Area" in a step toward full Community membership. These changes are happening already.

In addition, despite political opposition and recent disruptions in the foreign currency exchanges, more members are now ratifying the two accords signed by the heads of governments last December at Maastricht — the Treaty of Economic and Monetary Union and the Treaty on Political Union. These treaties will haul Europe into an even closer economic, social, and political union.

With 380 million people and a high per-capita income, the E.C. will be the largest single market in the world. Europe's new treaties will go further toward creating a unified market than the proposed North American Free Trade Agreement (NAFTA) between the United States, Mexico, and Canada.

The new European economy will challenge the U.S. free-market approach to creating a growth economy. In contrast to NAFTA, the European economic union will emphasize government intervention, industrial and social welfare policies, and consensus between "social partners" (the telling European term for employers and workers).

For those of us who have endured the nightmare of Thatcherism first hand, the European social model sounds like a cavalry coming to the rescue, a point of view endorsed every time Margaret Thatcher and her allies denounce current European developments. Her political spectre moved the U.K. government to opt out of the social provisions agreed to by the other eleven members states at the Maastricht Council.

Because of these social provisions, the E.C. offers some progressive gains. If the European model's emphasis on social justice bears fruit, U.S. progressives could build on it. How successful the E.C. will be as a vehicle for progressives is uncertain. But without a doubt, an integrated Europe will challenge United States and Japanese economic dominance.

THE MOVE TOWARD UNITY

The E.C.'s origins are partly political. After the two world wars, European nations — particularly France and Germany, which had been at war with each other for generations — hoped to prevent further conflicts by creating a European community.

The desire to avoid war still drives the E.C., and the ghastly war in nearby former Yugoslavia has provided a jolt. Yet Europe's fear of losing international competitiveness, and its own growing internal trade, have driven the move toward unity. In 1958, only 36% of current E.C. countries' trade was among member states. By 1990, this had risen to 60%, and trade with former colonial partners had collapsed.

The objective of the single market is to allow goods and services, capital, and labor to move freely among E.C. countries. Before 1992, the ability of businesses to trade between England and France, for example, was far more constrained than trading between New York and New Jersey, even though European states are the size of smaller U.S. states. Imagine the regulatory burden of the U.S. economy if every time you crossed from New York to New Jersey you had to stop, exchange currencies, and pass through a border control.

The single market will remove these costly bureaucratic and technical barriers. By the end of December, E.C.

countries will have unified close to 300 measures, ranging from removing border controls and abolishing trade document requirements to establishing community-wide technical standards and recognizing professional qualifications. Public authorities are also encouraging European business to stop thinking of national boundaries to their operations and to think instead of Manchester, Munich, and Madrid as one market.

The single market is far more than a removal of trade barriers. It is the beginning of an economic and monetary union, a more socially cohesive Europe capable of joint projects in such areas as research and development and environmental action.

Jacques Delors, president of the European Commission, refers to this as the "European social model." Delors, former French socialist cabinet minister, told the congress of the European Trade Union Confederation in May 1991 that he envisions reconciling economic efficiency and social justice. The Single European Act of 1986 and the Social Charter of 1989 enshrine these goals, and they are reinforced further by the yet-to-be ratified Maastricht treaties.

IN CONTRAST TO NAFTA, THE EUROPEAN ECONOMIC UNION WILL EMPHASIZE GOVERNMENT INTERVENTION, INDUSTRIAL AND SOCIAL WELFARE POLICIES, AND CONSENSUS BETWEEN "SOCIAL PARTNERS."

The E.C. vision stands in sharp contrast to the United States' laissez-faire capitalism. Supporters — European socialists, trade unions, and Christian Democrats — believe that Europe should improve its international competitiveness through better product quality and higher productivity rather than cheap labor. They conceive of a high-wage, high-tech economy. This economy would be open to market forces, but with a high degree of social protection and substantial support for business activity through education and training, research and development, and support for industries and regions.

Not all participating governments wholly share this vision. Chief opposition comes from the British Tory government, which retains its ideological links with laissez-faire capitalism. Hence the British refused to sign the Social Chapter of the Maastricht treaty. Moreover, the Germans, who have long been the financial bedrock of the Community, are increasingly skittish as the cost of unifying East and West Germany mounts. The tensions generated by compromise have alienated a wide range of interest groups. This opposition was apparent in the Danish rejection of the Maastricht treaties and the large number voting against them in France.

A EUROPEAN INDUSTRIAL POLICY

Despite these hesitations, the vision of a single market should prevail. The Single European Act lays the foundation for a broader industrial policy. Major European socialist parties and the Christian Democrats (who form the main right-of-center groups in Germany, Italy, the Netherlands, and Belgium) support a Europe-wide industrial policy.

A common research and development program is crucial. Both business and national governments believe European industry must restructure to compete successfully with U.S. and Japanese firms. This fear motivates the single market program.

European firms have lost ground in some high-technology markets. While they are strong in telecommunications equipment, advanced manufacturing equipment, and software, they are weak in semi-conductors, computers, and consumer electronics. European production, for example, supplies only two-thirds of Europe's demand for computers, with American-owned firms accounting for 60% of that. Japanese companies dominate the semi-conductor market. In these areas, Europe is running high trade deficits. In electronics, for example, Europe's deficit with Japan was 31 billion ECU ($39 billion) in 1989, and with the United States it was 7 billion ECU ($9 billion.)

As Europe is creating a single market with standard regulations, it is trying to create a community with fewer disparities between low-wage and high-wage nations. Europeans call this promoting "economic and social cohesion." To do this, the E.C. believes it must shift investment and funds from rich to poor regions of the community.

Portugal is one of the poorer countries of Western Europe. Its standard of living has been climbing, but its gross domestic product per person, one measure of standard of living, is only 55% of the E.C. average. Portugal is a beneficiary of the E.C.'s main program to address this disparity — the Regional Development Fund — which is used primarily to finance infrastructure projects in poorer areas.

The Social Charter, adopted in 1989 by all members except the United Kingdom, will also help alleviate disparities between rich and poor. It states minimum social needs in such areas as employment conditions, health and safety, and the right to company information and consultation. While many supporters of the European economic model, including the governments of Germany and Denmark, regard commitment to the Social Charter as essential to the whole economic package, others, such as the United Kingdom government and some employer organizations in other member states, disagree. The E.C.'s official position, however, remains that social justice is necessary to economic development.

Economic pressures also lead richer E.C. nations to favor the Social Charter's principles. Germany, Denmark, and the Netherlands are worried about the dangers of "social dumping," or companies locating in the less-well-off countries to take advantage of the poor working conditions in the less-regulated regions of Europe. The richer nations argue that fair business competition demands similar wages, benefits, and regulations. German firms, for example, are willing to compete with Portuguese firms as long as the goods conform to minimum technical standards and their workers earn fair wages and benefits as agreed to by the Community. If the Maastricht treaties are ratified, the support of richer countries improves the chances of successfully implementing the Social Charter.

DEVELOPING DEMOCRACY

The Treaty on European Political Union is less far-reaching than its grand title suggests. It grants the Community slightly more power in education, transportation, and culture, previously the exclusive preserve of national governments. It also makes coordinating foreign policy an E.C. objective. But the treaty does not give effective decision-making power to any supranational body. The representatives of the national governments in the Council of Ministers will still make the ultimate decision. Indeed, in many respects, the power of this body in relation to other E.C. institutions will increase.

The Treaty on Economic and Monetary Union (EMU) proposes changes that would dramatically centralize macroeconomic policy. Once a single market is created, the presence of 11 separate currencies begins to look decidedly out of place. Different national currencies with their attendant transaction costs and uncertainties will remain the most obvious barrier to a truly unified market. With a single currency, one central body must control exchange rate policy and monetary policy. The treaty sets out a timetable for creating a European central bank, irrevocably locking currency exchange rates and establishing a single currency by the end of the 1990s. The recent turmoil in the international money markets and the United Kingdom's suspension of its membership in the EMU have raised serious questions about the timetable for these developments. But for many people, the same events have underlined the need for a more stable monetary regime better able to resist the attacks of speculators.

Neither treaty creates avenues for democratic participation in the policy that many Europeans wanted. They do not, for example, increase substantially the powers of the directly elected European parliament. Both progressives and the conservative right lament the unaccountable power that the new central bankers may assume.

CAN THE E.C. SUCCEED?

How successful will the new European economic model be? A definitive answer is impossible. On the one hand, eliminating internal trade barriers will enlarge market size. One official report, subject to some criticism, estimates that these changes will expand Europe's gross domestic product by 3%-6%. Eliminating currency fluctuations

THE NEW EUROPEAN ECONOMY

1958 The E.C. established. Its main elements are the creation of a free trade area and development of a common agricultural policy. Includes Belgium, France, Italy, Luxembourg, Netherlands, West Germany.

1973 Denmark, Ireland, and the United Kingdom join E.C.

1979 European Monetary System (EMS) begins. Its objective is to create exchange rate stability in Europe.

1981 Greece joins E.C.

1986 Single European Act signed by E.C. members. The Act aims to create a single market by abolishing non-tariff barriers. It also sets objectives of Economic and Monetary Union. Portugal and Spain join E.C.

1989 E.C. members, except Britain, adopt Social Charter. Its aim is to ensure minimum standards at work and facilitate labor mobility.

1991 E.C. members agree to Maastricht treaty. This combines two treaties for an Economic and Monetary Union and European Political Union.

1992 The Single European Market completed. E.C. members due to ratify Maastricht treaty. Danish referendum rejects, Irish and French accept.

1995 Austria, Switzerland, Sweden, Norway, and Finland scheduled to join E.C.

1997 European Monetary Union (EMU) to establish centralized monetary institutions and precisely fix exchange rates.

2000 Eastern European countries and Turkey scheduled to join E.C.

and creating R&D programs and associated policies designed to promote a high-wage, technically advanced economy will also aid growth.

On the other hand, with Germany leading the way, a single European monetary policy will keep the money supply in check and inflation low. Germans largely perceive their strict monetary discipline as the source of their economic success. Low inflation and high interest rates typically lead to high unemployment that will particularly hurt countries such as Italy, which now holds loose monetary reins. The proposed Regional Development Fund alone cannot solve these problems. It is underfunded and the richer states resist increasing its size.

If the new European model succeeds, U.S.-based businesses will face added competitive pressures. Faced with a European as well as a Japanese challenge, U.S. businesses will undoubtedly push to cut workers' living standards. To respond, unions and progressive movements don't have to oppose trade and promote protectionism. Rather, they can support an E.C. high-wage model.

U.S. progressives can also draw some encouragement from labor movements across Europe. The new European social model has emerged in part because those on the left have supported it. The weight of left-of-center opinion across the continent has always recognized the economic logic driving integration. Progressives decided it was best to recognize that the political and institutional developments at a European level gave them the opportunity to influence the process.

The British Labor party, which until the 1980s was generally anti-European, has undergone a spectacular conversion on this point. Its previous anti-European stance was partly a consequence of the movement's isolationism and partly a concern about the lack of democratic accountability of a European state. Now Labor draws strength from its closer association with other European movements. Many doubts remain, as was evident from the stance adopted by some on the left during the referendum campaigns in Denmark and France. But the general line of development is clear.

Increasing numbers of people hope to develop a socialist program at a European level. So far socialists cannot agree on a European-wide socialist party, and trade unions of various European nations have not agreed how to work together. But parties and unions have agreed on the elements of a common program emphasizing democracy within European Community institutions, including those determining economic policy and a Social Action program, and countering the growing threat of racism and fascism. The events of 1992 are clearing the ground for a number of battles, and significant progressive gains are possible.

STATISTICAL APPENDIX

GROSS DOMESTIC
PRODUCT

TRADE, INVESTMENT,
GOVERNMENT SPENDING

WORKFORCE & WAGES

UNEMPLOYMENT

INFLATION, INTEREST
RATES, AND DEBT

DATA NOTES & SOURCES

TABLE 1: GROSS DOMESTIC PRODUCT (Billions of 1987 dollars, unless otherwise noted)

Year	Real GDP Growth Rate (%)	GDP 1987 dollars	Personal consumption spending	Gross private investment	Govt. pur-chases	Exports	Imports	Popula-tion (millions)	GDP Per Capita
	1	2	3	4	5	6	7	8	9
1945	-4.0	1,603	715	83	829	41	64	139.9	11,453
1946	-20.6	1,272	779	196	271	81	49	141.4	8,997
1947	-1.5	1,253	793	199	219	97	47	144.1	8,692
1948	3.8	1,300	813	230	241	73	55	146.6	8,866
1949	0.4	1,306	831	187	269	77	54	149.2	8,751
1950	8.7	1,419	874	256	285	70	64	151.7	9,352
1951	9.9	1,558	895	256	397	85	68	154.3	10,101
1952	4.3	1,625	923	232	468	83	75	157.0	10,353
1953	3.7	1,686	963	240	490	79	82	159.6	10,563
1954	-0.7	1,674	987	234	455	82	79	162.4	10,307
1955	5.6	1,768	1,047	285	442	91	91	165.3	10,699
1956	2.0	1,804	1,079	282	444	103	98	168.2	10,722
1957	1.9	1,838	1,104	267	465	112	103	171.3	10,733
1958	-0.5	1,829	1,122	246	476	97	109	174.1	10,504
1959	5.5	1,929	1,179	283	475	74	96	177.8	10,846
1960	2.2	1,971	1,211	283	477	88	96	180.7	10,908
1961	2.7	2,024	1,238	282	502	90	95	183.7	11,017
1962	5.2	2,128	1,293	306	524	95	106	186.5	11,408
1963	4.1	2,216	1,342	327	536	102	108	189.2	11,708
1964	5.6	2,341	1,417	356	549	115	113	191.9	12,198
1965	5.5	2,471	1,497	388	567	118	125	194.3	12,715
1966	5.9	2,616	1,574	401	622	126	144	196.6	13,310
1967	2.6	2,685	1,622	391	668	130	154	198.7	13,513
1968	4.2	2,797	1,708	417	687	140	178	200.7	13,935
1969	2.7	2,873	1,771	437	682	148	189	202.7	14,175
1970	0.0	2,874	1,814	424	666	161	196	205.1	14,015
1971	2.9	2,956	1,874	455	652	162	208	207.7	14,234
1972	5.1	3,107	1,978	510	653	174	230	209.9	14,803
1973	5.2	3,269	2,067	554	644	210	244	211.9	15,425
1974	-0.6	3,248	2,054	512	655	234	238	213.9	15,188
1975	-0.8	3,222	2,098	452	664	233	210	216.0	14,917
1976	4.9	3,381	2,207	495	659	243	250	218.0	15,506
1977	4.5	3,533	2,297	566	664	247	275	220.2	16,043
1978	4.8	3,704	2,392	627	677	270	300	222.6	16,639
1979	2.5	3,797	2,448	656	689	294	304	225.1	16,871
1980	-0.5	3,776	2,447	603	704	321	290	227.7	16,583
1981	1.8	3,843	2,477	607	713	326	304	230.0	16,712
1982	-2.2	3,760	2,504	558	724	297	304	232.2	16,195
1983	3.9	3,907	2,619	595	744	286	342	234.3	16,673
1984	6.2	4,149	2,746	690	767	306	428	236.3	17,553
1985	3.2	4,280	2,866	724	813	309	455	238.5	17,947
1986	2.9	4,405	2,969	727	855	330	485	240.7	18,302
1987	3.1	4,540	3,052	723	882	364	507	242.8	18,698
1988	3.9	4,719	3,162	753	887	422	526	245.0	19,258
1989	2.5	4,838	3,223	754	904	472	545	247.3	19,560
1990	1.2	4,897	3,273	741	933	510	565	249.9	19,594
1991	-0.7	4,861	3,259	684	946	543	562	252.7	19,237
1992	2.6	4,986	3,341	726	945	578	612	255.5	19,515
1993	2.9	5,133	3,452	805	939	596	676	258.2	19,880

TABLE 2: TRADE, INVESTMENT, GOVERNMENT SPENDING (Billions of 1987 dollars, unless otherwise noted)

Year	Merch-andise Trade Balance	Nominal Trade-Weighted Value of US $	Gross Business Fixed Investment	Gross Residential Invest-ment	After-tax Corporate Profits	Manufact. Capacity Utili-zation Rate (%)	Govt. Transfer Payments Purchases	Federal Govt. Purchases	State & Local Govt.
	10	11	12	13	14	15	16	17	18
1945			87	13	68		33	746	83
1946	39,014		124	53	95		58	188	91
1947	51,573		143	67	109		54	108	103
1948	26,906		150	81	116	82.5	49	125	110
1949	25,484		135	75	95	74.2	54	141	125
1950	5,289		146	102	123	82.8	65	137	134
1951	13,400		155	85	103	85.8	49	252	136
1952	11,193		154	84	93	85.4	51	321	138
1953	6,114		165	87	95	89.3	53	348	145
1954	10,879		162	94	94	80.1	62	288	157
1955	12,280		178	109	118	87.0	65	257	169
1956	19,851		189	99	116	86.1	68	254	175
1957	25,352		190	93	108	83.6	77	264	185
1958	13,608		169	95	91	75.0	92	265	201
1959	4,482		165	118	112	81.6	107	223	163
1960	18,775		173	109	107	80.1	112	212	171
1961	21,166		172	110	109	77.3	128	223	184
1962	17,006		185	121	134	81.4	131	246	193
1963	19,394		192	135	144	83.5	136	247	207
1964	24,922		214	142	162	85.6	140	247	223
1965	17,855		251	137	188	89.5	148	251	241
1966	13,383		277	124	192	91.1	161	285	262
1967	12,925	120.0	271	120	181	87.2	185	316	281
1968	2,073	122.1	280	136	174	87.2	204	324	301
1969	1,879	122.4	296	140	154	86.8	215	311	314
1970	7,621	121.1	292	132	126	79.7	245	293	330
1971	(6,339)	117.8	287	168	148	78.2	279	280	349
1972	(17,437)	109.1	312	198	167	83.7	301	290	366
1973	2,331	99.1	357	197	172	88.1	324	278	382
1974	(12,685)	101.4	356	156	121	83.8	347	271	393
1975	18,799	98.5	317	135	150	73.2	400	273	405
1976	(18,933)	105.7	329	166	165	78.5	412	271	410
1977	(58,283)	103.4	364	202	192	82.8	414	277	413
1978	(59,112)	92.4	413	214	202	85.1	416	283	421
1979	(43,137)	88.1	449	207	179	85.4	418	281	421
1980	(35,155)	87.4	438	165	128	80.2	438	288	411
1981	(35,021)	103.4	455	152	126	78.8	451	301	400
1982	(42,950)	116.6	434	124	104	72.8	474	314	402
1983	(76,534)	125.3	421	174	154	74.9	494	333	411
1984	(122,994)	138.2	490	199	186	80.4	489	340	426
1985	(128,986)	143.0	522	202	194	79.5	506	363	452
1986	(150,376)	112.2	500	226	171	79.1	528	381	482
1987	(159,557)	96.9	498	225	193	81.6	532	385	497
1988	(121,915)	92.7	531	223	219	83.6	544	372	511
1989	(105,967)	98.6	540	214	203	83.1	564	368	525
1990	(94,611)	89.1	546	195	210	81.1	591	371	540
1991	(61,251)	89.8	514	170	200	77.8	602	372	545
1992	(77,842)	86.6	529	197	211	78.8	691	363	553
1993		93.2	591	214	224	81.1	711	349	561

TABLE 3: WORKFORCE & WAGES

Year	Civilian labor force over 16* (millions)	Total Employment over 16* (millions)	Female Employment over 16 (millions)	% of Civilian Jobs Held by Women	Labor Force Union-ized (%)	Average Gross Weekly Earnings (1987 dollars)	Change from a Year Earlier (%)	Average Bargained Pay Increases (%)
	19	20	21	22	23	24	25	26
1945	53.86	52.82			12.6			
1946	57.52	55.25			13.3			
1947	59.35	57.04	16.05	28.1	14.6	230.73		
1948	60.62	58.34	16.62	28.5	15.0	230.73	0.0	
1949	61.29	57.65	16.72	29.0	14.7	238.97	3.6	
1950	62.21	58.92	17.34	29.4	14.8	250.74	4.9	
1951	62.02	59.96	18.18	30.3	15.8	253.10	0.9	
1952	62.14	60.25	18.57	30.8	16.3	258.98	2.3	
1953 6	63.02	61.18	18.75	30.6	17.9	269.58	4.1	
1954	63.64	60.11	18.49	30.8	17.9	271.93	0.9	3.1
1955	65.02	62.17	19.55	31.4	17.8	287.24	5.6	5.4
1956	66.55	63.80	20.42	32.0	18.5	295.48	2.9	5.4
1957	66.93	64.07	20.71	32.3	18.4	295.48	0.0	4.9
1958	67.64	63.04	20.61	32.7	18.1	294.30	-0.4	3.9
1959	68.37	64.63	21.16	32.7	18.2	307.54	4.5	3.9
1960 6	69.63	65.78	21.87	33.3	18.1	309.60	0.7	3.2
1961	70.46	65.75	22.09	33.6	17.3	313.82	1.4	2.8
1962 6	70.61	66.70	22.53	33.8	17.6	323.16	3.0	2.9
1963	71.83	67.76	23.11	34.1	17.6	328.40	1.6	3.0
1964	73.09	69.31	23.83	34.4	18.0	334.68	1.9	3.2
1965	74.46	71.09	24.75	34.8	18.5	344.23	2.9	3.8
1966	75.77	72.90	25.98	35.6	19.2	346.48	0.7	4.8
1967	77.35	74.37	26.89	36.2	19.7	346.38	0.0	5.6
1968	78.74	75.92	27.81	36.6	20.3	351.67	1.5	7.2
1969	80.73	77.90	29.08	37.3	20.4	354.76	0.9	8.0
1970	82.77	78.68	29.69	37.7	20.8	350.84	-1.1	10.0
1971	84.38	79.37	29.98	37.8		357.10	1.8	12.2
1972 6	87.03	82.15	31.26	38.0	20.9	372.05	4.2	6.3
1973 6	89.43	85.06	32.72	38.5		371.99	0.0	5.5
1974	91.95	86.79	33.77	38.9	21.6	356.61	-4.1	9.0
1975	93.78	85.85	33.99	39.6	28.9	345.30	-3.2	10.0
1976	96.16	88.75	35.62	40.1	20.3	350.28	1.4	8.5
1977	99.01	92.02	37.29	40.5		354.30	1.1	8.0
1978 6	102.25	96.05	39.57	41.2		354.91	0.2	7.3
1979	104.96	98.82	41.22	41.7		344.10	-3.0	7.7
1980	106.94	99.30	42.12	42.4	23.2	324.12	-5.8	9.5
1981	108.67	100.40	43.00	42.8		318.93	-1.6	9.8
1982	110.20	99.53	43.26	43.5	21.9	314.62	-1.4	3.8
1983	111.55	100.83	44.05	43.7	20.1	320.16	1.8	2.6
1984	113.54	105.01	45.92	43.7	18.8	320.20	0.0	2.4
1985	115.46	107.15	47.26	44.1	18.0	315.77	-1.4	2.3
1986 6	117.83	109.60	48.71	44.4	17.5	315.98	0.1	1.2
1987	119.87	112.44	50.33	44.8	17.0	312.50	-1.1	2.2
1988	121.67	114.97	51.70	45.0	16.8	309.23	-1.0	2.5
1989	123.87	117.34	53.03	45.2	16.4	306.21	-1.0	2.7
1990	124.79	117.91	53.48	45.4	16.1	300.17	-2.0	4.2
1991	125.30	116.88	53.28	45.6	16.1	295.24	-1.5	4.2
1992	126.98	117.60	53.79	45.7	15.8	294.69	-0.2	2.9
1993	128.04	119.31	54.61	45.8	16.8	293.74	-0.3	2.3

Over 14 before 1947

TABLE 4: UNEMPLOYMENT

Year	All civilian workers	White	White Males	White Females	Black	Black Males	Black Females	All 16-19 Years	Average Unemployment Duration (weeks)
					(black and other before 1972)				
	27	28	29	30	31	32	33	34	35
1950	5.3	4.9	4.7	5.3	9.0	9.4	8.4	12.2	12.1
1951	3.3	3.1	2.6	4.2	5.3	4.9	6.1	8.2	9.7
1952	3.0	2.8	2.5	3.3	5.4	5.2	5.7	8.5	8.4
1953	2.9	2.7	2.5	3.1	4.5	4.8	4.1	7.6	8.0
1954	5.5	5.0	4.8	5.5	9.9	10.3	9.2	12.6	11.8
1955	4.4	3.9	3.7	4.3	8.7	8.8	8.5	11.0	13.0
1956	4.1	3.6	3.4	4.2	8.3	7.9	8.9	11.1	11.3
1957	4.3	3.8	3.6	4.3	7.9	8.3	7.3	11.6	10.5
1958	6.8	6.1	6.1	6.2	12.6	13.7	10.8	15.9	13.9
1959	5.5	4.8	4.6	5.3	10.7	11.5	9.4	14.6	14.4
1960	5.5	5.0	4.8	5.3	10.2	10.7	9.4	14.7	12.8
1961	6.7	6.0	5.7	6.5	12.4	12.8	11.9	16.8	15.6
1962	5.5	4.9	4.6	5.5	10.9	10.9	11.0	14.7	14.7
1963	5.7	5.0	4.7	5.8	10.8	10.5	11.2	17.2	14.0
1964	5.2	4.6	4.1	5.5	9.6	8.9	10.7	16.2	13.3
1965	4.5	4.1	3.6	5.0	8.1	7.4	9.2	14.8	11.8
1966	3.8	3.4	2.8	4.3	7.3	6.3	8.7	12.8	10.4
1967	3.8	3.4	2.7	4.6	7.4	6.0	9.1	12.9	8.7
1968	3.6	3.2	2.6	4.3	6.7	5.6	8.3	12.7	8.4
1969	3.5	3.1	2.5	4.2	6.4	5.3	7.8	12.2	7.8
1970	4.9	4.5	4.0	5.4	8.2	7.3	9.3	15.3	8.6
1971	5.9	5.4	4.9	6.3	9.9	9.1	10.9	16.9	11.3
1972	5.6	5.1	4.5	5.9	10.4	9.3	11.8		
1973	4.9	4.3	3.8	5.3	9.4	8.0	11.1	14.5	10.0
1974	5.6	5.0	4.4	6.1	10.5	9.8	11.3	16.0	9.8
1975	8.5	7.8	7.2	8.6	14.8	14.8	14.8	19.9	14.2
1976	7.7	7.0	6.4	7.9	14.0	13.7	14.3	19.0	15.8
1977	7.1	6.2	5.5	7.3	14.0	13.3	14.9	17.8	14.3
1978	6.1	5.2	4.6	6.2	12.8	11.8	13.8	16.4	11.9
1979	5.8	5.1	4.5	5.9	12.3	11.4	13.3	16.1	10.8
1980	7.1	6.3	6.1	6.5	14.3	14.5	14.0	17.8	11.9
1981	7.6	6.7	6.5	6.9	15.6	15.7	15.6	19.6	13.7
1982	9.7	8.6	8.8	8.3	18.9	20.1	17.6	23.2	15.6
1983	9.6	8.4	8.8	7.9	19.5	20.3	18.6	22.4	20.0
1984	7.5	6.5	6.4	6.5	15.9	16.4	15.4	18.9	18.2
1985	7.2	6.2	6.1	6.4	15.1	15.3	14.9	18.6	15.6
1986	7.0	6.0	6.0	6.1	14.5	14.8	14.2	18.3	15.0
1987	6.2	5.3	5.4	5.2	13.0	12.7	13.2	16.9	14.5
1988	5.5	4.7	4.7	4.7	11.7	11.7	11.7	15.3	13.5
1989	5.3	4.5	4.5	4.5	11.4	11.5	11.4	15.0	11.9
1990	5.5	4.7	4.8	4.6	11.3	11.8	10.8	15.5	12.1
1991	6.7	6.0	6.4	5.5	12.4	12.9	11.9	18.6	13.8
1992	7.4	6.5	6.9	6.0	14.1	15.2	13.0	20.0	17.9
1993	6.8	6.0	6.2	5.7	12.9	13.8	12.0	19.0	18.1

TABLE 5: INFLATION, INTEREST RATES, DEBT

Year	Consumer Price Index CPI (%)	Infla-tion from CPI (%)	Growth of money supply	Prime interest rate (%)	Real prime rate (ex post) (%)	New home mortgage yields (%)	Federal Surplus/Deficit (billions of 1987 $)	Federal debt held by public, as % of GDP
	36	37	38	39	40	41	42	43
1945	18.0	2.3		1.50	-0.77		-300.4	110.9
1946	19.5	8.3		1.50	-6.83		-92.6	113.8
1947	22.3	14.4		1.50	-12.85		20.4	100.6
1948	24.1	8.1		1.60	-6.47		55.6	87.7
1949	23.8	-1.2		1.90	3.14	4.3	2.9	81.6
1950	24.1	1.3		2.00	0.73	4.2	-14.6	82.4
1951	26.0	7.9		2.56	-5.32	4.2	26.7	68.4
1952	26.5	1.9		3.00	1.07	4.3	-6.4	63.1
1953	26.7	0.8		3.17	2.41	4.6	-27.7	60.0
1954	26.9	0.7		3.05	2.30	4.6	-5.1	61.0
1955	26.8	-0.4		3.16	3.53	4.6	-12.7	58.9
1956	27.2	1.5		3.77	2.27	4.8	16.3	53.4
1957	28.1	3.3		4.20	0.89	5.4	13.7	50.0
1958	28.9	2.8		3.83	0.98	5.5	-11.0	50.5
1959	29.1	0.7		4.48	3.78	5.7	-50.0	47.5
1960	29.6	1.7	4.9	4.82	3.10	6.2	1.2	46.2
1961	29.9	1.0	7.4	4.50	3.48	5.8	-12.5	44.8
1962	30.2	1.0	8.1	4.50	3.49	5.6	-26.7	43.4
1963	30.6	1.3	8.4	4.50	3.17	5.9	-17.8	42.1
1964	31.0	1.3	8.0	4.50	3.19	5.8	-21.6	39.6
1965	31.5	1.6	8.1	4.54	2.92	5.8	-5.0	37.1
1966	32.4	2.9	4.5	5.63	2.77	6.3	-13.0	34.2
1967	33.4	3.1	9.3	5.61	2.52	6.5	-29.3	32.8
1968	34.8	4.2	8.0	6.30	2.10	7.0	-82.3	32.6
1969	36.7	5.5	4.1	7.96	2.50	7.8	9.9	29.0
1970	38.8	5.7	6.5	7.91	2.18	8.5	-8.2	28.0
1971	40.5	4.4	13.5	5.72	1.33	7.7	-64.5	27.6
1972	41.8	3.2	13.0	5.25	2.04	7.6	-63.6	26.7
1973	44.4	6.2	6.9	8.03	1.80	8.0	-38.1	25.3
1974	49.3	11.0	5.5	10.81	-0.22	8.9	-14.1	23.6
1975	53.8	9.1	12.6	7.86	-1.26	9.0	-112.3	24.9
1976	56.9	5.8	13.7	6.84	1.07	9.0	-147.1	27.0
1977	60.6	6.5	10.6	6.83	0.32	9.0	-100.7	27.8
1978	65.2	7.6	7.9	9.06	1.46	9.6	-103.1	27.2
1979	72.6	11.3	7.8	12.67	1.32	10.8	-62.9	25.7
1980	82.4	13.5	8.9	15.27	1.77	12.7	-101.7	26.2
1981	90.9	10.3	10.0	18.87	8.55	14.7	-98.7	25.9
1982	96.5	6.2	8.9	14.86	8.69	15.1	-150.7	29.2
1983	99.6	3.2	12.0	10.79	7.57	12.6	-237.0	33.2
1984	103.9	4.3	8.7	12.04	7.72	12.4	-202.7	34.4
1985	107.6	3.6	8.3	9.93	6.36	11.6	-224.1	37.1
1986	109.6	1.9	9.5	8.33	6.47	10.2	-229.3	40.7
1987	113.6	3.6	3.6	8.21	4.56	9.3	-149.8	41.6
1988	118.3	4.1	5.5	9.32	5.18	9.2	-149.0	41.8
1989	124.0	4.8	5.0	10.87	6.05	10.1	-139.7	41.7
1990	130.7	5.4	3.5	10.01	4.60	10.1	-192.4	43.5
1991	136.2	4.2	3.0	8.46	4.25	9.3	-224.8	47.0
1992	140.3	3.0	1.4	6.25	3.23	8.2	-235.1	49.7
1993	144.5	3.0	1.6	6.00	3.00	7.2	-200.2	

CONTRIBUTORS

(in order of appearance)

D&S Collective member John Miller teaches economics at Wheaton College.

D&S Associate Teresa Amott teaches economics at Bucknell University.

Edwin Melendez directs the Gastón Institute for Latino Research and Community Development at UMass-Boston.

D&S Collective member Randy Albelda teaches economics at UMass-Boston.

D&S Collective member Chris Tilly teaches policy and planning at UMass-Lowell.

David M. Gordon teaches economics at the New School for Social Research in New York City and is co-author of *After the Waste Land: A Democratic Economics for the Year 2000.*

D&S Collective member Gretchen McClain is a research associate at the Tellus Institute.

Catherine Lynde teaches economics at UMass-Boston.

D&S Associate Ronald Kwan is a doctoral candidate in economics at Harvard University.

D&S Associate David Levine teaches industrial relations at the University of California-Berkeley.

D&S Collective member Bryan Snyder teaches economics at Bentley College.

Martin H. Wolfson teaches economics at the University of Notre Dame.

Max Sawicky is an economist with the Economic Policy Institute.

Betsy Reed is a *D&S* editor.

Doug Orr teaches economics at Eastern Washington University.

D&S Associate Robert Pollin teaches economics at the University of California-Riverside.

Catherine Hill is a research associate at the Project on Regional and Industrial Economics at Rutgers University. Ann Markusen is the Project's director.

Arthur MacEwan, a founding editor of *Dollars and Sense*, teaches economics at UMass-Boston.

Marc Breslow is a *D&S* editor.

Mike Coyne, a consultant in Brussels, previously taught economics at DeMontfort University, England.

Francis Green teaches economics at the University of Leicester, England.